THE LOOK AND SHAPE OF ENGLAND

THE LOOK AND SHAPE OF ENGLAND

*How Politics Has Influenced its Appearance
Over the Last Century*

Nigel Moor

Book Guild Publishing
Sussex, England

First published in Great Britain in 2010 by
The Book Guild Ltd
Pavilion View
19 New Road
Brighton, BN1 1UF

Typesetting in Garamond by
YHT Ltd, London

Printed in Great Britain by
CPI Antony Rowe

A catalogue record for this book is available from
The British Library.

ISBN 978 1 84624 439 1

Contents

Acknowledgements

This book describes how there has always been a strong political character to spatial planning and that this is increasing. Today, faced with the issues generated by global warming, it is even more important that this is understood, particularly by a younger generation unfamiliar with the political history.

I have worked on this book for almost a decade and during that time my wife Christine has helped enormously with the research. I would also like to acknowledge the late Tony Greenwood (since 1970 Lord Greenwood of Rossendale), a member of Harold Wilson's cabinet who encouraged my interest in politics; *Building Magazine*, where as planning correspondent between 1979 and 1996 I had a ringside seat on the Thatcher era; Bob Langton, a long-standing property journalist who introduced me to the world of property; and Councillor Ann Ducker MBE, leader of South Oxfordshire District Council, who by including me in her cabinet gave me an experience of practical politics. Finally I thank Book Guild Publishing for sharing my commitment to the book.

The book is dedicated to my three daughters, Sarah, Vanessa and Katherine, in the hope that it will help them understand what has preoccupied me for so long. This book will be published shortly after the 2010 general election and I can predict with considerable confidence that the next decade will exert as much if not greater an influence on the look and shape of England as the preceding ones have.

Picture Acknowledgements

The author and publishers acknowledge the co-operation of the following for allowing the inclusion of the photographs that illustrate this book.

1. Creative Commons Attribution 2.0 Licence taken by Adrian Pingstone. 2. Punch Ltd. 3. London County Council The County of London Plan 1943. 4. The Museum of London. 5. Malcolm D. Moor. 6. Osborn, F.J. & Whittacker, A. (1977) *New Towns* London Leonard Hill. 7. Creative Commons Attribution 2.0 Licence taken by C. Ford. 8. Moor, N. & Langton, R. (1978) *Planning For New Homes*. 10. The Daily Telegraph. 11. Building Magazine. 12, 13 & 14 Malcolm D. Moor. 15. Creative Commons Attribution 2.0 Licence taken by zakgollop. 16. Heron International. 19. Building Magazine.

Photographs 9, 17, 18 & 20 were taken by the author.

Acknowledgement for Betjeman – Collected Poems: 'The Planaster's Vision' from Collected Poems, by John Betjeman © 1955, 1958, 1962, 1964, 1968, 1970, 1979, 1981, 1982, 2001. Reproduced by permission of John Murray (Publishers).

Abbreviations

AAP	Area Action Plan
BPF	British Property Federation
CBI	Confederation of British Industry
CIL	Community Infrastructure Levy
CPRE	Campaign to Protect Rural England
DCLG	Department for Communities and Local Government
DEA	Department of Economic Affairs
DEFRA	Department for the Environment, Food and Rural Affairs
DETR	Department of the Environment, Transport and the Regions
DLR	Docklands Light Railway
DoE	Department of the Environment
DPD	Development Plan Document
DTI	Department of Trade and Industry
DTLGR	Department of Transport, Local Government and the Regions
EEC	European Economic Community
EiP	Examination in Public
ERM	Exchange Rate Mechanism
EU	European Union
GLC	Greater London Council
HCA	Homes and Communities Agency
HPDG	Housing & Planning Delivery Grant
IDeA	Improvement and Development Agency
IMF	International Monetary Fund
IPC	Infrastructure Planning Commission
IPPR	Institute for Public Policy Research
LAMS	land acquisition and management scheme
LDD	Local Development Document
LDF	Local Development Framework
LDP	Local Strategic Partnership
LGA	Local Government Association

MAFF	Ministry of Agriculture, Fisheries and Food
MoHLG	Ministry of Housing and Local Government
NEDC	National Economic Development Council
NHS	National Health Service
NPS	national policy statement
ODPM	Office of the Deputy Prime Minister
PAG	Planning Advisory Group
PGS	planning gain supplement
PIU	Performance and Innovation Unit
POS	Planning Officers Society
PPG	Planning Policy Guidance Note
RDA	Regional Development Agencies
RDC	Rural Development Commission
RIBA	Royal Institute of British Architects
RICS	Royal Institution of Chartered Surveyors
RLB	Regional Leaders' Boards
RPG	Regional Planning Guidance Note
RSA	Royal Society of Arts
RSS	Regional Spatial Strategy
RTPI	Royal Town Planning Institute
SNP	Scottish National Party
TCPA	Town and Country Planning Association
UDC	Urban Development Corporation

1

Introduction: The Politics of Development

Politics and Planning

In election year 1983, the then Prime Minister Margaret Thatcher stood on a piece of urban wasteland on Teesside and vowed that her Conservative government would remove the scourge of decay from the inner cities. The changes that she and her ministers ushered in that year radically altered planning and environmental policies for the rest of the decade. The soaring skyscrapers of Canary Wharf, which can be glimpsed from as far as away as the M11 at Fiddler's Hamlet in rural Essex, became the most graphic symbol of these policies which established Enterprise Zones and deregulated planning controls. Other politicians have been responsible for similar dramatic effects. Around most large provincial towns, some six or more kilometres from the town centre are the post-war estates of bungalows and terraced and semi-detached two-storey dwellings, often set in large grassy areas with generous gardens and roadways. These are the 'homes for heroes' and were built by Nye Bevan, a member of Clem Attlee's post-war cabinet. More famous for his founding role in the formation of the National Health Service (NHS), but one million of these houses were built on his watch as Housing and Health Minister. Nearer the town centre, built on bomb sites and cleared areas, where Victorian houses, factories and yards have been demolished, rise blocks of prefabricated flats, often at high density. These were the result of Macmillan's housing boom when he was Housing Minister in Churchill's Cabinet once the Conservatives got back into office in 1951 and Churchill tasked him with beating Labour's housing record. The look and shape of England in the twenty-first century results from decisions made by politicians – both at national level and at local level – during the hundred years that we have had planning controls.

In thinking about the appearance of England, it is worth keeping in mind a mental image of a typical city, and how it has grown in the twentieth century. Although not replicated throughout the country, it is recognisable to anyone travelling across a large urban area. The late Professor Peter Self, the father of the author and social commentator Will Self, described in his book *Cities in Flood* (1961) the typical city form. At its historic core were the main business, shopping and entertainment areas, and the transport terminals. Near the centre, and adjoining the railways and river or canals were a high proportion of the industries housed in ageing buildings developed in the nineteenth century, together with rows of old slum dwellings. Much of this land was redeveloped at the end of the twentieth century, encouraged by successive governments' inner-urban programmes.

The city has expanded from this historic central core, which at the beginning of the twentieth century was its whole entity, in roughly concentric circles. The first main distinguishable circle contains the 'by law' housing, built under the impetus of the sanitary legislation of the mid-nineteenth century, and still standing and habitable in many areas such as Newcastle, Gateshead, Liverpool and Manchester. The ring also contains the big houses of the Victorian merchants, large numbers of which have been converted into flats, offices, bars and hotels. Next comes the ring of suburbia, initially of the 1920s and 1930s, and then, after the Second World War, of the housing estates encouraged by Nye Bevan and Harold Macmillan when both were Housing Ministers in their successive governments of the late 1940s and 1950s – in the latter case sometimes containing system-built blocks of flats.

Beyond that, if the city is ringed by a green belt, is a zone of half-town and half-country, containing the residences of the more wealthy, living in large detached dwellings or converted farmhouses with large gardens. Less well off people here dwell in bungalows or caravans on large plots, at one time worked as smallholdings. Beyond this area are the satellite towns and villages linked to the city by train and motorway. The concentric rings give the appearance of an organic growth with the experienced observer able to date the buildings in each ring, like an arboriculturist examining the rings of a felled tree. But the growth is not organic, but the result of decisions taken by central and local politicians over a hundred years of planning control.

The determination of Oxford City Council to build for its housing needs in the green belt around the city, pleas for yet more airport capacity at Heathrow, or the plans by the major retail operators to open even more superstores, have a resonance because these are the issues that have confronted politicians almost since the beginning of planning control. Concerns about global warming and energy reserves mean that spatial planning has become even more important, but the choices are political decisions. Much

INTRODUCTION: THE POLITICS OF DEVELOPMENT

The soaring skyscrapers of Canary Wharf, which can be glimpsed from as far away as the M11 at Fiddler's Hamlet in rural Essex, became the most graphic symbol of the policies which established enterprise zones and deregulated planning controls.

© Creative Commons Attribution 2.0 Licence taken by Adrian Pingstone

that is written on the subject of spatial planning has an academic or pseudo-scientific gloss, but this book looks at the politics of it, and particularly the personalities of the politicians who have had the levers of power and made the decisions that they have. At the same time, the book places planning and environmental politics within an overall political context so as to understand the relationship between decisions taken about the environment and the other political tensions and themes that characterise every political administration during its time in office.

Before 1997, planning policy was formulated by a relatively small number of agencies. These comprised the national UK government, central government offices in the English regions and in Scotland, Wales and Northern Ireland, and local government. Devolution to the Celtic countries and decentralisation to the English regions since 1997 has complicated the planning framework. This book therefore deals with the evolution

3

of planning policy and ideology in England where arrangements for self-government are still in transition, and not finally resolved, when compared with the Celtic fringe, and also where the objectives for local government of the major political parties are most polarised. Regional planning does exist in England but is in a state of flux, and may not survive a change of government.

Politics is part of spatial planning, which is distinguished from other professional and technical services provided through local government by displaying a political–professional spectrum that continually exhibits a tension between these two traits. In this introduction the three political levels at which spatial planning operates are examined: the national, the regional and the local. Central to the role of planning below the national level is the role of elected councillors within the spatial planning system and the extent to which political ideologies influence their decision-making. Central government delegates to these politicians the power to take planning decisions and to understand the political influences on councillors, the evolution of the spatial planning system in England is reviewed. However at the sub-national level there is more and more evidence of a change taking place and politics being relegated while a discourse within a political–professional elite of senior members and officers takes centre stage. Modernising initiatives from central government which wishes to see a more 'managerialist' culture within local government are encouraging this trend, which could suggest that local politicians will have less say in the future over the look and shape of England.

A Political Overview of Spatial Planning

Spatial planning in England has had a legislative basis for a hundred years. It has evolved from a system predicated on the control of land use as introduced by the reforming 1908 Liberal government through the Housing, Town Planning etc. Act 1909, the comprehensive measures introduced by the 1947 Act, to the more holistic, community-based system of spatial planning introduced through the Planning and Compulsory Purchase Act 2004. Looking back over more than 50 years, planning has had its successes and its failures. Those least successful aspects, critics would assert, include the sprawling housing estates built in the 1960s and 1970s, town centres isolated from their communities by inner ring roads and modern buildings built with no reference to their surroundings. Preservation of our best landscapes through National Parks and Areas of Outstanding Natural

Beauty, best buildings and townscapes preserved through listed building and conservation area controls, and urban sprawl curbed by green belts are often asserted to be the successes. All of this has had a political dimension. Leach (2002) has explored the British political tradition and identified the tensions between the free market and the state in political thinking and practice. These tensions occur in spatial planning and throughout the period since 1909 there have been ideological differences between the major political parties as to the objectives and financial mechanisms and means of control of the system. Tewdwr-Jones (2002) dispels the myth that planning is essentially technical and value-free and asserts that on the contrary it is essentially political. Moor (1983) observed the increasing role of the market in the planning system, and the increasing politicisation of spatial planning (1999). The erosion of planning during the Thatcher era has been evaluated by Montgomery and Thornley (1990), while Evans (2004) explores the ideological background to the emergence of Thatcherism. Rydin (2003) asserts the necessity for spatial planning as a means of avoiding anarchy and disorder in the economic system.

Corkindale (2004) argues the need to introduce more economic valuation and cost-benefit into spatial planning, particularly so as to cost emissions and improve sustainability. He draws important parallels between the 1947 Act and the nationalisation of industry carried out by the Labour administration of 1945–51. They have to do with the role of the state in the management of economic enterprise, where it shields public enterprise from competition and subsidises inefficiencies for political reasons. As a result, factor prices become distorted and this leads to inappropriate resource allocation. Where land development rights are nationalised, the arbitrariness and lack of transparency inherent in the exercise of administrative discretion over the granting of planning permission are likely to result in a pattern of land development that is economically inefficient.

Parliament has delegated the decision-making role to the Secretary of State, who in turn has delegated to local planning authorities and their councillors, and the discretion of the decision-makers has been robustly upheld by the courts, which have shown no wish to usurp the decision-making, particularly in the period since the introduction of the Human Rights Act in 2000. However, by means of delegation, the decision-making is shared with officers, who are increasingly members of a professional institute specialising in the built environment. Since the advent of a New Labour government there has been a strong reforming agenda in local government aimed at improving the quality and delivery of council services including town planning.

Following a major review of the planning system by New Labour (Department of Transport, Local Government and the Regions, 2001), the Planning and Compulsory Purchase Act 2004 introduced a new approach to spatial planning in the form of the Local Development Framework (LDF). Although the government has made it clear that it is committed to the well-established principle of a plan-led system, and that decisions on proposals for development or change of use should not be arbitrary, the new spatial planning system is intended to go beyond traditional land use planning so as to bring together and integrate policies for the development and use of land with other policies and programmes which influence the nature of places and how they function. Advice to local planning authorities is that they should take account of the principles and characteristics of other relevant strategies and programmes when preparing local development documents and in particular the core strategy introduced within the LDF. The LDF is seen as a key component in the delivery of the Community Strategy, setting out its spatial aspects where appropriate and providing a long-term spatial vision, and local planning authorities are encouraged to liaise closely with their Local Strategic Partnerships (LDPs) to ensure that the community strategy contains realistic assumptions about the statutory constraints and the resources available to the local planning authority (Department for Communities and Local Government, 2006).

These changes can be viewed as carrying forward into the planning system the principles set out in The Local Government Act 2000 that enshrined in law the community leadership role of local authorities. The duty to produce a Community Strategy, combined with the establishment of LDPs, provides a vehicle for establishing and delivering a shared vision for local areas (Moor, 2004). The Local Government Act 2000 also introduced a new ethical framework aimed at ensuring 'high standards of conduct in local government' and required all authorities to adopt a members' code of conduct based on a national model, which councillors must sign up to.

Modernising Planning: Proposed Changes

Alongside these legislative changes, the New Labour government introduced what it termed a 'modernising' agenda for spatial planning. The Green Paper *Planning: Delivering a Fundamental Change* (Department of Transport, Local Government and the Regions, 2001) comprises a critique of the whole spatial planning system, but specific criticisms of interest to this subject are as follows.

- Speed of decision-making. This is both slow and variable between local authorities. Over 90 per cent of councils fail to meet the target that 80 per cent of planning applications should on average be decided within eight weeks.
- Planning committees can make decisions on planning applications without the applicants or significant objectors having an opportunity to present their case.
- Elected councillors serving on planning committees are often insufficiently well trained to undertake their important duties.
- The regional planning bodies charged with preparing Regional Spatial Strategies (RSSs) should demonstrate that they are representative of key regional interests – groups comprised solely of local authorities will not be acceptable. If directly elected assemblies are established, it is envisaged that they, as democratically accountable bodies, would take over the regional planning role.
- Local authorities are not achieving the targets for processing planning applications that have been set. These targets will be monitored through the Best Value regime and will be one of the principal ways in which the performance of local planning authorities will be judged.
- To speed up decision-making, authorities should delegate decisions to officers as far as practicable. To encourage this process, a new target of delegation of 90 per cent of decisions has been set for 2002–03, and will be monitored through Best Value.
- It is clearly right that some decisions should be decided by elected members, but this can be a cause of unnecessary delay where committees meet infrequently, and authorities should review their committee cycles to ensure that the targets can be met.
- Elected members need to become more expert, and councillors should undergo training before they sit on planning committees.
- Best Value imposes a duty of continuous improvement in service delivery on local authorities. Government will intervene where there is persistent failure and in the case of poorly performing planning services action may include:
  - negotiated or imposed peer or external support;
  - transfer of the processing of planning applications to an arms-length body, another local authority or a private-sector contractor.

Among those contributing to the evidence base for this Green Paper were the academics Manns and Wood (2002) who had carried out a survey of local authorities that had allowed the public to address the development control committees. They describe the critical role that these committees play in the British town and country planning system, by providing the opportunity for democratically elected councillors to scrutinise development proposals, balance a wide range of material factors and reach a decision. These committees provide a degree of local accountability and are the only point at which members of the public can physically witness, and in some cases contribute their views in person to, those decisions. They also point out that in 2002 all local authorities in England and Wales had delegated decision-making powers from full council to some form of development control committee, and most delegate further powers to officers. At that time, the Best Value target of 70 per cent of decisions on planning applications to be dealt with under delegated powers by chief planning officers was the guideline. However, the Green Paper proposed that this target be increased to 90 per cent.

This target has been justified on grounds of efficiency and predictability of decision-making, but given added emphasis by the use of planning delivery grants to reward those local planning authorities achieving these targets with substantial sums from the central Exchequer. These grants have been used to finance the capital and revenue costs for local authorities of employing planning staff. This has produced a tension in the planning process. On the one hand, the government is keen to speed up the determination of planning applications to assist business interests and encourage investment. On the other, it wishes to open up local government and make decision-making more open, transparent and democratic. As Manns and Wood (2002) caution, these forces are pulling in opposite directions, and current indications are that speed and efficiency may triumph over openness and accountability.

In addition there are other pressures at work that may limit the discretion of councillors in the planning process. The Local Government Association (LGA), the business sector and the voluntary sector published, in July 2000, *The Planning Users Concordat* in which the delegation of more decisions to officers was commended. Subsequently, in March 2004, the LGA Planning Executive, together with the Planning Officers Society (POS), endorsed the following approach:

> The LGA and POS favour moving towards a more widely adopted approach where only applications that cannot be determined by officers are determined by

committee. We wish to see councillors accepting the principle of decision making only in such cases.

The Barker review of planning (2004) commissioned by the Chancellor of the Exchequer, and the Department of Communities and Local Government (2007) document on the role of councillors in planning have advocated that training be made compulsory for councillors on planning committees. The authors of the latter document saw divergence between officers and elected members in their decisions on planning applications as a threat to the integrity of the planning system. Further support for this approach has come from the British Property Federation (BPF) who, in evidence (2008) to the Communities and Local Government Committee's inquiry into planning skills, proposed that councillors must have training in areas such as commercial awareness and development economics.

The report of the Committee has been published and despite the almost unanimous view of professional organisations such as the BPF, the Royal Institution of Chartered Surveyors (RICS), the Town and Country Planning Association (TCPA), the Royal Town Planning Institute (RTPI) and the POS that councillors who are local cabinet members in charge of planning policy or who serve on planning committees should receive some form of compulsory or mandatory training provision, the Committee disagreed and supported the view of the Housing Minister who argued that the role that an elected person brings to the function is not that of the professional but to take advice from the professionals and then, just as ministers have to, make a judgement. Trevor Roberts Associates, who gave evidence to the Committee, best summed up the role of the councillor: 'The system rests on the basis that the technical specialist can be challenged by a non-specialist, so that there are checks and balances and that the decisions being made reflect the needs and desires of the wider community' (Trevor Roberts Associates 2008). However, despite the support that the role of councillors periodically obtains, over nearly a decade the government's modernising agenda has continued to marginalise the role of councillors within the planning system.

These pressures suggest a diminishing role for local autonomy in spatial planning, and Jenkins (2006) sees this as part of an ever-increasing centralisation in local government initiated by Margaret Thatcher and Michael Heseltine when in government between 1979 and 1983. However, pressures from competing directions are evident. Of particular importance is the changing style of governance in local government. Rhodes (1997) has examined these changing styles of governance. The responsibilities introduced by The Local Government Act 2000 and the duty to produce a

Community Strategy suggest that spatial planning, rather than continuing as a quasi-legal silo within the council, has to be integrated into the community vision strategy developed at a political level (Moor, 2004). The requirement for the production of a Statement of Community Involvement and a Core Strategy introduced by the Planning and Compulsory Purchase Act 2004 again suggests a more clearly focused political agenda for spatial planning. These changes suggest that once the Core Strategy has been agreed, there will be little discretion left to councillors on how individual planning applications might be determined.

Political Ideologies and Spatial Planning

The term ideology, Leach (2002) asserts, may be loosely defined as any system of ideas and norms directing political and social action. An ideology involves firstly an interconnected set of ideas that forms a perspective on the world, and secondly ideologies have implications for political behaviour – they are 'action-orientated', and in this sense, not being pure theory, they should be related to practical politics.

From its inception as part of the welfare reform programme introduced by the 1908 Liberal government, and through the inter-war years, spatial planning was promoted as being necessary to avoid urban sprawl and to protect the countryside by seers such as Abercrombie, Osborn and Sharp, and literary figures such as Betjeman, but the inter-war governments were reluctant to legislate for a system that was both comprehensive and compulsory. A series of interim legislative measures was the outcome until the outbreak of the Second World War finally produced a consensus within government that a compulsory and comprehensive system was necessary. The outcome was the 1947 Act introduced by the Attlee government.

In Britain, leading Labour and Conservative politicians in the post-Second World War era increasingly shared the same assumptions, and often the same remedies. The term 'Butskellism' was coined (from the names of Labour and Conservative Chancellors Gaitskell and Butler) to describe the similar approach of both major parties to economic management.

This approach had become so widely accepted and unchallenged that at the time it was not even perceived as 'ideological', but a widely prevailing consensus does not necessarily imply the end of ideology, but rather the dominance of a particular ideology, which for a time becomes the ruling political orthodoxy. Spatial planning, having emerged in the Second World

War as part of the Keynesian approach to economic management, was also part of that Keynesian collective consensus.

This consensus was first challenged in the initial years of the Heath Conservative government in 1970–71. It was the misfortune of this government that the Conservatives' reception to economic liberalism coincided with the worst post-war economic crisis yet encountered. Heath's retreat from economic liberalism and the ignominy of the three-day week marked a watershed in the ideology of the Conservative Party and ignited the spark that led to Margaret Thatcher's bid for the leadership. Tutored in the views of Friedrich. A. Von Hayek (*The Road to Serfdom*, 1944) by Sir Keith Joseph, after her leadership victory in 1975 Thatcher's own free-market convictions became manifest in her speeches.

The Thatcher governments broke with the post-war consensus, and following her loss of leadership the Conservatives attempted to revert to the pragmatic flexibility in pursuit of power that had marked the two decades after the end of the Second World War. By promoting an approach to decision-making that was predicated on local plans adopted by local planning authorities, the Major government tried to revert to a universal planning system that was perceived as a strong line of defence against change. New Labour however, borrowing a Thatcherite approach to economic management, if not to the management of the public services, appeared willing to move to a planning system that abandoned the principle of a universal planning system covering the country. The 'eco-towns' can be viewed as a hark-back to the simplified planning regimes introduced by the Thatcher government as an alternative approach to development control and administrative discretion.

Three Political Levels

Politics in planning operates at three recognisable levels. The first is at the national level. Because the British town and country planning system is one of the most centralised in the world, planning policy features among the other major areas of domestic policy, such as health and education, and is therefore susceptible to the ideology of the political party in power. The provision of national planning policy from central government to local government to shape land use policy and development has been a central feature since the advent of the modern planning system after the end of the Second World War.

Secondly, there is the preparation of development plans. The resultant policies within development plans act as an agreed set of principles to guide decision-makers on the future of the built and natural environment and as a means through which development opportunities are advertised to the private sector. Agreement on these policies is essentially a political act, and in the new more managerial system of local government introduced by New Labour, these policies are endorsed by council cabinet or executive – which is now the main political body within local government – both before and after public consultation.

Thirdly, there is the control of the system. This has been delegated to local government with advice from central government and legal parameters established by courts of law, and this, in turn has predominantly been delegated to professional planning officers, responsible for determining applications for planning permission from households and companies. A minority, but an important minority, because they are usually the more controversial, larger or complex applications, are determined by planning committees made up of local elected members representing wards in the council's areas. Traditionally these decisions, because they are quasi-judicial, are not 'whipped' in a party political sense, but inevitably local political issues come to the fore in this decision-making. Even though they now determine perhaps as many as 90 per cent of applications, some professional planning officers still find it irksome when their recommendations are overturned by planning committee members. One reader, writing in *Planning Magazine* (2005), suggested that 'It must be dispiriting for officers to find their careful recommendations overturned so lightly and so often by members', and was subsequently loudly rebuked by a council member who responded by observing that,

> Planning is usually subjective and is always very personal to those concerned. It is also one of the sole areas left where members feel that they can help their electors. You may get unusual decisions from members, officers and the inspectorate, but that is the system we live with.
>
> (*Planning Magazine* 2005)

One of the earliest academics to explore this issue was Professor Gordon Cherry, whose book *The Politics of Town Planning* was published in 1982. His conclusions were rather tentative: 'Planning is an activity which is about choices, and it establishes goals of a kind which ultimately must win political approval. Planning may not of itself be political, but it eventually operates in a political framework.' (Cherry, 1982). A contemporary planning academic, Mark Tewdwr-Jones (2002), is much more forthright: 'First, let us dispel a myth that planning is essentially technical and value free; it is neither, and anyone within practice who thinks they are performing such a job are deluding themselves and others'. Patsy Healey (2007) strives to reflect political initiatives in her goal of a relational planning for our times which reflects urban complexity and spatial strategies, and predicts a recognition of the condition of dynamic instability in governance processes. Her study of transformation in the 'Cambridge sub-region' identifies the power of spatial strategy to shape attention and maintain a degree of local control over the scale and form of urban development in the face of external pressures, although there is little discussion of the role of councillors in this process.

This book will trace briefly from the early days the intellectual case for a system of planning control, the evolution of the post-war consensus, which chimed with a common Keynesian view of economic management by the two major political parties, and how the Thatcher legacy broke down this consensus as it attempted to expose planning to the same deregulatory pressures as the rest of the economic system. Reforms and innovations introduced by the Blair government brought about more changes which in turn caused a reaction among the opposition parties. The interaction between politics and the planning system is explored initially through a historical review of the evolution of planning. This begins in its formative period before the Second World War, when luminaries such as Sir Patrick Abercrombie and Dr Thomas Sharp fulminated against ribbon development and the crassness of so much speculative estate building.

The Role of Councillors

More than 40 years ago, Bernard Crick wrote *In Defence of Politics*, first published in 1962, to defend the art of politics from those who sought to denigrate it. Against the orthodoxies of the time – Fabian centralism on the Left and the one-party Conservatism on the Right, he sought to return to a much older tradition of political thinking, centred on active and participatory citizenship in a pluralistic political community. He defined politics in this way: 'Politics, then, can be simply defined as the activity by which differing interests within a given unit of rule are conciliated by giving them a share in power in proportion to their importance to the welfare and the survival of the whole community' (Crick, 1982). Councillors at the local level are part of this political matrix. Strong support for the positive role of councillors in spatial planning was given by Lord Nolan in his report on standards in public life (1997). Councillors were seen as exercising quite properly two roles in the planning system. They determine applications, arriving at a decision on granting or refusing permission by using planning criteria and by excluding non-planning considerations. They also act as representatives of public opinion in their communities. There has always been some tension in this dual role, but it was minimised when public opinion was broadly in favour of, or at least neutral to, development. The tension has, however, become more acute as opposition to development projects has grown. As politicians, local councillors must listen and be responsive to the views of their constituents. As members of the planning committee, they must make a decision using only planning criteria. This may be a delicate balance to achieve.

Nolan noted that one approach to this difficulty might be to reduce the scope of councillor involvement in the planning process, but he concluded that the result, although well intentioned, creates immense difficulties. Among those he identified was the view that planning is a 'quasi-judicial' process. Nolan disagreed, and argued that if planning decisions by local authorities were to be regarded as quasi-legal decisions in which councillors played a role similar to that of inquiry inspectors or judges, there would be no point in involving councillors in such decisions – they might as well be taken by planning officers, or by inspectors. Another difficulty was the assumption that councillors cannot be trusted to arrive at a sound decision or, more insidiously, that they are more likely than officers to succumb to corruption or improper influence. Nolan took a robust approach to these concerns. Planning, he concluded, was not an exact science; there will always be a balance between various planning criteria. There is therefore nothing intrinsically wrong if planning committees do not invariably follow the advice of officers. Planning officers exist to advise planning committees, which are entitled to reach their own decisions by attaching different weight to the various planning criteria that are relevant to an application. If a decision is thought to be perverse, a planning officer should so advise the committee, but respect the committee's decision. Providing elected members are fully and properly briefed, they are particularly well equipped to make planning decisions *because* of their representative role, not *despite* it. Finally, attempting to divorce the political role of councillors from their planning function is unlikely to succeed. It is also undemocratic and impractical to try to prevent councillors from discussing applications with whomever they want.

Nolan concluded that planning decisions are not legal judgements. They are administrative decisions, taken within a framework of law and practice, and his view has been upheld by the courts. The effect of this is not that planning decisions are free from legal constraints, but that the constraints are different. Decisions must still be free from bias caused by personal interest, but they need not be decisions that are taken judicially, based solely on a rational and impartial assessment of evidence. On the contrary, councillors must bring to planning decisions a sense of the community's needs and interests. That is why they are there. The Nolan Committee therefore accepted and understood the duty of elected members to listen to their constituents, together with an expectation that the vast majority of members will behave properly if they have the support of best practice guidelines and training, and effective external scrutiny if misconduct is suspected. A *Code of Best Practice in Planning Procedures* was recommended and subsequently adopted by the Standards Board for England.

Part of the evidence base that the Nolan Committee had access to was a study commissioned from the School of Planning, Oxford Brookes University, and published by the RTPI in March 1997. It was the first systematic, nationally-based study to be conducted into how elected members carry out their role and responsibilities in the planning system. Three of the issues examined by the study are of value here. These were firstly, how councillors, approach their work and role; secondly, what it is like serving on a planning committee; and thirdly, the issue of planning policy and decision-making.

Almost all members saw representing the people of their ward, making policy for the local authority as a whole and serving the public interest as major aspects of the job of being a local councillor. There was a slight tendency for chairs and sub-chairs of planning committees to give greater weight to the broader policy-making responsibility. Fewer than half of the whole sample mentioned representing the principles of the ward party as part of the job of a councillor. Backbenchers gave greater emphasis to ward responsibilities than did chairs and sub-chairs of planning committees.

The majority of the councillors agreed that the planning committee was one of the most popular positions for elected members in local government, but supplementary comments indicated that 'popularity' could be a misnomer for some councillors, and that serving on planning committees could be a 'mixed blessing'. Elected members felt obliged to become members of planning committees to maintain a watching brief on development in their locality. Councillors were caught between their wish to be seen to be 'doing things' and yet not being associated with policies and actions that were unpopular. It seems that the popularity of planning committees is related to the type of local authority, with shire district councillors more likely to see it as a key function, while in the larger county or unitary authorities, members find competing policy areas to be as or more interesting and popular.

Members frequently breach the framework of planning policies at the local level. There appeared to be a contradiction between the majority view

15

of councillors that Section 54A of the 1990 Act provided a change for the better in development planning and development control, and the evidence of officers that party politics come into play on some occasions in over half of the sample authorities (and that, in particular, there are some topics where party political views are especially strong and likely to be brought to bear on local decisions). Also, not surprisingly, backbenchers are more likely to adopt a ward perspective in making town planning decisions, as compared with senior councillors who are more aware and appreciative of agreed planning policies.

The Nolan Report stimulated a strong debate on the role of councillors following its publication, and in 2001 Matthew Taylor, then director of the Institute for Public Policy Research (IPPR) and now chief executive of the Royal Society of Arts (RSA), and Paul Wheeler, head of member development at the Improvement and Development Agency (IDeA), published a pamphlet entitled 'In Defence of Councillors'. The analysis contained in their essay is still relevant, and is an important guide to understanding the political influence on councillors.

Taylor and Wheeler (2001) assert that successive governments have put considerable energy into minimising the capacity of councillors to make decisions or wield power. As well as the executive reforms in the 2000 Local Government Act, the government has on the one hand tied up local authorities in a web of central regulations, targets and inspections, while on the other hand it has removed local authority functions and set up new bodies to drive priorities such as neighbourhood renewal and a variety of Action Zones. In addition, there is the emergence of the 'quango state' in which local decisions are made by executives and non-executives appointed by central government.

The managerialist critique of councillors tends to focus on two managerial attributes said to be lacking: namely, impartiality and expertise. It is argued that while the decisions made by councillors are clouded by political ambition, inflexible beliefs and internecine conflicts, the judgement of managers is evidence-based, objective and disinterested. Councillors are seen as part-time amateurs, while managers are seen as full-time professionals.

There are two main expressions of the rise of managerialism. These are a consumerist approach to service delivery and the requirements of Best Value targets together with the greater use of external management consultants. There is clearly a case for managerialism, for councillors not to be taking detailed operational decisions or using irrelevant or inappropriate political criteria to determine the allocation of local resources. However, much of the business of local government is about the political reconciliation of competing interests, and here political parties have a vital function in organising choices in elections and in ensuring that political accountability relates to the pursuit of broad values.

Taylor and Wheeler (2001) explain that although the social and cultural base of the political parties has been eroded, the control of these parties over the formal representative democratic process has, if anything, increased. Parties control who can be elected, and have first call on the accountability of politicians. This accountability is both downwards to the activists who campaign for and reselect the candidate, and upwards to the party hierarchy, whose patronage will determine the career prospects of the councillor. Particularly in councils run by their own party, councillors will be powerfully constrained by the patronage of the executive, and 'it will continue to be in party group meetings rather than public scrutiny sessions that the executive will be called to account by the majority group' (Taylor and Wheeler, 2001).

As part of the modernising planning agenda, the Department for Communities and Local Government commissioned a report on councillor involvement in planning decisions, which was published in 2007. The conclusions were that better and more regular training for local authority councillors and greater involvement in forward and strategic planning would improve the predictability and quality of local planning decisions. The report can be seen as part of the managerialist agenda described by Taylor and Wheeler, for the researchers – undeterred by the conclusions of the Nolan Report – caution that 'There can also be an inherent conflict between the representative role of Councillors and their 'quasi-judicial' role in determining planning applications' (Department for Communities and Local Government, 2007). The authors expand on these concerns in their comments on the new local governance that envisages the backbencher performing a scrutiny role on the executive as well as being a champion on behalf of his or her ward. When considered in the context of planning committees and development control decision-making, this may suggest a potential conflict, with backbenchers increasingly championing community and ward interests, utilising the planning application process as a way of challenging the executive's policies.

These concerns about the role of members on planning committees also emerged in the Barker Review of housing supply (2004). The background to the Review was that while demand for housing is increasing for a number of reasons, the construction of new houses in the UK is falling and is at historically low levels. Among a large number of recommendations that cover all aspects of the supply of housing, some relate to the role of elected members in the planning system. The Review proposes three alternative routes to gaining planning permission, as follows:

17

- Existing route – applicants seek either outline or detailed planning permission. The application is considered and determined by councillors (or delegated to officers for determination). If outline permission is granted, then applicants re-run the process for detailed permission.
- Outline-only route – applicants would put forward an outline proposal with greater detail than currently found in an outline application. If acceptable, permission would be granted by councillors who would identify reserved matters. That would mark the end of the councillors' involvement in the proposals, as officers would be charged with ensuring that reserved matters were addressed in a satisfactory manner.
- Design code route – under this route, applicants would put forward a proposal which was supported by a design code. Codes would be prepared by applicants and the local authority. Councillors would consider this information and satisfy themselves that the code was consistent with planning guidance; if so, a Local Development Order would be adopted essentially to grant planning permission for that development, subject to compliance with the design code. Officers would then ensure that the development as implemented complied with the design code.

No decisions have been made on these recommendations, but the Barker Review continues, and they can be seen as part of an evolving discourse which perceives councillor involvement in the planning process as obstructive, unpredictable and lacking in consistency, contributing towards an overall national failure to achieve economic, environmental and social goals. Against this background, it is important to try and understand the current role of councillors in the spatial planning system.

The Ideological Political Spectrum

Robert Leach (2002) provides a useful typology of the ideological influences on British politics. Despite the problems of ambiguity and inconsistencies, Leach employs the conventional Left–Right political spectrum, which places communism on the far Left, socialists and social democrats on the moderate Left with liberals in the Centre, conservatives on the moderate Right and fascists on the far Right. Feminism and the Green movement are difficult to locate on the Left–Right spectrum, and some would argue that Left and

Right describe the old politics, while these new movements represent a new politics, which is more appropriately viewed as a discourse (which could also include the politics of pressure and protest, such as the campaigners against new roads or airport expansion).

Attitudes towards the state have been a massive theme in British politics, particularly for the mainstream ideologies of liberalism, conservatism and socialism. Nineteenth-century liberalism sought to uphold the liberty of the individual against the encroachment of the state, while the new liberalism of the early twentieth century attempted to reconcile this individual liberty with state-inspired social reform. The first planning legislation, in 1909, was part of this reforming agenda. During the 1930s, town planning legislation mirrored the conflicting ideologies that were unsuccessfully reconciled in the various attempts of national or coalition governments, and there was no consensus that would permit a comprehensive regulated system of town and country planning control. The experiences of the Second World War and the apparent success of a planned economy provided the impetus for a dominant British interpretation of socialism which involved the growth of state intervention to provide public services, including a comprehensive system of plan making and planning control. That survived until the Thatcher government sought to re-draw the boundary between the public and private spheres.

Following Thatcherism, the post-war Keynesian consensus has not been restored, but there has been the emergence of a professional elite discourse which advocates a large amount of centralised control of public services including spatial planning, within a neo-liberal, market-orientated economy. The main opposition to this centralism is beginning to emerge from an advocacy of localism predicated on both green and community politics.

An alternative approach to England's political history is offered by David Marquand (2008). He identifies in twentieth-century politics four rich traditions that stretch back into the past and it is these that have dominated politics rather than conservatism and socialism. The first is 'Whig paternalism', best exemplified in the career of Stanley Baldwin, who became Prime Minister in June 1935, and now most closely associated with the 'one nation' wing of the Conservative Party. The second is 'Tory nationalism', which is a tradition binding Lord Salisbury, Enoch Powell and Margaret Thatcher. The third is 'democratic collectivism' characterised by the traditions of the Fabian Society and Labour planners such as Stafford Cripps and Hugh Dalton, who believed that rationalism and the intervention of the state would deliver a fairer and more prosperous society. The fourth, and in Marquand's view the least successful, but the one he admires most, is 'democratic republicanism', which he attributes to the philosophers Milton, Mill and Tawney, emphasising civil liberties, public participation and local democracy.

The Ideological Issues

From the historical review in this book, I have identified the ideological issues that distinguish the major political parties in their approach to planning policies, and which still divide the parties. The planning controversies that feature in the daily press are usually about these issues, and an understanding of how the political parties have come to their respective views on these issues is important to anyone who wants to understand the look and shape of contemporary England. I explore these issues in Chapter 13 and show how the political parties have come to their respective views, but here I briefly set out the contrasting views.

Sustainability and Global Warming

John Major was the first head of a G7 government to announce that he would attend the Rio Earth Summit in June 1992, at which the British government committed to both cutting the emission of greenhouse gases and biodiversity. Environment Secretary John Gummer introduced the Environment Act in 1995, and the White Paper on sustainable development. New Labour has maintained and expanded the legislation so that in policy terms sustainability is at the centre of national planning policy. Gordon Brown launched the eco towns initiative as a demonstration of how necessary additional housing could be harnessed to innovations in energy saving and improved sustainability in terms of design and layout. The majority of the initial launches of eco towns were located in Conservative-controlled local authority areas, and the ferocity of the opposition now threatens to derail the scheme as promoters question whether the eco towns have an assured political future. The central issue is how to reconcile urban expansion – the European Union (EU) predicts that Great Britain will later this century overtake Germany as the largest member state in terms of population – with the commitments made at Rio.

Housing Land and House Building

During the past 40 years both major parties in power have failed to address the housing issue, and particularly that of affordability. Under Gordon Brown and his economic advisor Kate Barker, New Labour envisaged the private sector, in a deregulated planning regime, being able to step up housing production, but the 'credit crunch' has placed a large question mark over that approach.

Development Betterment and Planning Gain

The ideological issue is: how can the financial benefits that emanate from a planning decision be equably distributed not only to the owner of the land that benefits from the decision but to the community that has transferred the benefit? All the major parties since the 1909 Act have attempted a betterment levy concept. The absence of this tax has influenced the attitude of decision-makers to development. The Labour Party has tried on four occasions to legislate for this betterment and, notwithstanding the disappearance of Labour's Clause Four nationalisation aspirations under Blair, the collection of development betterment remains a leitmotif for the party.

A further difficulty is the lack of precision and fairness in the present system of acquiring from a developer reasonable payments for on- or off-site infrastructure facilities necessitated by a development and other planning gains which might be thought necessary to facilitate such a development. At the moment, such payments are negotiated on a case by case basis, normally through the medium of planning agreements. Again, various governments have wrestled with this issue, and the Barker Review of housing delivery has sought to try and introduce a tariff approach to infrastructure contributions, which the Conservatives appear willing to support.

Delivery and Implementation

The means by which development, particularly in the field of housing, can be most efficiently and equably delivered has been a major issue between the parties. The Labour Party ushered in the 'new towns' by means of the development corporations while the Conservatives used similar agencies to deliver the urban regeneration of the inner cities in the 1980s. Opposition in the shires prevented the use of the concept outside the cities. New Labour, impatient of the lack of delivery of new housing, now brings forward new town-style development corporations in the growth areas that bypass local planning authorities. Local authorities have often been regarded as inadequate for this task, particularly in areas of substantial growth, but there are differences as to the form, composition and political accountability of new agencies tasked with regeneration.

Local Autonomy and Local Government

The autonomy that can be delegated to local planning authorities and to elected members by central government in the making of planning policy and the planning decisions that are taken is a major difference between the parties. The Liberal Democrats have supported localism, and at varying times the Conservatives have championed local autonomy, but Blair continued the micro-management of local government begun by Margaret Thatcher. In opposition, parties have championed local autonomy but, as Jenkins (2006) has observed, centralisation remains a powerful force.

Regional Government

Throughout the political history of spatial planning, the Conservatives have resisted moves for regional government. There has been a long-standing fear that if regional democratic bodies were based on existing major provincial cities, such authorities would tend to fall under Labour control. New Labour implemented its devolution manifesto for Scotland and Wales and in England now champions a model based on the regional development agencies rather than the regional assemblies that are to be wound up by 2010 in the Planning Reform Bill 2007. The Conservatives have consistently opposed regional government and have pledged to repeal the legislation (Cameron, 2008).

Green Belt Policy

Green belt policy was first advanced by professionals such as Professor Patrick Abercombie in 1944 as part of the County of London Plan, and introduced to London in the Town & Country Planning Act 1947. After the 1947 Act, most policy development concerning green belts has come from Conservative administrations (1955, 1988 and 1995). Even during the Thatcher era, green belt policy was not seriously challenged. The concept has had widespread popular support. Its effects are apparent around England's towns and cities which mainly have the same built-up edges that they had at the end of 1939. This control, it might be argued, also ensured that the rich and powerful who lived in the countryside had their rural ambience safeguarded. Labour has often appeared ambivalent towards the policy, particularly in its concerns regarding housing needs, and the new quango Natural England has promised a policy review.

Community Politics

Early government attempts at public participation in the 1970s now look contrived and patronising. The Liberal revival since that date owed much to community politics. Against a current background of concern about global warming and sustainability and the rise of Green parties elsewhere in Europe, is this a possible portent of political changes in England? The means by which emissions can be curbed is likely to be a further area of difference between the parties.

Modernising Planning

This has been the central thrust of New Labour thinking on planning since their election success in 1997. New Labour inherited a system of local government traumatised by the Thatcher years, and has helped local government to regain its confidence. However, the modernising agenda threatens to marginalise the role of many councillors, and raises important questions of local autonomy.

New Forms of Local Governance

Planning decisions are part of the bedrock of local democracy. Many councillors come into local government because of an interest in planning or because of a previous involvement in a planning issue or controversy. There have been few examples where councils have been prepared to delegate planning decisions to local area committees. Oxford City Council which operates an area-based committee structure for the majority of its services is an exception. There is now a huge tension between the search on the one hand for new forms of local governance and for speed and efficiency on the other.

Visionary Planning

These issues on which there are differences between the major political parties in their approach to planning show that an understanding of the politics of planning is an essential basis from which to appreciate contemporary England and the country that it has become. At the same time as I have studied these issues, I have also been struck by the discourse that has emerged. David Dutton, in his seminal book *British Politics Since 1945* explores the convergent and contrasting views of political historians as to whether, after 1945, there was a consensus among the political parties (Dutton, 1997). His conclusion is that bearing in mind that the duty of opposition parties is to oppose, the post-war consensus can most clearly be seen not in relation to the two political parties, nor even as between governments and opposition, but in terms of the fundamental continuity between the government elites of the two parties, alternating in power in succession to one another. This has a particular resonance in spatial planning and is currently evident in Prime Minister Gordon Brown's search for an agreed planning governance which can deliver the three million additional dwellings identified as needed in the Barker Report.

Politics now permeates planning at every level. Whether it is the publication of a planning policy statement, which aims fundamentally to alter the lifestyle of a community, the decision of a county environmental committee on the direction of growth, or the decision of a shire district council such as West Berkshire on the planning application from an international giant such as Vodafone for a massive new office campus in the countryside outside Newbury, these are all essentially *political* acts. Officers advise, but the link between planning decisions and political considerations is now absolute.

It was not always like this. Planning's founding fathers thought politics should be kept out of the process. Thomas Sharp, in his prefatory note to *Oxford Replanned* published in 1948 exclaimed,

> The task has proved to be an onerous one, and now that it is completed I cannot with certainty expect that the result will be generally acceptable even in its main features, let alone in all its details. Indeed I know very well that some of the suggestions I make will rouse bitter opposition in some quarters. But, whatever one may suggest, that is unavoidable in a city where there are so many strong and opposing interests. If I had allowed my mind to dwell on them, both the responsibility of advancing proposals which will, perhaps, leave their mark for good or ill on this old and famous city, and the powerful nature of the possible opposition to them, might so have intimidated me that it might have seemed better to play for safety. But I have not attempted to play for safety. With a full sense of the responsibility that has been placed on me, I have suggested whatever measures seem to me to be necessary, without regard to the power of those who may be affected by them.

It is worth spending a few moments examining Sharp's career because he was probably the epitome of the idealistic planner, fiercely independent and suspicious of political interests, but also a popular writer and well known in his day. Educated at council schools, he had worked in local government before becoming a lecturer in town and country planning at Durham University. During the 1930s he published a number of influential books in which he bemoaned the suburban sprawl that was creeping across England's countryside. *Town And Countryside* (1931) and *English Panorama* (1936) are polemic and attracted a wide audience. During the Second World War, he prepared plans for the rebuilding of Durham and Exeter and in May 1945 was instructed by Oxford City Council to prepare a report on the planning and development of the city. The council was required to prepare a development plan under the Town and Country Planning Act 1947, and to that end commissioned Sharp to advise it. Sharp's report on the city (*Oxford Replanned*) was published as a lavishly illustrated book by the Architectural Press in 1948. His main recommendations were that the car factories should be moved to a more favourable location elsewhere in the country, that the High should be bypassed by a Merton Mall and that the city should expand the shopping area near Carfax rather than develop suburban satellites. They were inevitably controversial but, during his time at Oxford, Sharp became a friend of and was championed by John Betjeman who, during the critical two years 1946 to 1948, was secretary of the Oxford Preservation Trust – then as now a leading ginger group in Oxford. Sir John was to describe Sharp as 'our most sensitive and controversial town planner'. John Edwards, the Oxford City deputy town clerk, thought otherwise (Hillier, 2002). He stated:

> Through his inability to compromise, and his bluntness in argument and inability to suffer fools gladly, [Sharp] was unable to fit in with the process of planning by committee. Perhaps it was TS's misfortune to have been born too late; the age which produced Brunel and Telford might have found him better employment than our own was able to.

Betjeman's friendship with Thomas Sharp was quite surprising for in 1945 John Murray had published the fourth volume of his poems entitled *New Bats In Old Belfries* published by John Murray which included the poem: 'The Planaster's Vision'. The second verse reflects the Poet Laureate's long-held suspicion of bureaucracy and administrative planning and his scepticism of the new breed of planner that had emerged during the war excited by the redevelopment possibilities created by the widespread devastation caused by the blitz:

> I have a Vision of The Future, chum,
> The workers' flats in fields of soya beans
> Tower up like silver pencils, score on score:

And Surging Millions hear the Challenge come
From microphones in communal canteens
'No Right! No Wrong! All's perfect, evermore.'

Perhaps Betjeman was attracted to Sharp's no-nonsense approach as he had, like Betjeman in the 1930s, raised his voice in protest against the ongoing suburban sprawl, but Betjeman in his poem acutely touches on the essence of the ethos of the professional town planner: the need for a 'Vision' to guide future development. It is of course this tendency that brings the planner hard up against politics, particularly at a local level, where decisions are taken often with an eye on the next election rather than a decade hence.

Betjeman and Sharp did eventually cross swords later in 1949 at a debate held in the village hall of Letcombe, Berkshire, which was broadcast live on BBC radio. Betjeman had taken up the cause of the villagers who wanted a public inquiry into proposals by the Wantage rural district council to shift the population to a larger adjacent village. Sharp, who supported this move, said of the village, 'It is a slum, a rural slum'.

Many influences have been at work, the following being key:

Margaret Thatcher's Legacy

When Prime Minister Margaret Thatcher capped local authorities, encouraged the contracting-out of many services formerly carried out by local authorities and privatised the councils' housing stock, many councillors found that serving on the planning committee was one of the few arenas left where they had any influence, and preferable to the managerial demands made on members by being on public amenity and public protection committees. A high profile on the planning committee could ensure re-election. This has been encouraged by the increasing practice of allowing local residents, parish councils and applicants to address committees. The officer's report can frequently be sidelined while committee members and the public engage in, often entertaining, debate.

The Professionalism of Members

Many leading local politicians spend an inordinate amount of time on council business. Early retirement for many has meant that they have both the time and the financial independence to devote a great many hours to local government. Such politicians can often be seen at their desks before the council staff arrive. In essence this professionalism is encouraged by the changes that Tony Blair brought to local government with directly elected mayors and cabinet-style decision-taking, with many local members taking on the role of constituency backbenchers with little influence on actual policy-making. In this milieu the planning portfolio holder is as much a full-time planner as the chief officer. This point is given added emphasis by the government's decision that all elected members will be given guidance on their planning training needs depending on their particular role. This is in response to the Nolan Report (1997) that recommended that 'all members of an authority's planning committee should receive training in the system'.

Public Involvement

Public participation emerged in the 1970s but the public has never shown much interest in the difficult and time-consuming task of actually preparing plans. However, in this last decade they have shown every interest in the actual business of *taking* planning decisions. No local politician can ignore the groundswell of opposition that 'nimbyism' can provoke.

Hung Councils

Many local authorities in England are hung, with no party in overall control. This provides a fertile ground for all sorts of local alliances as councillors from different parties find common cause in pursuit of a local agenda. In Oxfordshire, where for 20 years no overall party had absolute control, the county council's initial decision was to direct the major growth of Didcot – a town originally signalled for expansion in Sir Patrick Abercrombie's South East Plan published during the Second World War – to the north-east of the town. This was contrary to the advice of the environment director and was decided by a single vote. The Labour group supported the local Labour Didcot councillor who proposed the motion, and a number of neighbouring Tory councillors were also in support. Subsequently the decision was reversed when elections introduced new cross-party alliances.

A rueful commentary on this increasing politicisation was contained in an interview with former chief planning officer Derek Kingaby who retired in 2001:

> Politicians have seized control in a much firmer way. The result was that heads rolled if you disagreed. There was a general sense that professional planners basically had to learn that whereas before honesty and being forthright were seen as worthwhile qualities, they were no longer qualities that were going to serve your best interests.
>
> (Dewar, 2004)

He bemoaned that local politicians' objectives are nearly always short-term and that they would not take difficult decisions: 'They will put them off. That is no way forward and not what planning is all about'.

The Role of the Courts

Traditionally the courts have been very reluctant to be seen to interfere with the administration of the planning system. Lord Hoffman's speech in the Tesco case (House of Lords, 1995) succinctly summed up the position: 'If there is one principle of planning law more firmly settled than any other, it is that matters of planning judgement are within the exclusive province of the local planning authority or the Secretary of State'.

This autonomy, allied with the tendency of the courts to widen the scope of what constitutes a material consideration in the determination of the planning application, has given enormous discretion to the decision-taker, whether it be planning officer, planning committee or planning inspector. This has proved particularly the case in the controversial area of planning gain.

Planning Gain

In April 1982, the RTPI endorsed the following definition:

> A Planning Gain is a benefit which accrues when, in connection with the obtaining of a planning permission, a developer incurs some additional expenditure or other liability beyond that required to meet normally accepted planning standards in providing a benefit he would not otherwise choose to provide, but which the Local Planning Authority has justifiable planning grounds for seeking to achieve.
>
> (Royal Town Planning Institute, 1982)

This is as good a working definition as any and illustrates how local planning authorities have tried to widen the definition of planning gain to include community benefits, rather than to be tied down to the narrow requirements of access or drainage to a site. At each stage, government has sought to try and restrict the definition by setting down precise criteria. The courts, on the other hand, through judicial authority, have ever-widened the scope of planning gain, and planning authorities armed with Section 54A of the 1990 Act strive to introduce extensive shopping lists of planning gain through Local Plan policies.

In previous guidance in 1991 the government actually tried to ban the use of the expression 'planning gain', stating that the term had no statutory significance and was not found in the planning acts. Despite these strictures, the expression has not been lost from the vocabulary of planning. The planning system is adversarial and planning gain has a justification to both applicant and local planning authority.

Section 54a of the 1990 Act

So we have the paradoxical situation that on the one hand through Section 54a of the 1990 Act, and now retained as Section 386 of the 2004 Act, the role of the development plan was elevated to its current pre-eminence, while on the other hand planning decisions are increasingly taken with an eye to their political significance, whether it is a 'call-in' by the Secretary of State or an application approved by the planning committee of a shire district against officers' advice.

It is also worth remembering that the introduction of the plan-led system came through a political decision. During the passage of the Bill through Parliament, the Labour opposition was critical of what they saw as lukewarm support by the then Conservative government for the role of development plans in decision-taking. The Tory response – Section 54a – surprised everyone by its unequivocal support for the planning system.

Human Rights Act

When the Human Rights Act 1998 came into force, many in the planning and legal professions thought that the Act paved the way for the creation of a truly independent planning inspectorate or environmental court. This view was encouraged by the High Court judgement in the Alconbury cases when the judges ruled that the planning system was incompatible with the Human Rights Act. The High Court ruled that the Secretary of State's planning powers denied protestors and developers the right to a fair trial, and were thus incompatible with Article 6 of the Act. 'He cannot be both policy-maker and decision-maker' said Lord Justice Tuckey and Mr Justice Harrison, the two judges assigned to the cases. As is now well known, the Law Lords did not support that judgement, and there was sufficient judicial control of the process to ensure compliance with the European Convention. Lord Nolan summarised the central issue as follows:

> In the relatively small and populous island which we occupy, the decisions made by the Secretary of State will often have acute social, economic and environmental implications. A degree of central control is essential to the orderly use and

development of town and country. Parliament has entrusted the requisite degree of control to the Secretary of State, and it is to Parliament that he must account for his exercise of it. To substitute for the Secretary of State an independent and impartial body with no central electoral accountability would not only be a recipe for chaos: it would be profoundly undemocratic.

Many who are critical of the Law Lords' decision have described it as both pragmatic and politically expedient: 'Their lordships have decided that the planning process is essentially administrative and not judicial' (Holgate and Gilbey, 2001). The implications of the judgement are the importance to the spatial planning system of democratically elected councillors.

Local Government Management

Local government at district level moved extraordinarily quickly to implement the changes that the government stipulated in the 2000 Local Government Act. Many councils now have in place a structure of cabinet and leader. Decisions on planning applications remain with the planning committee but planning policy formulation clearly resides within the cabinet.

Modernising Planning

Planning ministers have pledged to modernise the planning system. Politicians when they first come into office pledge to reform planning but after a while frustration creeps in as the system proves extremely resistant to change. But now, as economic difficulties loom, the Treasury (which is pro-development, to boost the economy), has become fretful of the apparent lack of progress in reforming the planning system and is perceived as the force behind many of the changes introduced by the 2004 Planning and Compulsory Purchase Act.

Community Involvement

The 2004 Act has placed much greater emphasis on community involvement in the preparation of the Core Strategy and the other documents to be included in the LDF. This in turn brings ward members much more into the planning debate, requiring them to face the difficult choices which in an earlier age were left to the salaried officers.

Election of Officers

In these twisting currents full of hard rocks and shifting sands, what role should the professional planner take? Traditionally the political affiliation, if any, of an officer played no part in the selection process for a top job in local government. But in the new era of streamlined local government on the Blair model, perhaps the chief planning officer should be elected. Would a mandate from the electorate enhance his or her ability to drive through sustainable planning policies? Clearly there is a dilemma here. Planners who enter local government do so expecting to offer impartial professional advice to elected members, but the ground rules have changed.

As the planning process becomes more politicised, planners will need to decide whether they can actually make a recommendation or whether their role is to set out the planning implications of different decisions. Many planners will be content to accept that role but others may consider that their training and experience is not being properly channelled.

Or is there a third way? Ken Livingstone as a directly elected mayor took a high profile on many planning issues in London ranging from affordable housing to a high buildings policy. Planning policy and major planning decisions now emanate directly from the Mayor's Office, and Boris Johnson, in his opposition to high buildings, was able to capitalise on this in his 2008 London election campaign. In the section on the role of the councillor (see pp. 13), I described the pressures that are increasingly limiting the discretion of the councillor in planning decision-making. The role of elected mayor effectively transfers a large part of planning policy to a politician and reduces the influence of professional planners. The debate that this stimulated in London suggests that a system under which a series of candidates vie for the position of mayor would spark a greater interest in the democratic process and a more powerful debate about issues, particularly those to do with spatial planning. The White Paper *Communities in Control: Real People, Real Power*, launched in July 2008, supports the directly-elected mayor model, already in operation in 12 towns in addition to London, and wishes to see more mayors directly elected. The document also proposes to amend the 'Widdicombe' rules which forbid council workers above a certain salary band from being active in party politics. This would allow senior management to openly declare their political loyalties.

Lord Heseltine (2008) has said that if English cities are to become 'great' again, they must be handed back powers from central government, and be governed by elected leaders. He said that government should compel local authorities to take on the mayoral role and hand back decisions over funding that are currently in control of quangos such as the Housing Corporation and the regional development agencies. He argued that local authorities need to be trusted again so that the civil spirit that had characterised the great English cities could be reinvigorated. He also contrasted the current system of local government with a highly paid chief executive and a poorly paid council leader as 'ludicrous'.

Third Party Rights

The lack of any third party right of appeal against the grant of planning permission, other than judicial review (which is extremely difficult to achieve) means that objectors to a planning proposal must concentrate their efforts on persuading committee members to oppose, particularly where a proposal has the professional recommendation of support from the planning officer. Planning committee members, petitioned continually by objectors, can see their role on the committee as representing these third-party interests, rather than necessarily exercising the planning judgement of the decision-taker – the role delegated to them by the Secretary of State.

The Growth of Judicial Intervention

Two methods exist whereby the High Court can be called on to review the legality of a planning decision. Firstly there is the statutory right to challenge the decisions of the Secretary of State or local planning authority, although the opportunities to challenge the latter are very limited. Secondly, where there is no statutory right, the jurisdiction of the High Court applies and planning decisions can be challenged by way of an application for judicial review.

These factors have all contributed to the political nature of what is now spatial planning but for several decades the planning system was less politicised than now. A glance back at the origins of statutory spatial planning is revealing.

Consensus

Prior to the Second World War, the impetus for a comprehensive system of town and country planning was led by a professional elite who had tried to make work a partial and tentative system first put into place in 1909 by the Liberal government. After the Second World War both the major political parties, by then the Conservatives and Labour, agreed on the need and means to rebuild the nation, and planning was awarded a central role in that task. It was part of the wide range of economic and social policies described as the 'post-war Keynesian consensus'. The two parties differed on the financial means to introduce this planning system but this was not to fundamentally disturb this shared approach which was part of a political consensus which characterised British politics until the rise of Thatcherism.

As in so many other areas of British life, Thatcherism broke the mould and ushered in a market-led approach, which introduced New Right ideology into local government: 'What the Thatcherites left untouched was central government's control of how much of the 42 per cent of national income it takes in tax is spent' (Field, 2008). John Major's premiership appeared to signal a changed climate for the planning process that would have encouraged localism but under the Blair government since 1997, and accelerated under Brown, planning is to be increasingly market-led in the New Labour economic model that has borrowed much of the New Right economic thinking. For the Conservatives this shift on the part of New Labour poses many problems. David Cameron wishes to position the party in the political centre with a strong positive environmental agenda which recognises the issues raised by climate change and resource depletion, but his core constituency vote wishes to see a more discretionary, localised planning system not dominated by a central government agenda. This has produced latterly a commitment to "localism" (Cameron, 2008).

An administrative system born in wartime would of necessity display strong centralising instincts, but despite the adoption of New Conservative economic measures in planning, central government (whether Conservative or New Labour led) has continued to keep a tight rein on the planning activities of local government. Right-wing economists would see this as a paradox and evidence of a continuing Keynesian influence at the heart of planning. Others wish to see the preparation of plans be made more transparent and decision-taking more rooted in the communities that elect local politicians. As Simon Jenkins has argued in his influential book *Thatcher & Sons* (2006): 'The localist route to democratic revival is plausible.' However, in this introductory chapter I have demonstrated that despite the support for the role of councillors sitting on development committees evidenced in Lord Nolan's report and the judgement in the Alconbury case, competing voices such as the Barker Report see the involvement of councillors as obstructive and time-consuming. The government's modernising agenda for planning threatens to marginalise their role. There has been much criticism (Michell, 2008) of government initiatives that threaten the democratic accountability of planning decision-making – for example, transferring powers to unelected quangos and a new quango to decide on major projects such as power stations and airports – but with regard to the delegation of planning decisions to officers, councillors appear to have 'sleep-walked' into a situation where far fewer planning applications are determined by councillors than ten years ago.

Conclusions

All the political parties face a series of challenges that will determine their policies. I would summarise these as follows:

- England is now a post-industrial society having to earn a living in a rapidly changing world economy.
- Our way of life is more prosperous, households are greater in number but smaller in size, we are more car-based and we make huge demands on land for housing, work, shopping, leisure and travel.
- Urban renewal is required so that our society is more inclusive and sustainable.
- As consumers we want user-friendly services 24 hours a day, seven days a week, and via modern technology.
- As citizens we question more but want to own the decisions made in our name.

My own conclusions are that the over-centralised, visionary approach has had its day and the essentially political character of planning decisions as well as the preparation of plans must be made more transparent. Decision-taking must be more rooted in the communities that elect local politicians.

The challenge for politicians will be to demonstrate that they can take decisions looking to the longer term rather than short-term electoral advantage, and dispel the scepticism of the professional planning elite who have argued for almost a hundred years that only they are capable of this attribute. In his book *Profiles in Courage* (1956) published when he was a young senator, John F. Kennedy wrote thoughtfully and persuasively about political courage:

To be courageous, these stories makes clear, requires no exceptional qualifica- tions, no magic formula, no special combination of time, place and circumstance.

It is an opportunity that sooner or later is presented to us all. Politics merely furnishes one arena which imposes special tests of courage.

Political courage in planning requires local politicians to be prepared to take big decisions which may be locally unpopular, and for politicians in central government to resist the micro-management that has characterised so much of the politics of planning, has prevented the emergence of vigorous local democracy that characterised Victorian England, and which can now be experienced in Germany and Scandinavia.

References

Betjeman, J. (1945) *New Bats in Old Belfries*, Vol 4. London: John Murray.

British Property Federation (2008) *Evidence to the Communities and Local Government Committee's Inquiry into Planning Skills*, London: BPF, 7 May.

Cameron, D. (2008) Speech to LGA Conference, July.

Cherry, G. (1982) *The Politics Of Town Planning*. London: Longman, p. 71.

Corkindale, J. (2004) *The Land Use Planning System*. London: The Institute of Economic Affairs.

Crick, B. (1982) *In Defence of Politics*, 2nd edn. London: Penguin, p. 21.

Department for Communities and Local Government (2006) *Planning Policy Statement 12: Local Development Frameworks*, 2nd edn. London: DCLG.

Department for Communities and Local Government (2007) *Councillor Involvement in Planning Decisions*. London: DCLG, p. 14.

Department of Transport, Local Government and the Regions (2001) *Planning, Delivering a Fundamental Change*, Green Paper. London: HMSO.

Dewar, D. (2004) Interview with Derek Kingaby, *Planning Magazine*, 10 December, p. 13.

Dutton, D. (1997) *British Politics Since 1945*, 2nd edn. London: Blackwell, p. 10.

Evans, E. (2004) *Thatcher and Thatcherism*. London: Routledge.

Field, F. (2008) Government must be cut down to size, *Daily Telegraph*, 4 July.

Healey, P. (2007) *Urban Complexity and Spatial Strategies*. London: Routledge, p. 173.

Heseltine, M. (2008) Keynote address to Regeneration & Renewal Northern Summit, Manchester, 23 October.

Hillier, B. (2002) *John Betjeman: New Fame, New Love*. London: John Murray.

Holgate, D. and Gilbey, I. (2001) Business as usual, *Estates Gazette*, 19 May, pp 218–19.

House of Lords (1995) Judgement of Tesco Stores Ltd v Secretary of State for the Environment 2 *All ER* 636. London: House of Lords.

Jenkins, S. (2006) *Thatcher & Sons*. London: Allen Lane.

Kennedy, J.F. (1956) *Profiles in Courage*. New York: Harper, p. 225.

Leach, R. (2002) *Political Ideology in Britain*. London: Palgrave.

Local Government Association (2000) *The Planning User's Concordat*, July. London: LGA.

Marquand, D. (2008) *Britain Since 1918: The Strange Career of British Democracy*. London: Weidenfeld & Nicholson.

Mitchell, K. (2008) Speech to South East England Regional Assembly, 16 July.

Montgomery, J. and Thornley, A. (1990) *Radical Planning Initiatives*, Aldershot: Gower.

Moor, N. (1983) *The Planner and the Market*. London: George Godwin.

Moor, N. (1999) *The Paradox of Planning Politics*, *Planning*, September, p. 10.

Moor, N. (2004) Delivering the community vision, paper delivered to the Planning Summer School, University of Reading 3–6 September.

Nolan, Lord (1997) *Third Report of the Committee on Standards in Public Life: Standards of Conduct in Local Government*. London: The Stationery Office.

Office of the Deputy Prime Minister (2004) *The Barker Review of Land Use Planning*. London: ODPM.

Planning Magazine (2005) Correspondence of Andy Hey and George Reynolds, 4 November and 9 December.

Rhodes, R.A.W. (1997) *Understanding Governance: Policy Networks, Governance, Reflexibility and Accountability*. Buckingham: Open University Press.

Royal Town Planning Institute (1982) *Planning Gain*. London: RTPI.

Rydin, Y. (2003) *Urban & Environmental Planning in the UK*. London: Palgrave Macmillan.

School of Planning Oxford Brookes University (1997) *The Role of Elected Members in Plan Making & Development Control*. London: RTPI.

Self, P. (1961) *Cities in Flood*, 2nd edn. London Faber & Faber.

Sharp, T. (1948) *Oxford Replanned*. London: The Architectural Press.

Taylor, M. and Wheeler, P. (2001) *In Defence of Councillors*. London: Improvement and Development Agency, p. 32.

Tewdwr-Jones, M. (2002) *The Planning Polity*. London: Routledge.

Trevor Roberts Associates (2008) *Evidence to the Select Committee on Communities and Local Government*, The Eleventh Report of the Communities and Local Government Committee. London: HOC Publications.

Von Hayek, F. (1944) *The Road to Surfdom*. Chicago: University of Chicago Press.

Further reading

Department for Communities and Local Government (2006) *Planning Policy Statement 12: Local Development Frameworks*, 2nd edn. London: DCLG.

Manns, S. and Wood, C. (2002) Public speaking at the development control committee, *Journal of Planning Law*, pp. 382–97.

2

The Early Years: 1909–1939, Planning Comes of Age

The Liberal Reforms

Town planning as a legislative arm of modern government developed from public health and housing policies in the nineteenth century. Population increase and the growth of towns led to public health problems and legislation was passed (e.g. the 1875 Public Health Act) allowing local authorities to make and enforce building bylaws for controlling street width and the height, construction and layout of buildings. Improvements though they were, the bylaws created dreary and ugly towns. More imaginative experiments under private patronage took place at Saltaire (1853), Bourneville (1878) and Port Sunlight (1887). The Garden City Association was founded by Ebenezer Howard in 1889 (it subsequently renamed itself the Town & Country Planning Association, TCPA) a year after the publication of his book *Tomorrow, a Peaceful Path to Real Reform*, republished in 1902 as *Garden Cities of Tomorrow*. The Association, not surprisingly, campaigned for the introduction of garden cities, the first of which was begun at Letchworth in 1903. Aided by the capable architect Raymond Unwin, this scheme, and even more convincingly Hampstead Garden Suburb, begun in North London in 1907, set new standards of layout by adapting to contours and natural features, and embracing comparatively low densities with sizeable back gardens. But it was not until the reforming Liberal government of 1908 that the first legislation bearing the description 'town planning' came onto the statue book in the shape of The Housing, Town Planning etc. Act which was finally enacted in 1909. The legislation was drafted on German experience of town extension plans which contained the rudimentary zoning of land uses as well as laying down a pattern of new roads. From the 1870s, cities in many German states had legal powers to plan and control town extensions, and Britain was perceived as lagging behind its continental rival.

The most remarkable visual feature of England before the First World

War was how compact its cities and towns were compared with the sprawling city regions of the twenty-first century. Post-1918 development in the Manchester conurbation, by way of example, spread over five times the area covered by earlier development, although it only contains 25 per cent more people (Self, 1961). The impetus for planning at this time was not a desire to control the endless growth of new development, which became a preoccupation in the 1930s, but was more rooted in social reform and the need for housing for the working class. In the first decade of the 1900s there was a dramatic fall in newly-built houses from 150,000 to 100,000. Both David Lloyd George and Winston Churchill (then in the Liberal government) after the 1906 Liberal election victory thought that a platform of social reform would protect the Liberal Party from the threat posed by the recently established Labour Party, which had set out to attract support from the working classes. The Liberal programme included a state pension for the first time and the Planning Bill. Despite Victorian improvements to drainage and sanitary reform, diseases caused by overcrowding and poverty were still rife, and the average life expectancy was just over 50. But there was a promise of better times ahead. The first purpose-built cinemas were appearing, Selfridges opened in London, Woolworth's launched in Liverpool, while the first rugby match was played at Twickenham.

The Housing, Town Planning etc. Act 1909

This Act was introduced by John Burns, the president of the Local Government Board (a Cabinet post earlier spurned by Winston Churchill who instead went to the Board of Trade), who on being appointed the first 'working man' Cabinet member in 1905 is reputed to have said to his leader, Cambell-Bannerman, 'Sir, 'Enry, you never did a more popular thing in your life' (Jenkins, 2001). Introducing the second reading of the Bill, Burns explained to the House of Commons:

> The object of the Bill is to provide a domestic condition for the people in which their physical health, their morals, their character and their whole social condition can be improved by what we hope to secure in this Bill. The Bill aims in broad outline at, and hopes to secure, the home healthy, the house beautiful, the town pleasant, the city dignified and the suburb salubrious.
>
> (Hansard 1908)

One of its first objectives would be to ban the building of back-to-back houses, which were such a feature of industrial England.

The Bill was indeed popular and was carried by 128 votes to 20. A dissenting voice was Mr Hicks-Beach who felt that working-class housing should be a burden borne by the Exchequer rather than local rates. Much of the Bill dealt with health and housing but local authorities were encouraged to control the development of new housing areas. A leader in the *Daily Graphic* for 6 April 1909 (Heap, 1975) declared:

> So far as Town Planning is concerned there is more to be said for the proposals of the Bill. If we could be sure that local authorities would always take a far-seeing view of the future requirements of our towns we should all be glad to give them large powers of control. Unfortunately, the men who now sit upon municipal councils do not inspire very much confidence as regards the present, and still less as regards the future.

This leader was singularly prophetic for it was a recurring anxiety of governments through to the Second World War that local authorities could not be trusted to prepare town planning schemes without detailed parliamentary approval. As a consequence the legislation was unnecessarily complex and, as we will see, achieved very little in the face of the massive inter-war building boom.

However, the Bill empowered local authorities to make town planning schemes (which had to be approved by central government) with the general object of securing proper sanitary conditions, amenity and convenience in connection with the laying out and use of land. The new control was an optional exercise for local authorities and, even when used, it could only be applied to the developing fringes or suburbs of established towns. The open countryside was not included in the scope of the Act and unsurprisingly, given the extent of consultation required, few schemes were actually completed under the 1909 Act.

Section 58 provided for the payment of compensation to owners whose property was injuriously affected by the scheme, but for the first time in English legislation it authorised the local authorities to recover betterment from anyone whose property was increased in value by the scheme. Only three schemes affecting a total area of less than 10,000 acres were completed by 1919. One example was the Ruislip-Northwood scheme in North London approved by the Board in 1914. It was notable for including a clause enabling the authority to control the external appearance of buildings. Another prepared for East Birmingham showed a few proposed new roads and road widenings, some playing fields and allotments, industrial areas and residential areas with maximum densities varying between 30 and 45 dwellings to the hectare (12 and 18 houses to the acre). What the 1909 Act did not do was establish a means of implementing the planning schemes. The expectation was that the housing would be put up in accordance with the bylaw regulations, for which formal permission was necessary. Essentially the Act was perceived as a vehicle by which local authorities could supply new working-class housing.

Indeed there has been a perception that these early town planning controls were not altruistically promoted for the good of the people as a whole, but primarily because the interests of the ruling classes were threatened by the lack of planning, which caused congestion and lower productivity. This is to underestimate the reforming zeal of the Liberal administration. In April 1909 the Chancellor, Lloyd George, had introduced his 'People's Budget', and a central aim was to provide the finance for the ambitious social agenda. One of the features was a 20 per cent tax on the increase in land value that resulted when land in urban areas inflated massively in price because of the general increase in the prosperity of the community. It was fiercely criticised by the landowners, and peers like the Duke of Westminster complained that Lloyd George would reduce them to poverty (Morgan, 1981). The House of Lords threw out the budget and this impasse ultimately led, following a further election which the Liberals won, to the Parliament Act which curbed the powers of the second chamber and asserted the primacy of the Commons over the House of Lords. In retrospect we can see that this first systematic attempt to introduce planning control was part of a broad reforming movement to improve social and economic conditions, and town planning was seen for much of the twentieth century until the Thatcherite revolution as a component of the social welfare programme

One important development stimulated by the 1909 Act was the formation of the Town Planning Institute in 1914, with articles of association signed in September. Earlier meetings had been held in 1913 of a small group of people from four other professions (architecture, municipal engineering, law and surveying), the purpose being to advance the study of town planning and civic design. From these humble beginnings the new profession grew.

Although the 1909 Act had little effect on the form of the built environment, its importance was that it was the embryo from which planning law was to grow. It introduced the concept that building should be guided by the plan, the crucial role of local authorities, that planning should be added to their executive powers over housing and public health, and the need for compensation and betterment in relation to the profits made from development.

The Tudor Walters Report

Published at the end of the First World War in 1918, this report on the design of low-cost housing had a huge impact on the appearance of England. It recommended development of single family housing at about 12 houses per net residential acre (30 per hectare), which was only 25 per cent of the density of the old bylaw housing. The conclusions of the report were heavily influenced by the work of Barry Parker and Raymond Unwin, who were the dominant professional figures of the Garden City movement. They first came to prominence in 1902 with their scheme for Rowntree's industrial village of New Earswick, were successful in the competition to design Letchworth New Town in 1903, and shortly after in 1906 the Hampstead Garden Suburb. Both Fabians, they had been much influenced by the ideas of Ebenezer Howard, particularly the need to plan for green belts around new development. Their design influence can be seen in the public housing schemes of the 1920s and 1930s, for example the vast Wythenshawe estate built south of Manchester in 1930. As we shall see shortly, these estates, built at relatively low densities, had their critics who were concerned at the loss of countryside represented by this development. The standards recommended by the Tudor Walters Report did not extend to the 2 million houses built by speculative builders between the two world wars, so that the council houses built at this time were larger and of better quality than the privately built houses.

The Housing & Town Planning Act 1919

The first revision came after the First World War in 1919, enacted by Lloyd George's peacetime coalition, as The Housing & Town Planning Act 1919. This removed the necessity of obtaining the consent of the Local Government Board to make a planning scheme (but this was only a temporary reprieve) and of laying schemes before Parliament. Section 45 first introduced the principle of interim development, which secured that, during the preparation of the scheme, development of land could continue and developers would be eligible to claim compensation if their buildings had to be demolished or their property injuriously affected. Section 46 of the 1919 Act also tried to increase its coverage by introducing a new principle which placed on borough and urban district councils with a population anticipated to exceed 20,000 an obligation to prepare planning schemes within a given period. The driving force behind the legislation was again the housing crisis: three million people lived in overcrowded dwellings, 70,000 houses were unfit for habitation and another 300,000 were seriously defective (McCallum 1946). Planning and housing legislation were so interlinked at this time that it is helpful to briefly summarise housing performance and the shifting policy towards council house subsidies. Over this next decade council house building, and then the era of the 'spec' builder, were to define the character of most English cities and towns.

Homes for Heroes

From 1919 as part of the move to deal with the housing crisis and nick-named in the popular press as 'Homes for Heroes', generous subsidies were paid to local authorities and in the following four years 170,000 houses were built. In 1923 The Chamberlain Act reversed this and subsidies were now aimed at the private sector, and although 360,000 private dwellings were built, the number of council houses fell to 75,000. Council housing in the 1920s was occupied by white-collar and skilled manual workers. The poorest looked to private renting. The first Labour government in 1924 increased subsidies and more than 500,00 council houses were built before the subsidies were abolished in 1932. The Greenwood Housing Act in that year replaced the general subsidy by subsidies linking council housing with slum clearance, and for the first time poorer families began to get access to council houses, but the size and quality was materially reduced. This was also the era of the spec builder and in just four years from 1932 to 1936 nearly 4 million houses were built by small private builders. This compared with 250,000 houses built under the Greenwood slum clearance schemes.

Interim Development

This concept of interim development was carried forward right through the 1930s and was only abandoned in 1943 because of wartime bombing, when planning authorities were given the power directly to enforce their development control decisions before proposals for the area concerned had received final approval. It was as if, despite the acceptance of the need for planning, successive governments were afraid to slow down the house-building boom for fear of censure from the electorate. This approach was also a reflection of the weakness of the administrative structure that existed for the control of the planning system. Outside the county boroughs which administered the large urban areas, the administrative unit was the district council. These were often small and poorly financed. At a time of slump and major unemployment, the local authorities did not, and probably could not, ignore the jobs created by new house-building nor the additional rate income. Ten years after the 1932 Act, only 5 per cent of England was covered by approved planning schemes, but no less than 73 per cent was covered by declarations of intent to prepare a plan, so conferring interim control powers on the local authorities concerned. There was also the failure to confront the issue of compensation but that of course continues to bedevil planning control to the present day.

One of the perceived defects of the 1932 Act was that a departure from the allocation in an approved town planning scheme required a modification to the scheme itself. As we will see, there was agreement in the 1940s on the need for a universal and mandatory system of development plans, and that these plans needed to be flexible so as to respond to the need for new development.

The concept of interim development which had been an expedient in the 1930s became a central feature of the new legislation. Development rights were nationalised but the plans became indicative rather than legally binding. The grant of planning permission was the principal means of conferring the right of development, rather than allocation in a development plan.

The 1919 Act was notable for its acceptance of state subsidies for housing, which led to the era of large-scale council housing estates at low densities, which had been recommended by the influential Tudor Walters Report. Suburban development taking the form of semi-detached houses or short terraces became the dominant feature of new house-building for the next two decades, stimulated by railway and bus route development, and in the case of private housing, the building society movement.

Further Legislation 1923–1929

There was further legislation by the Conservatives with Neville Chamberlain as Minister of Health under Prime Minister Stanley Baldwin in 1923, 1925 and 1929 but the underlying concept of a town planning scheme to be prepared in areas of growth but only after enormously complicated consultation was little changed. The 1929 Act brought in the county councils to take part in planning, but other than a number of regional advisory plans prepared by consultants such as Patrick Abercrombie, Thomas Adams and Thomas Mawson, in which counties were involved, this legislative innovation achieved little.

Arterial Roads

After more than a decade of wrangling about the sort of authorities needed for the task, by 1924 good progress had been made with the London Arterial Roads programme which included Eastern Avenue, the London–Southend Road, the London–Tilbury Road, the North Circular and the Great West Road. Despite this progress, which had begun to give London the shape and form we now recognise, concern was expressed about the ribbon development that accompanied this arterial road-building, and was clearly destroying the main traffic function of the roads. The Greater London Regional Planning Committee had been set up in 1927 by the Minister of Health, Neville Chamberlain, to consider planning problems as they applied to the London region. Technical adviser to the committee was Raymond Unwin, and almost single-handed he campaigned against the frontage development and sprawl that the construction of the arterial roads had unwittingly unleashed. Unwin's reward would come in 1935 with The Restriction of Ribbon Development Act.

Urban Sprawl

A year earlier, on 8 August 1928, a cartoon was published in the popular magazine *Punch*, which showed Mr Punch sitting on a bench on a hillside, a newspaper in his hands, while below him the towers and spires of a historic city were being engulfed by the smoking chimneys of innumerable factories. Standing beside him, his walking stick pointing to the panorama below, was a severe, broad-shouldered man, an American tourist. He asks, 'Pardon, me, sir, but can you put me wise to the name of this thriving burg?' Mr Punch replies, 'I regret to say, sir, that this is Oxford.' The publication of the cartoon had been prompted by the news that a trust had been formed to protect the beauties of Oxford and its environs, and had appealed for a sum of £250,000 to purchase the land required for this purpose. The formation of the trust reflected the anguish at the time that nothing other than land ownership could control the urban expansion then occurring. Between 1921 and 1941 the population of Oxford almost doubled, nearly entirely predicated on the growth of the car industry. The development of the car industry was an accident beginning with William Morris working out of a former barracks off the High Street, and then at Cowley introducing the mass production techniques brought over from Detroit.

Oxford's plight was not unique, and urban development was taking place

Between 1921 and 1941 the population of Oxford almost doubled, nearly entirely predicated on the growth of the car industry.

TWENTY YEARS ON?

AMERICAN TOURIST. "PARDON, ME, SIR, BUT CAN YOU PUT ME WISE TO THE NAME OF THIS THRIVING INDUSTRIAL BURG?"

MR. PUNCH. "I REGRET TO SAY, SIR, THAT THIS IS OXFORD."

[A Trust has been formed to protect the beauties of Oxford and its environs, and has appealed for a sum of £250,000 to purchase the land required for this purpose. Donations should be sent to the account of the Oxford Preservation Trust, Barclays Bank, High Street, Oxford.]

■ Familiar story . . . This cartoon appeared in *Punch* on August 8, 1928 on a massive scale – most of it outside town planning schemes. The implications of the Tudor Walters Report, which recommended a maximum density of 12 dwellings to the acre, meant that the enormous new council estates would be built on greenfield land on the edge of towns and cities. Derived from the Bourneville and Letchworth model estates, the 12-to-the-acre semi-detached became the standardised home of the inter-war period. Farming had collapsed after the First World War, with the import of cheap foodstuffs, and land was cheap. Land on the edge of towns was also made accessible to the city centres by the new trolley and motor buses. In addition, a drift of industry to the London area accentuated by depression and unemployment in the heavy industries of the North intensified this growth in London and the Home Counties. The scale was enormous. Some 4.5 million new houses were built between the two wars. Thomas Sharp lampooned this approach to residential density: 'The population of all the Russias could easily be housed in the areas now zoned for building in England. Actual figures are not available. If they were they would make humorous reading in Bedlam' (Sharp, 1932).

After the First World War and through into the 1930s, the greatest physical change to England's appearance was the growth of the suburb. The suburb was not new (London and the provincial cities and towns had expanded into the surrounding countryside in the nineteenth century), but what was new was the unparalleled scale and pace of the change. From 1915 until 1932 the London Metropolitan Railway Company published a guide to the new housing estates being built along the railway line out from London into the villages and small towns of Middlesex. 'Metroland' was the name coined by the railway company for this suburban area beyond London, and subsequently immortalised in the poems of John Betjeman. At the time there were critics who regarded the low-density estates as sprawl, and one of the most vocal was Thomas Sharp. His polemic, *English Panorama*, was published by Dent in 1936, and it was a plea for a planned and clear-sighted approach to the control of growth, and the preservation of England's countryside of hedgerows and trees. He described the countryside as now pushed away from the town, behind miles of vague and disorderly suburbia. Earlier, in 1932, his first book *Town and Countryside* was published in which he showed how the 1909 Act had consolidated the idea of the 'garden city' of the garden back-front-and-side. Houses must not now be built in continuous streets and so the town was to be no longer a town, but a loose collection of country cottages, and the looser and the more countrified the better. Sharp was a maverick and he upset the planning and architectural establishment by calling these developments 'snob planning', but in his advocacy of urbanism and higher densities and his appreciation of townscape he was years ahead of his contemporaries.

The Town & Country Planning Act 1932

The governments of the 1930s had much on their minds (Wright, 1966). The Conservatives had been swept into power by the landslide victory of 1931, when Labour was only able to win 52 seats. It was not to win a parliamentary majority for 14 years. The electorate was unforgiving to the political party blamed for the Depression, but the anxiety of the government was with two enormous concerns. The first was the drift to war. In July 1932, with German unemployment at over 4 million, Hitler's National Socialists surged to 230 seats with 37 per cent of the vote and Hitler achieved power a year later in July 1933. The other was unemployment in this country. In the serious slump of the 1930s, unemployment reached over 2.5 million under the short-lived Labour administration of 1929–31.

The national government formed by Ramsay MacDonald, Stanley Baldwin and Neville Chamberlain introduced the Town & Country Planning Act 1932. Sir Edward Hilton Young moved the second motion. Its scope was ambitious. It extended planning powers virtually across the whole of the country, but reintroduced the obligation, removed by the 1919 Act, for local authorities to obtain ministerial consent to prepare planning schemes and for schemes to be laid before Parliament before coming into operation. Other than from landowners, there was little opposition in the House of Commons. Unemployment stood at nearly 3 million and there was an adverse balance of trade. Members were therefore ready to support some boldness in fields less exacting than trade or foreign policy: 'The Town and Country Planning Bill seemed modestly bold' (McCallum, 1946).

The 1932 Act itself was considerably more complicated than any of its predecessors. The reason for this was that the legislation, having originated in the realm of public health in the early part of the century, preserved in large part the methodology of that legislation. The clauses were so arranged as to seek to lay down in great detail, and with considerable precision, what might and might not be done in various parts of the area concerned.

The system was comprehensive and in that sense it could be said to have provided the basis for the modern-day planning system but it did not require applications for planning permission. While the local authority had powers to demolish development that did not comply with its scheme, many developers gambled that an authority might fail to get a scheme approved by parliament or, where a scheme was approved, the authority would not jeopardise political support by seeking to demolish buildings.

It is important to appreciate the reasons for the failure of the legislation because, as we will see, these had a significant impact on the political response of the wartime Cabinet and anticipated the post-war legislation that ushered in the 1947 Town & Country Planning Act.

There were two fundamental criticisms. The first concerned what Lewis Keeble has called 'a state of perpetual interim development'. A scheme was as binding upon a local authority as on developers, and could only be varied by going through the inordinately lengthy and complicated procedure entailed in preparing the original scheme. 'Small wonder', remarked Keeble,

> that local authorities were loath to have their schemes finally approved and brought into operation, but preferred on the whole to continue in a state of what has been called perpetual interim development, during which they were free to vary and modify their development control policy as seemed fit, and during which, too, they were immune from claims from compensation, the only corresponding disadvantage being that they could not force compliance with the scheme upon those who chose to ignore it.
>
> (Keeble, 1961)

The other criticism was that in truth the schemes achieved little. Barry Cullingworth (1964) noted:

> Furthermore, most schemes in fact did little more than accept and ratify existing trends of development, since any attempt at a more radical solution would have involved the planning authority in compensation they could not afford to pay. In most cases the zones were so widely drawn as to place hardly more restrictions on the developer than if there had been no scheme at all. Indeed in the half of the country covered by draft planning schemes in 1937 there was sufficient land zoned for housing to accommodate 350 million people.

The late Professor Myles Wright in a series of lectures to the Royal Society of Arts in July 1966 (Wright, 1966) summed up the disappointments of this era:

> The reformers of 1920–30 made exactly the same miscalculations as did their successors of 1945–65. In particular, they greatly underestimated the scale of post-war development and overestimated the amount of attention which the public would consent to give to the forward planning of their environment.

We shall see in the next chapters to what extent this criticism of the 1945–65 period was valid, but in the 1930s, despite the great indignation expressed by Clough William Ellis, Thomas Sharp, the Campaign to Protect Rural England (CPRE) and others (including John Betjeman), tremendous damage was done to the countryside for 10–15 miles around the larger cities.

The Restriction of Ribbon Development Act 1935

It was significant that the most effective piece of restrictive planning legislation during the inter-war period was not part of any town planning scheme. This was the Restriction of Ribbon Development Act introduced in 1935 which was administered by the Ministry of Transport. Its purpose was to prevent the spread of development along the edges of arterial and trunk roads, a process which was rapidly becoming serious. It did have an impact and to this day one can see where ribbons of development were arrested by the legislation.

Green Belt Scheme

Another innovation that did not require legislation was the launch by the London County Council, at the request of the Regional Planning Committee, of a green belt scheme in 1935. The council proposed to make grants to neighbouring county councils to preserve land for recreation, and were prepared to spend as much as £2 million over three years. It was the beginning of a policy that would eventually create a girdle of parkland around London and protect that area against new building, but it was soon found that the existing powers of the authorities had to be supplemented. A Bill was presented to allow land to be acquired by agreement or declared to be part of the green belt, and to provide that no such land should be sold or built on without the consent of the minister. In due course this Bill became the Green Belt (London and Home Counties) Act 1938.

The Prospect of World War

The planning legislation of the 1920s and 1930s achieved little but as the prospect of war became more imminent, a new concern was to provide the greatest impetus to a more effective planning system. As in so many spheres,

Winston Churchill was to prove particularly prophetic. He warned of the vulnerability to air attack of the huge sprawl that London and the Home Counties had become. From the back benches in his House of Commons speeches in 1934 (Jenkins, 2001), he spoke on 30 July of London being 'the greatest target in the world, a kind of tremendous, fat, valuable cow tied up to attract the beast of prey'. On 28 November he said, 'We must expect that under the pressure of continuous air attack upon London at least three or four million people would be driven out into the open country around the Metropolis'.

The Excessive Growth of London

Throughout the troubled decade of the 1930s London was growing and changing rapidly. In 1939 the population of Greater London including the Home Counties was close to 9 million. About a fifth of all the people in Great Britain lived within a radius of 15 miles from Charing Cross.

Three years earlier in 1936 Sir Malcolm Stewart, the Commissioner for the Special Areas (areas of high unemployment in the North East, West Cumberland and South Wales where the Commissioner had executive powers to facilitate economic development) called attention in his third report to the excessive growth of London and suggested that further extension of industry should be controlled.

Neville Chamberlain, Chancellor of the Exchequer, in a debate in the House of Commons on the report (Hansard, 1936) in November 1936 said there was nothing very revolutionary in the proposal to control further factory extension in Greater London because this would only be an extension of the practice common in town and country planning schemes. As we have seen, this was rather a flattering picture of the effectiveness of these schemes. However, in a subsequent debate in March 1937 on the report (Hansard, 1937) the then Minister of Labour remarked, 'this extension is occurring not merely in London but in the other great cities and it gives rise to grave problems, not merely of industry, but of health, communication, vulnerability from the air, and other problems that go far beyond the issue raised by Sir Malcolm Stewart'. In the event the recommendation of Sir Stewart was heeded and a Royal Commission was appointed in 1937 with Sir Montague Barlow as chairman. Chamberlain was a lifelong tireless campaigner for planning, and for the Garden City principle. It was not surprising that one of his first decisions as Prime Minister should have been to create the Commission from whose report the rest of the story flows.

Significantly the wide terms of reference included vulnerability from the air. These were:

> to inquire into the causes which have influenced the present geographical distribution of the industrial population of Great Britain and the probable direction of any change in that distribution in the future; to consider what social, economic, or strategical disadvantages arise from the concentration of industries or of the industrial population in large towns or in particular areas of the country; and to report what remedial measures if any should be taken in the national interest.
>
> (Ministry of Town & Country Planning, 1950: 8)

The report of the Commission was presented to Parliament in January 1940 and the recommendations were to have a profound impact on the evolution of the planning system in England in the post-war period. They are considered in the next chapter, but I conclude this chapter with a reflection that notwithstanding the pioneering planning legislation of the last Liberal government before the First World War, the efforts of the subsequent national government to extend the coverage of planning control and the enormous urban growth in England during the two decades following that war (one third of all the houses in England had been built since 1918), the major impetus to the evolution of a more effective post-war planning system was the realisation of the risk to the country posed by Hitler and the Luftwaffe, because of the sprawl that London had become.

References

Cullingworth, J.B. (1964) *Town & Country Planning in England & Wales.* London: George Allen & Unwin, p. 20.

Hansard (1908) *Parliamentary Debates,* 12 May, col. 958.

Hansard (1936) *Parliamentary Debates,* 17 November, col. 1595.

Hansard (1937) *Parliamentary Debates,* 9 March, cols 1026–27.

Heap, D. (1975) *The Land and The Development.* London: Sweet & Maxwell, p. 3.

Jenkins, R. (2001) *Churchill.* London: Macmillan.

Keeble, L. (1961) *Town Planning At The Crossroads.* London: The Estates Gazette, p. 23.

McCallum, I.R.M. (1946) *Physical Planning.* London The Architectural Press pp. 3, 9.

Ministry of Town & Country Planning (1950) *Report of the Committee on Qualifications of Planners,* Cmnd 8059. London: HMSO.

Morgan, K.O. (1981) *David Lloyd George*. Cardiff: University of Wales Press, p. 29.

Self, P. (1961) *Cities in Flood*. London: Faber & Faber, p. 23.

Sharp, T. (1932) *Town And Countryside*. Oxford: Oxford University Press, p. 221.

Wright, M. (1966) The planning of cities and regions, *Journal of the Royal Society of Arts*, p. 650.

3

The Wartime Consensus: the Impact of War on the Planning System

A Second Chance

In the prefatory note to the first edition of his classic book, *Town Planning*, written in December 1939, shortly after the outbreak of war, Thomas Sharp (1940) perceptively observed that if the country was to avoid the tragic muddle and mess that followed the last war, it was essential 'that we got our minds clear now as to what should be the basis of our future policy in the building of towns and in carrying through the widespread improvements that are necessary in the countryside'. Intellectuals such as Sharp, the architect Maxwell Fry, the author J.B. Priestley and the scientist Julian Huxley all caught the mood of the country and helped shape that mood which was to prove an overwhelming determination that at the end of the war the disappointments that had followed the First World War should not be repeated. It is no exaggeration to describe the progress of planning legislation during the war as heroic. Looking back nearly 70 years later, what is quite remarkable is that during these desperate months and years so much energy and intellect was devoted to what Sharp thought necessary: the basis of a future planning policy for the country.

The Barlow Report

The Barlow Commission's report was presented to Parliament in January 1940 – some four months after the start of the Second World War and five months in advance of the 'Inquest on Norway' House of Commons debate on 7 and 8 May 1940 when Winston Churchill became Prime Minister and leader of the wartime Cabinet, which included Labour MPs Clement Attlee, Ernest Bevin and Arthur Greenwood. As his deputy, Attlee was effectively in charge of domestic policy allowing Churchill to concentrate on his role as war leader.

On 7 September 1940, the first major air attack on London involving nearly 400 enemy bombers and fighters took place: 'From the moment of this first big attack on London the interest of the British people in planning was awakened; it began in fervent hope and determination to use the damage done by bombs to good purpose' (McCallum, 1946). The bombing, and fear of much greater damage to come, finally convinced the government that the existing system of war-building control was inadequate, and one month later Lord Reith – the moving spirit behind the success of the pre-war BBC – set up a small group to consider the problems of guiding land use after the war and post-war reconstruction. The terms of reference for this small group were laid down by the Lord Privy Seal (1942):

> It is clear that the reconstruction of town and country after the war raises great problems and gives a great opportunity. The Minister of Works and Buildings has, therefore, been charged by the Government with the responsibility of consulting the departments and organisations concerned with a view to reporting to the Cabinet the appropriate methods and machinery for dealing with the issues involved.

The Scott and Uthwatt Reports

In the debate which took place in the House of Lords the same month, Lord Reith left no one in doubt of his sincerity, high purpose and resolve. As expected he set a fast pace. On 29 January he announced in the Lords that the main obstructions to planning, those which concerned compensation and betterment, were to be inquired into by an expert committee. This emanated from a recommendation of the Barlow Commission which had taken evidence on the subject. The Commission also considered that agriculture was beyond its terms of reference and a further committee, the Committee on Land Utilisation in Rural Areas, with Lord Justice Scott as chairman and the famous geographer Sir Dudley Stamp as deputy chairman, was appointed by Lord Reith in October 1941. The joint secretary of the committee was Thomas Sharp, and he was subsequently credited for the concise and clear language of the report. It was perhaps no coincidence that despite the protests of the TCPA, and the assurances of the chairman, recommendations for higher-density flat-building and critical comments on policies for population dispersal remained in the report. Sharp, as a joint secretary, was clearly going to have the last word.

The following year, in August 1942, the Scott Committee reported and the following month the Uthwatt Committee's final report appeared. It is appropriate here to summarise its findings together with those of the Barlow Report because, as all students of planning know, they underpinned the basis of the planning system that was evolving by the end of the war. The committees recommended:

(i)   that planning control should be extended immediately to the whole country;

(ii) that there should be a national policy for industrial location and population distribution;

(iii) that a central planning authority should be set up with the following objectives:

(a) redevelopment of congested urban areas;

(b) decentralisation or dispersal from such areas of industries and industrial population;

(c) encouragement of a reasonable balance of industrial development and appropriate industrial diversification throughout the divisions or regions of Great Britain;

(d) examination of how far garden cities or garden suburbs, satellite towns, trading estates, further development of existing small towns or centres, or other methods should be encouraged to accommodate decentralised or dispersed industry and workers;

(e) research and collection of information relating to the location of industry and the various natural resources – land, agriculture, amenities etc. – that may be affected by industrial location;

(f) correlation of local town and country planning schemes in the national interest.

In December of that year the Japanese attacked the United States fleet lying in Pearl Harbour.

The Ministry of Works & Planning

The beginning of 1942 proved to be unpredictable as far as planning matters were concerned. On 11 February, the Ministry of Works and Buildings was renamed the Ministry of Works and Planning and the planning powers of the Minister of Health, Mr Ernest Brown, were transferred to Lord Reith, who was charged with the welding of all physical reconstruction into a single and consistent whole and the execution of the main recommendations of the Barlow Report. Lord Reith's speech of that day expressed a full determination, a full sincerity of interest in planning. A fortnight later on 22 February he was gone, having lost his portfolio in the government reshuffle of that day to Lord Portal. In his *History of the Second World War* Winston Churchill (1951) gives no explanation for the change, nor does Roy Jenkins (2001) in his biography of Churchill. Before going to the House of Lords Reith had briefly been an MP, and shortly before the election early in 1940 that had been engineered for him, he confided to Churchill, then First Lord of the Admiralty, that he was rather frightened of the Commons. Churchill replied: 'Not nearly as frightened as they are of you' (Seatrobe, 2009). Reith was a powerful, domineering figure and it may have been no more than a clash of personalities but in any event he was to resurface after the war when Lewis Silkin, appointed by Clement Attlee as Minister of Planning, appointed Reith to deliver the new towns programme.

Lord Portal appears to have got off to a good start because on 27 February he received a memo from Churchill praising him for the 'impressive White Paper you have just issued about training for the building industry . . . I am glad that you are taking timely steps to plan for it, and are planning with courage and wide vision. I wish your scheme every success' (Churchill, 1951). Such memos on domestic issues from Churchill were rare as, understandably, he was preoccupied with the war effort, but as we will see later in this chapter he was to intervene to significant effect in the debate on the 1944 Planning White Paper.

At the end of the year, to some dissatisfaction because there had been no government response to the Scott and Uthwatt reports, Lord Portal announced that a separate Ministry of Town and Country Planning was to be set up to take over from the Ministry of Works and Planning. In that same year the Beveridge Report, which proposed that existing schemes of welfare support should be consolidated into a universal national scheme, was published, and its acceptance firmly established the emergence of the welfare state with which spatial planning was to be irrevocably linked.

The Town and Country (Interim Development) Act 1943

On 26 January 1943, Sir William Jowitt, having been appointed the previous month as Minister Without Portfolio (but charged with post-war reconstruction), to succeed Arthur Greenwood who had lost his job in the 1942 government reshuffle, moved the second reading of the Ministry of Town and Country Planning Bill. The second reading was approved but without much enthusiasm for the Bill implied that the minister's job would be to administer the Town and Country Planning Act 1932 and members thought that something much bigger was required. There were further ministerial changes. Mr W.S. Morrison became minister on 5 February 1943 and moved the second reading of the Town and Country (Interim Development) Bill three months later on 11 May 1943. The Bill became an Act on 22 October and all land in England and Wales came at long last under planning control. On 12 November Lord Woolton became Minister of Reconstruction and with his previous proven good record as Minister of Food (the originator of the famous meat-free vegetarian Woolton pie), it was thought that he would allocate work shrewdly and maintain a brisk pace.

The County of London Plan 1943

While the war was still on the London County Council turned towards the future. 'The war has given us a great opportunity' declared Lord Latham in the introduction to the County of London Plan, 1944 'and by the bitter destruction of many acres of buildings has made easier the realisation of our dreams . . . The fate of London in the post-war years will be one of the signs by which posterity will judge us'. The authors of the County of London Plan, J.H. Forshaw, the council's architect, and Sir Professor Patrick Abercrombie, had assembled a talented team of young town planners and came forward with a bold, ambitious plan for the metropolis involving ring roads, the decentralisation of industry and new residential communities. An innovative feature prepared by Arthur Ling and D.K. Johnson, who were to become leading planning academics in the post-war period, was a social and functional analysis of the 'world city'. They recommended that 'recognition of the existing community structure of London must be implicit in any main reconstruction proposals'. The diagram illustrating this analysis has become a planning classic with its faintly psychedelic character.

The County of London Plan 1943. The diagram illustrating the community structure of London has become a planning classic with its faintly psychedelic character.

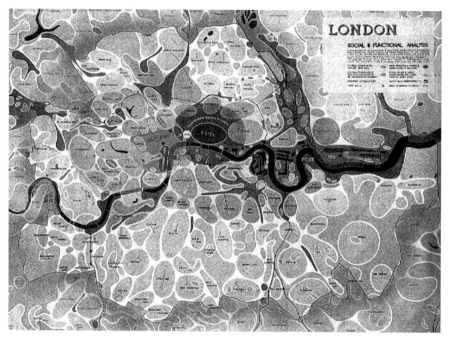

© London County Council The County of London Plan 1943

Civic Diagnosis

Others too saw the bombing as an opportunity to make good the past's mistakes. In July 1943, W.S. Morrison, the then Minister of Town and Country Planning, opened at the Housing Centre in London an exhibition of plans for the redevelopment of Hull which had been severely bombed. The study had been led by the architect and planner Max Lock who had pioneered the concept of 'civic diagnosis' which involved exhaustive physical and social surveys of the plan area. In a preface to the exhibition Lock wrote that 'Hitler has at least brought us to our senses in that we find the cleared and cleaned up spaces a relief. In them we have hope for the future, opportunities to be taken or lost'. These open spaces, he opined, 'begin to ventilate the congestion of our cities and maybe also of our imagination' (Lock, 1943).

Transition

Between 1943 and 1948, planning was legally in a peculiar position. The principal Act remained the Act of 1932 and theoretically all the local authorities in the country were engaged in preparing schemes under powers conferred by it, while all such schemes, if completed, would have attracted compensation and betterment on the basis of the 1932 Act.

> Yet all concerned knew that new and radical legislation was on the way and made use of the flexibility possible when working in a state of interim development. The position of those few Authorities which had operative schemes must have been more difficult, for such schemes did not cease to have effect until 1st July, 1948.
>
> (Keeble, 1961)

The Town & Country Planning Act 1944

In May 1944, Lord Woolton published his White Paper, *Employment Policy*, of which an important part dealt with the location of industry and which proved in due course to be a much more important document than it first appeared, for it was to underpin the 1945 Distribution of Industry Act. In June, not long after the Normandy landings, the White Paper *Control of Land Use* and the Town & Country Planning Bill 1944 were presented to Parliament on the same day. The Bill gave local authorities a much simpler procedure for buying land for redevelopment and some financial help for blitzed towns towards meeting the cost. The land was to be bought at 1939 values, which aroused great opposition from landowning interests. The Prime Minister intervened and when the Act received royal assent in November, the valuation was improved by 30 per cent to owner-occupiers.

An innovative feature of the Act was, for the first time, systematic protection for historic buildings. From 1941 to 1945 Sir John Summerson was the deputy director of the National Buildings Record which prepared lists of historic buildings at risk of bombing. Many of the early photographs in the collection were Summerson's own. At the beginning of the Blitz, as he said, 'it seemed now a good deal more important to record buildings than to write about them' (Massingberd, 1999).

At the year end, Lord Portal went – almost as suddenly as his predecessor – and Mr Duncan Sandys became Minister of Works and Planning. Almost at the same time, in 1944, Patrick Abercrombie's plan for Greater London was published and submitted to the minister, and was distributed by the latter to all the constituent local authorities. The plan was immediately taken as an interim basis for planning decisions until a complete review could be carried out. As I have noted, it represented the most advanced attempt to plan in physical terms on virtually a regional scale. Reflecting Churchill's concerns about the sprawl of London, this bold document involved the planned dispersal of over a million Londoners from the congested inner urban ring across the new green belt, which would limit the further growth of the conurbation, into planned satellite towns – the famous London 'new towns'. The New Towns Committee, under the chairmanship of Lord Reith, subsequently provided a detailed prescription for the location and form of such new towns, essential features being that they should be some distance from existing urban areas and should be largely self-contained for work and living.

Elsewhere the new legislation was a spur to those authorities willing to think about the future of their areas once the war was won. Although published after the end of the war in 1947, the fieldwork for the Middlesborough Survey and Plan had taken place during the war. The author, Max Lock, and his team that included the sociologist Ruth Glass and the young planner Frank Layfield, who was to become a leading planning silk and the author of a report on London's planning in the 1970s, had been working in cramped conditions and with limited resources during the war years. The plan gave special weight to sociological factors and included a precise concept of neighbourhoods, defined and demarcated in terms of a multiple index of living conditions. The neighbourhood concept mirrored that used in Abercrombie's Greater London Plan.

Land Ownership and Compensation

Even while the flying bombs were falling on London, debate raged within the coalition government concerning land ownership and the compensation issues raised by the White Paper *Control of Land Use*. That debate rages to the present day and it is useful to set out the ideological differences between the Conservatives and Labour over whether power should lie ultimately in the market or with the state. The position is well summarised by Rodney Lowe in his book *The Welfare State in Britain since 1945* (Lowe, 1993):

> Three particular issues were to guide policymakers. First, should betterment (the large increase in the value of land once it has been granted planning permission) be enjoyed by the private landowner or by the community? Secondly, how could a

steady supply of land for development be ensured, especially if the owner were to be denied betterment? Thirdly, how successfully could central and local government adjust to, and discharge, their new positive responsibilities? Both would acquire considerably more power as the rights of private property declined. Officials would also have rapidly to develop new skills if local government were to draft development plans (and consequently to anticipate the future economic and social needs of each locality) and central government were (in the absence of clear market criteria) to value land in order to impose a tax on betterment.

Lowe comments that in order to maintain political unity, the coalition's 1944 White Paper sought to resolve these problems by steering a middle course between the traditional Labour and Conservative preferences for the nationalisation of, and a free market in, land. It rejected the outright nationalisation of land or of development rights (as recommended by Uthwatt) but, while thus defending private ownership, it agreed that no land should be developed without planning permission. Owners should be compensated for the loss of any anticipated profit from the unrestricted development of their land. Should they thereafter be granted planning permission, however, they should be subject to a betterment tax equivalent to 80 per cent of the increased value of their land. Finally, the White Paper proposed a land commission to oversee both the levying of this tax and the payment of compensation. The authors of the White Paper were fully aware of the political sensitivity of these proposals but felt that they had steered a middle course which would command support from both main political parties. This proved not to be the case and as the end of the war approached and the election of the summer of 1945 beckoned, the White Paper was shelved.

Election

The wartime coalition broke up on VE Day in May 1945. Churchill wanted it to continue until Japan had been defeated but Attlee sensed electoral victory and Churchill had no choice but to disband the coalition and form a caretaker government until the election. Labour was uniquely linked in the popular mind with the new social agenda that had emerged during the war. The election took place in July and the Labour Party led by Attlee won a landslide victory. On 26 July, Churchill issued a brief and dignified farewell statement which was read on the *Nine O'Clock News*: 'Immense responsibilities abroad and at home fall upon the new government, and we must all hope that they will be successful in bearing them' (Jenkins, 2001).

Semi-utopian Socialism

The Labour political historian Ben Pimlott (1992), in his biography of Harold Wilson, sagely summed up the appeal of Labour to the electorate:

> Labour at the end of the Second World War offered an extension, rather than a rejection, of existing domestic policies. It embraced the employment, health, education and social plans of the wartime coalition, and sought to consolidate them. Pragmatic schemes, based on recent Whitehall experience, were propagated in the language of semi-utopian socialism.

The new government, as far as planning was concerned, started with the advantage that it had a wealth of information and ideas emanating from the stream of reports that had been published during the war years. Looking back over that period it is still extraordinary that a country facing fearful odds and in a struggle for its survival should nonetheless have the foresight to consider and plan for post-war reconstruction. We examine the consequences in the next chapter, but at this point it is worth noting the increasing confidence of the professional planner in putting forward ideas and proposals for reconstruction.

As Lowe (1993) has commented: 'Before the war, only three per cent of land had been effectively subject to planning permission. After the war, no land could be developed without prior consent from local or central government'. This was a revolutionary restriction on the traditional rights of private property and, together with the Beveridge Report and the Keynesian input into the 1944 Employment Policy White Paper, may be seen as a classic example of the confidence of 'disinterested experts that they could use the dislocation of war to realise reforms long championed by informal opinion'.

The end of the war and a new government laid the basis for a radical new approach to town planning control in England.

References

Churchill, W. (1951) *The Second World War*, Vol IV, *The Hinge of Fate*. London: Cassell & Son, p. 742.

Jenkins, R. (2001) *Churchill*. London: Macmillan, p. 799.

Keeble, L. (1961) Town planning at the crossroads, *Estates Gazette*, p. 33.

Lord Privy Seal (1942) *Report of an Expert Committee on Compensation and Betterment*, Cmnd 6386. London: HMSO.

Lock, M. (1943) *Civic Diagnosis*. Hull: Hull Regional Survey.

Lowe, R. (1993) *The Welfare State In Britain Since 1945*. London: Macmillan, p. 239.

Massingberd, H. (ed.) (1999) *The Daily Telegraph Fifth Book Of Obituaries: Twentieth-century Lives*. London: Macmillan, pp. 173–74.

McCallum, I.R. (1946) *Physical Planning*. London: The Architectural Press, p. 11.

Pimlott, B. (1992) *Harold Wilson*. London: Harper Collins, p. 348.

Seatrobe, J.B. (2009) Lord Reith, *Total Politics*, April p. 44.

Sharp. T. (1940) *Town Planning*. London: Pelican.

4

The Welfare State and the Role of Planning, 1945–1951

The Labour Government and its Personalities

Labour swept to an enormous landslide victory in the post-war election. The results declared on 26 July 1945 gave Labour 393 seats from nearly 12 million votes, the Conservatives only 213 seats from nearly 10 million: an overall majority, taking in a few Liberals and others, of 146. That afternoon Attlee began to form his Cabinet. As every Labour Prime Minister who succeeded him has had to do, Attlee had to balance the Left and Right wings of the party. Attlee, Dalton, Bevin and Morrison had all served in Churchill's wartime coalition and Attlee had probably more ministerial talent to choose from than at any other time in history. He and Morrison favoured a cautious approach to increased public ownership of the means of production but others wanted full steam ahead. Particularly leftish, Aneurin Bevan wanted to see a fulfilment of the pledges made in 1918 when Labour had agreed a clear socialist ideology and not just a continuation of the wartime coalition.

In a bold move Attlee made Nye Bevan, who during the war coalition had been an outsider, ever a critic of Churchill and his war leadership, Minister of Health. This ministry was responsible not only for health but for housing and in July 1945 the housing shortage was the most urgent social priority the new government faced. Yet before the election Labour had declared that it would split the two portfolios, merging housing with the Ministry of Town and Country Planning. Quite why Attlee went back on this sensible intention is not clear, although subsequently he concluded that the Minister of Town and County Planning was not really directly concerned with housing, but with betterment and compensation. As we shall see, Bevan's housing programme was one of the major physical changes of this first post-war government. Bevan, who had been responsible for housing as a councillor in Tredegar in the 1920s, took to his new role with energy and ability.

Although not in the Cabinet, Lewis Silkin became Minister of Town and Country Planning, charged by Attlee to secure consistency and continuity in the framing and execution of a national policy with regard to the use and development of land throughout England and Wales. In every sense, he hit the ground running. Prior to the 1945 election he had been the LCC (London County Council) housing chairman and, in a Fabian pamphlet of 1943, he had written that unless there is a National Plan and the Regional or Local Planning Authorities are very much larger than the existing ones, post-war planning will be as local and chaotic as it was before the war. Within two years he was the responsible minister and for a brief period the idea of national, comprehensive land planning held sway, until his separate ministry disappeared in 1951. It was a feature of Attlee that he picked whomever he thought the best man for the job and left him to get on with it (Jenkins, 2006).

The New Towns Act 1946

Abercrombie's Greater London Plan (1944) proposed a redistribution of London's population on a massive scale; more than a million people were to move, including 380,000 to eight or ten new satellite towns beyond the green belt. Although nothing had been said in the Labour Party manifesto before the election (this document, published in 1945, had been more or less a recycling of *Labour and the New Social Order* published in 1918), within nine months the government had introduced a New Towns Bill. There was surprisingly little opposition in Parliament and the Bill provided for the designation of sites for new towns and the setting up of Development Corporations. The Bill was based on the recommendations of a committee chaired by Lord Reith who had been rescued from the wilderness, where he had been dispatched by Churchill, to chair the New Towns Departmental Committee, which he launched with his usual energy and determination, publishing two reports in record time. This was just as well as in the places where they were to be built the new towns were very unpopular. To an extent, the possible sites for new towns had already been chosen in that the advisory and statutory plans published before 1946 had included proposals for them. Abercrombie's Greater London Plan had recommended ten sites.

The creation of the new towns was to be the responsibility of Development Corporations which were given powers to acquire land, to appoint officers and construction workers and in effect become large-scale developer landowners with some powers normally reserved to local authorities. They were not, however, to replace the local authorities and each town was to be made a separate county district for which the authority would be elected in the normal way. The loans advanced by the government were to be at the ordinary rate of interest on public loans, and were repayable over 60 years. Subsidies on housing were to be paid on much the same scale as to local authorities in general.

The government's original intention was to build up to 20 new towns, although in the event, between 1947 and 1950, 14 were started, of which 11 were in England. In the first of these, Stevenage in Hertfordshire, Professor Sir Peter Hall (2005) has related that people tore down the station names and replaced them by ones reading 'Silkingrad'. And when Silkin dared venture into a public meeting there, they let his car tyres down while he was speaking.

The Prefabs

The Second World War had interrupted a slum clearance programme begun in the 1930s and by 1945 housing had become the main issue of the day. The need for housing was immediate , and the prefab was born. Built of aluminium and steel in former aircraft factories, they could be taken to the site by lorry and assembled there, often by prisoners of war, in three days. The prefab had a modern kitchen, a gas cooker and fridge, hot running water and a modern bathroom. Meant to last for ten years, in many towns they survived, by necessity, for much longer.

The Town & Country Planning Act 1947

More complicated was the Bill that introduced the 1947 Act, which in effect nationalised development value, which meant that a person who was refused planning permission to develop land was not entitled to compensation. The government gave way on one issue only. This was that where compulsory purchase took place, the compensation was on the basis of current market value. Surprisingly at this stage, when compared with campaigns in 1932 and 1944, the opposition in Parliament was muted but this may have been because the Conservative Party was dejected after its massive loss – for as we shall see, once back in power in 1951, the Conservative administration lost no time in dismantling the compensation and betterment provisions.

The 1947 Act brought about a number of radical changes. Direct planning powers were removed from boroughs and district councils and vested in county councils and county boroughs. Plan-making was to be firmly based on a survey, analysis and plan system. Flexibility was built in, with an obligation to amend plans, if necessary, every five years. Approval of these plans, and amendments to them, was to come from the minister concerned and not via Parliament.

Control of development was to relate to all activities including the erection of new buildings, engineering works and material changes of use. A system of enforcement without compensation was directed against those that ignored the need for planning permission. The pre-war system whereby a proposal in accord with a zoning was more or less guaranteed a permission was removed, and the determination of planning applications was to be made not only with regard to the development plan but also to 'any other material considerations'. Power to impose conditions on planning permissions as thought fit was a further radical change. Another introduction was an appeal system for those unhappy with the planning decision to have their case reviewed by a planning inspector responsible to the minister. These parts of the 1947 Act have proved to be long-lived as they remain basically intact to this day. The Act introduced the discretionary element of decision-making which is such a unique feature of the English planning system, when compared with the more legalistic and codified systems in use in continental Europe.

Not long-lived but still a political issue nearly a century after the first planning act, was the new code for compensation and betterment. The details of this code were complicated but the basic concept was that if the process of selection of land for building thereby increased the value of an area of land then this notional development value belonged to the community and should be recouped from the developer. The 1947 Act therefore provided that in the case of permission to develop being granted, owners should pay the state a 'development charge' representing the monetary gain arising, and this charge was fixed at 100 per cent of the gain in value: 'This was perfectly logical and equitable; the only difficulty was that it did not work' wryly observes Professor Sir Peter Hall (1974). Additionally, if the planning process initiated by the 1947 Act meant that a landowner was deprived of development value which existed prior to the Act, then the developer should be compensated. A fund was set up to enable all claims to be met by a specific date – called the £300 million fund. As we have seen, the compulsory purchase of land was to be at existing use value, since development value had been effectively nationalised.

The provisions of the Act came into force on 1 July 1948 – the 'appointed day', and this is a date which will probably forever feature in the vocabulary of valuers and surveyors, for it marked a revolutionary day in land valuation. Lewis Silkin welcomed the 'appointed day' remarking that this was a date which would forever be a landmark in the history of planning in the country.

The Act remains basically intact to this day, although consolidated several times and totally relieved of its requirements for betterment. In some ways the Act was not fully tested in its early stages because until the final removal of building controls in 1954 and the emergence of the property boom in the late 1950s, private development activity was muted.

The introduction of the Act meant a large increase in the numbers of planning staff required by local authorities and the Ministry of Town and County Planning and its regional offices. But there was a sharp distinction between the counties where the new breed of professional, the county planning officer, held sway and the county boroughs where town planning remained under the aegis of the traditional regime of borough engineer and surveyor. And it was the plan-making sections of local planning authorities that recruited the most talented staff, leaving the development control work as the poor relation; a perception that still exists today.

The 1947 Act provided the framework for the present form of planning law. It repealed all previous legislation with the important exception of the Minister of Town and Country Planning which had been introduced during the war in 1943. In the immediate post-war period the centralisation of control arose because of three factors. The first was that many of the new planning authorities had had no real experience of planning as an activity of local government. The second was the drastic shortage of experienced and professionally qualified planning staff. The third was that the new Labour government was introducing a state-run economy with a consequent high level of centralisation.

Although the continuation of wartime controls after 1945 meant there was little private, speculative development, vast areas of cities in England were being changed by the government's policy on slum clearance. Local authorities could use two powers. The first was embodied in the Town and Country Planning Act 1944 which allowed authorities to acquire areas of bad layout and obsolete development and land for overspill. The second used powers under the Housing Act 1949 to acquire properties classified as 'slum' by the public health inspector. Prefabrication and the grant structure from central government ushered in large-scale redevelopment and the erection of high-rise blocks of flats, which ultimately attracted widespread disapproval from a public that became disillusioned with planning.

A central theme that characterised the 1947 Act and which was to cause so much difficulty in the speculative property boom that began in the late 1950s was the dichotomy between the strong negative powers of control bequeathed to the local planning authorities, which would regulate the private sector, and the weak positive powers. The assumption seemed to be that the good positive planning would be undertaken by the public building agencies – the local planning authorities and the new town Development Corporations.

The National Parks & Access to the Countryside Act 1949

Silkin's third town planning Bill concerned national parks. Once again the matter was of long standing and, as with the new towns, the Bill received little opposition and was passed in December 1949. Silkin's seat was abolished in a parliamentary boundary review and after the general election in 1950 he went to the Lords. Without a seat in the Cabinet, he had convinced his colleagues and piloted three major Bills through the House. But as we have seen, political opposition was muted, and most was internal from the Treasury, concerned at the huge reconstruction cost that the legislation promised.

Nye Bevan's Housing Programme

Nye Bevan does not feature in many accounts of the post-war planning regime. He is remembered for the introduction of the NHS but he should also be remembered for his housing programme. Beyond the inter-war sprawl of any large town will be found the post-war estates built at generous density, often to geometric layouts. These are Bevan's houses. One who remembers is the former Labour leader Lord Neil Kinnock who lived in one of Bevan's new bungalows in the minister's own town of Tredegar. He said it was 'like moving to Beverley Hills . . . People used to come just to look at it' (Harris, 1984). The scale of the housing problem was immense. Half a million homes had been destroyed or made uninhabitable by German air-raids, a further three million badly damaged and overall a quarter of the county's homes were damaged. There was also the baby 'boom' after the end of war. By 1951, despite all the difficulties of obtaining sufficient building materials in the years after the war, Bevan had built one million houses: 'They as well as the National Health Service are his memorial' (Campbell, 1987).

In his programme Bevan favoured local government because he thought it could be trusted to honour planning agreements, and the vast majority of building licenses (90 per cent in 1946 and still some 80 per cent in 1950) were reserved for the construction of high-quality council houses. He argued that the Labour government 'would be judged for a year or two by the number of houses we build, we shall be judged in ten year's time by the type of houses we build' (Foot, 1973). However, Bevan underestimated the public's disillusionment. The housing programme had started slowly and in 1946 there had been an extensive outbreak of squatting. Private building was restricted until 1951 when only 25,000 private houses were built compared to 237,000 in 1938 before the outbreak of war.

Despite his legacy, Bevan's socialist preference for public over private housing was not shared by the British public. The horrors of inter-war speculative housing had not dimmed their desire to own their own homes and later Harold Macmillan, in 1951–55 during his housing drive, made much more use of private builders. As we will see in subsequent chapters, the private house-building industry became very powerful and a vocal critic of the perceived complexity and slowness of town planning. With Bevan's death also died the dream of a socialist future where housing would become a universally provided social service like the NHS and equally accepted.

The government did not pursue the radical Uthwatt solution of actually taking the land needed for development. The private market was still needed but the 100 per cent charge had removed the incentive for it to work. By 1951 there was evidence that buyers were paying over the odds for land and this was inflationary. Thus, in 1953, the Conservatives scrapped the financial provisions of the 1947 Act.

By the end of the decade the main elements of a population distribution policy had emerged. Firstly, a better balance of industrial development between regions. Secondly, a policy for the relief of congested urban areas by the movement of population and industry to independent new settlements, physically separate. The statutory means to achieve these policies we have already examined but it is important to appreciate the facts and forecasts available at the time that informed this thinking. Repeatedly through the ensuing decades regional planning was sabotaged by the failure of long-term population forecasting. When Abercrombie was preparing his London Plan, the official projection available to him was that Britain's population, which was 46.6 million in 1940, would rise to 47.2 million in 1960 (the actual population in 1960 was 51 million), and therefore there would be little or no increase in population. The continual increase in real incomes with its attendant consequences in terms of the demand for space for housing, cars and leisure, along with the net inward migration from overseas from the mid-1950s onwards, was not foreseen.

Despite Labour's best efforts, by the end of the 1940s the country's political mood had changed and the impetus for further social change was lost. The election of 1950 gave Prime Minister Attlee only a narrow majority, and a further election in October 1951 saw the Conservatives sweep back to power, promising to lift the burdens of wartime controls.

The General Development Order 1950

David Kynaston titled his social history of this period *Austerity Britain* and those of us born in those years can still recall the rationing, the power cuts and the hard winter of 1947. By 1950 these vicissitudes had had their effect and the popularity of Labour was waning, but that year, in an attempt to claw back some popularity, Labour introduced a politically expedient change in legislation which was extravagantly labelled an 'experiment in freedom'. The 1950 Order defined in some detail a variety of minor developments which did not need planning permission, and the main beneficiaries were dwelling house extensions and alterations, and farm buildings. Operational development by statutory undertakers was also given extensive freedom. These changes, particularly those to do with the utilities, led to a rash of ill-thought-out development and were to prompt the 'Outrage' series of articles in the *Architectural Review* magazine some years later (and which are featured in the next chapter), but other than the farm building concessions, which have now been curtailed, they survive to this day.

The Festival of Britain

The final chapter of Labour's post-war government was an event conceived during the war years and which became an iconic emblem of the 1950s. The Festival of Britain transformed in 1951 the industrial wasteland of London's South Bank into an architectural and social extravaganza which proved enormously popular to all of those including myself who went there. Some 8.5 million people visited the exhibition, which was held from May to

September. A triumvirate of Herbert Morrison, the politician tasked by Attlee to deliver the project, General Lord Ismay, chairman of the Festival Committee and the director, Sir Gerald Barry, faced down the criticism and scepticism of critics, chief of which was Churchill, to ensure that the Festival opened its doors on time. Unlike the initial debacle of the Millennium Dome (overseen by Morrison's grandson Peter Mandelson nearly 50 years later), the Festival proved a genuine popular success. 'A tonic to the nation' was the phrase used by Sir Gerald Barry to epitomise its main aim, but in retrospect we can see that the Festival was a glimpse of the affluent future that Macmillan first characterised in a speech in July 1957: 'most of our people have never had it so good'.

The Festival was not only a sample of the consumer society to come but, in the piazza and pedestrian precinct, the espresso bars and community centres, the blocks of council flats and rows of little houses, and above all the office buildings, it exemplified the idea of the post-war welfare state (Banham and Hillier, 1976).

Incorporated into the Festival of Britain with the aim of demonstrating the planning and architectural possibilities of post-war reconstruction, the redevelopment of the Lansbury neighbourhood in the East End of London, named after the Labour leader George Lansbury, was planned and developed by the then London County Council as part of the Stepney–Poplar reconstruction area proposed in Sir Patrick Abercrombie's London Plan. The centrepiece of the scheme was the Chrisp Street shopping centre based on a pre-war street market. Designed by Frederick Gibberd, the pedestrianised precinct was the forerunner of many others in England developed in the next decade. In the middle of the square was a clock tower, which Gibberd intended to be also a watchtower, until it was subsequently closed for fear of suicides. London County Council was a complex machine and no less than ten committees were involved in Lansbury, and as a consequence in Gibberd's own words, 'the architecture was modest and lacking in excitement' (Banham and Hillier, 1976), but the environment was bright and cheerful. Despite scepticism at the time, the centre proved successful and is still a vibrant part of this East End neighbourhood, now more accessible through an extension of the Docklands railway.

After the closure of the Festival, the new Conservative government retained none of the buildings or structures other than the Festival Hall, which looked like pique on Churchill's part at the time because of its enormous popular success. Yet the event presented one of the numerous paradoxes that characterise the political history of planning, in that its state direction was to provide a template for the garden festivals and enterprise

The Festival of Britain transformed in 1951 the industrial wasteland of London's south bank into an architectural and social extravaganza.

74

zones that the Conservatives were to employ 30 years later to regenerate the inner city.

Stevenage: Future Townscape

Although initially not in terms of numbers built, but in offering a glimpse of a future lifestyle, the new town programme ushered in by Lewis Silkin in 1946 had a major impact on the English townscape of the 1950s. As noted earlier, the first town to be built was Stevenage in Hertfordshire, which would house Londoners relocated from the capital's bombed neighbour-hoods. Progress in building was slow. Local opposition was strong and the legal battles led all the way to the House of Lords before the adoption was ratified in 1947. The first residential area, Bedwell Park, was airy and open, with walkways and greenery designed to be integral to the whole concept. Queensway, the pedestrianised town centre, was finally opened by Queen Elizabeth II in 1959, and was the first traffic-free shopping centre in the country. The clock tower in the main square became an iconic symbol of the 'never had it so good' era of the late 1950s.

Elections

Labour had scraped back after the election in February 1950 with a small majority of six seats but in the following year Attlee was ill, Bevin had died and the Cabinet was divided, with Gaitskell the Chancellor at odds with Bevan over the introduction of prescription charges. The Conservatives under a reinvigorated Churchill kept the House of Commons sitting night after night. Exhausted Labour went to the polls again in October 1951 but this time the Tories, after an effective election campaign, returned with a small but sufficient majority and Churchill was able to form a Cabinet.

Labour's Legacy

Andrew Marr (2007), in his book *A History of Modern Britain*, when reviewing Attlee's record asks, 'The question was how aggressively socialist was the government's post-war agenda to be?' and concludes, 'The optimism shri-velled under economic and physical storms, and though much of the Attlee legacy survived for decades, it was nothing like the social transformation Labour socialists had hoped for'.

A comprehensive and compulsory system of town and country planning shorn of its betterment clauses is a lasting legacy of the Attlee post-war government. In the following years, governments led by either Labour or Conservatives used the system to modernise the infrastructure of the country until the Thatcher revolution which tried to dispense with it. The system survived this onslaught and emerged as a broader concept of spatial planning at the end of the century. It is now seen as a vehicle of both economic management and improved sustainability. In the next chapter we look at how planning played its part in the post-war housing and property boom.

References

Banham, M. and Hillier, B. (1976) *A Tonic to the Nation*. London: Thames & Hudson.

Campbell, J. (1987) *Nye Bevan*. London: Weidenfeld & Nicholson, p. 162.

Foot, M. (1973) *Aneurin Bevan*, vol. 2. London: Davis, Poynter, p. 82.

Hall, P. (1974) *Urban & Regional Planning*, 3rd edn. London: Routledge, p. 117.

Hall, P. (2005) Speech to the RTPI, 'Talking the talk, walking the walk: making paper plans real', p. 11. London: The Royal Town Planning Institute.

Harris, R. (1984) *The Making of Neil Kinnock*. London: Faber & Faber, p. 25.

Jenkins, S. (2006) *Thatcher & Sons*. London: Allen Lane, p. 106.

Marr, A. (2007) *A History of Modern Britain*. Basingstoke: Macmillan.

5

Conservatives Under Four Prime Ministers, 1951–1964: The Affluent Years

A Different Party

The general elections of 1950 and 1951 were the two mass plebiscites of British electoral history, opines Roy Jenkins (2001) in his biography of Churchill. In the first, 83.9 per cent of those eligible voted, higher than at any other election since the arrival of universal suffrage. Twenty moths later the turnout declined only to 82.6 per cent. Churchill was able to form a government in 1951 that ushered in 13 years of Conservative power under four different Prime Ministers, reinforced by two subsequent general election victories in 1955 under Anthony Eden and in 1959 under Harold Macmillan.

The Conservative Party that took office in 1951 was a very different one from that which had entered the war in coalition with Labour:

> The Labour governments refused to put the clock back and pursued a programme designed to consolidate and strengthen the social cohesion engendered by the war. And so successful were they in their aims that they even converted the Conservative Party. By 1951 there could simply be no return to the society of the 1930s: the Welfare State had been accepted.
>
> (Sked and Cook, 1979)

This was as true of land use planning as it was of the other components of the welfare state.

The Conservative government did not de-nationalise most of the sectors nationalised by Labour, maintaining for example public ownership of the mines and railways, but steel and road transport were de-nationalised in 1953. After 1951 the Conservatives retained most of the key policy measures introduced by Labour: nationalisation, the welfare state introduced after the Beveridge Report of 1942 through the 1946 National Insurance Act and the

1948 National Assistance Act, Keynesian demand management, central planning and a repudiation of laissez-faire economics. As during the war, Churchill was preoccupied with foreign policy (and his own future historical reputation) and gave Rab Butler, his Chancellor from 1951 to 1955, a free hand. Butler, who had written a document in 1947 on industrial policy, *The Industrial Chapter*, influenced policy for nearly 20 years. Social harmony would be promoted by a mixed economy using Keynesian demand management to secure full employment and cooperation with the unions to avoid industrial strife. Fiscal policy would be used to manage demand and ensure full employment. This continuity was remarked on by *The Economist* when in its issue of 13 February 1954 it invented the mythical composite personality of Mr Butskell – a combination of the names of Butler and his Labour predecessor Hugh Gaitskell; ever since, the hybrid concept of Butskellism has epitomised the consensus.

The 1950 election had seen an increase in the number of new younger Conservative MPs entering Parliament, including Edward Heath, Ian Macleod and Enoch Powell. They produced a policy document called *One Nation* and Rab Butler agree to write a foreword. It was published in October 1950 and greatly influenced future Conservative policy. It included a target that 300,000 houses a year should be built and this aspiration was adopted at the Party conference that year. Labour's housing programme had peaked in 1948 and the annual provision of housing had dropped since then. The target was to be a source of difficulty for Butler who as Chancellor after the 1951 election had to allocate a disproportionate amount of national resources to its achievement. However, during the election campaign the Conservatives campaigned on this platform to great effect. When the results were finally declared Churchill to his relief discovered that he had won a general election at last. Labour won a slightly higher percentage of the total vote, but much of this accumulated in large majorities in safe constituencies. The Conservatives were helped by the comparative lack of Liberal candidates. As a result, the Liberals only polled three-quarters of a million votes and the majority of Liberal supporters voted for the Conservatives. For the Liberals the election was an unmitigated disaster with only six MPs in the House. Their fortunes were not to revive until the end of the decade.

The next decade was to radically change the appearance of England for in 1951 there were no superstores, no shopping precincts, no prestige office buildings, no parking garages, no urban motorways, no towers and slab blocks of flats. The Conservatives had been elected because the electorate was tired and impatient of the shortages of the post-war years. They wanted change in their working and social lives, but these changes would also radically change the look of England.

The Dash for Housing

The other important feature of this political period was Churchill's choice of Harold Macmillan as Housing Minister to increase the pace of Nye Bevan's housing programme, but now with private builders as the instrument of change. Deeply affected by the dreadful levels of unemployment he had witnessed in his own Stockton-on-Tees constituency in the North East of England before the war, he was a 'one nation Tory' and was determined to achieve Churchill's housing pledge. His approach was essentially pragmatic. Before the war, in 1938, he had published a very influential book, *The Middle Way*, which advocated a combination of public sector and private enterprise which was regarded with deep suspicion by many of his colleagues.

Macmillan, whose real passion was international affairs, was reluctant to accept Churchill's offer of Minister of Housing, but eventually he accepted:

> Winston asked me if I could build 300,000 houses in a year, and if so, would I be Minister of Housing. I agree on condition that I could run it my way. We ran it in fact like a war department. You see I'd learnt a thing or two at the Ministry of Supply working with tycoons.
>
> (Dalton, 1961)

The word 'planning' was removed from the name of the ministry. In January 1951 Attlee had reorganised the department so that housing and local government functions were removed from the Ministry of Health where they had been grouped under Nye Bevan and grouped with planning (Lewis Silkin having been elevated to the House Of Lords); the consequent mixture was renamed the Ministry of Local Government and Planning. The new title, Minister of Housing and Local Government, seemed to many to be damaging as it appeared to diminish the status of planning, but in truth it did not affect its functions but demonstrated the commitment of the Conservatives to achieve their housing target.

Despite recurring balance of payments crises, Macmillan won a disproportionate share of scarce resources through Churchill's support and the fear that any shortfall in production targets might lead to a questioning of the Party's commitment to the welfare state and jeopardise its future electoral success. Macmillan's pragmatic approach to housing delivery is worth looking at in a little detail because it has lessons even now as government wrestles with a resurgent housing problem.

Unlike Nye Bevan, Macmillan did not discriminate against a particular sector. He encouraged council house building and record numbers were built in the years 1952 to 1956. Private building was encouraged as it had languished under Bevan. Building licenses were abolished in 1954 but earlier, in December 1952, Macmillan introduced the Town & County Planning Bill (the 1954 Act). The use of private land had been to a large extent frozen by the 100 per cent charge and he had decided to drop the concept of betterment and abolished the charge entirely. Oliver Marriott, in his groundbreaking book *The Property Boom*, published in 1967, quotes Macmillan:

> I know some people say that the development charge is all right in theory but it will not work in practice. I am sufficiently old-fashioned to believe that if there is something wrong with the theory (Ministerial cheers) . . . the people whom the Government must help are those who do things: the developers, the people who create wealth, whether they are humble or exalted.

Reading this quote more than 50 years later, it has an uncanny ring of Margaret Thatcher about it. Even this one nation Tory was impatient to get production moving. He also had a good team. His junior minister was Ernest Marples who he would eventually promote to Minister of Transport and would become more famous as the man who opened the M1 motorway. He was a cocky, self-made man who had made a fortune in construction and shouldered much of the administrative burden. The civil servant was Evelyn Sharp, a dedicated worker who would later be promoted to permanent secretary and who dominated the department as ministers came and went, achieving immortality in *The Crossman Diaries* when Richard Crossman described how, even in 1964, she still dominated proceedings.

Housing standards were changed to allow smaller houses to be built and licenses to private builders were much increased. Even the appeal system was not immune. Under Labour the percentage of appeals won had increased from about a third, where it traditionally rests, to 44 per cent, but by 1952 had increased to 54 per cent (a figure which would almost be reached subsequently in the Thatcher years) before falling to 33 per cent in 1956, by which time it was considered that the housing shortage had been resolved. The results were dramatic. In 1953, 327,000 houses were built and in 1954, 354,000. At the 1954 Tory Party conference Macmillan had a hero's welcome for having made housing a 'national crusade'.

Compensation and Betterment

Macmillan's approach to this issue was pragmatic rather than ideological but we need to understand it because subsequently there has been much criticism of his decision to abolish the development charge entirely. The charge was perceived by the Conservatives as an obstacle to increased private sector house-building. But having agreed this, if the main part of the planning system was to remain, some limit to compensation for planning restriction was essential, otherwise effective planning controls would become prohibitively expensive and the cost of compensation for restrictions, if paid at the market value, would be crippling.

The Conservatives came up with a bold initiative, which ideologically was all the more surprising given their resistance to the financial aspects of the planning Acts since before the war. The solution was to compensate only for the loss of development value which accrued in the past up to the appointed day in 1948 when the 1947 axe fell, but not for loss of development value accrued in the future. The advantages were that the government's liability for compensation was limited, and it was to be paid only if and when the owner of land suffered from planning restrictions which were in derogation of an owner's existing use rights. The drawback was that it established a dual market in land according to whether it was sold in the open market or acquired by a public authority. Public opposition brought about the Town & Country Planning Act 1959 which restored a fair market price as the basis for compensation for compulsory acquisition. As we will see, successive Labour governments would try and recover the betterment value. The Conservative position has been to accept the state ownership of development rights but fair market price as the basis for compensation and that betterment would be taxed through capital gains tax.

Town Development Act 1952

Land supply for housing was clearly a critical factor. Macmillan pinned his faith on the Town Development Act 1952. The aim was to encourage town development in that the exporting local authorities would get together with the receiving authorities so as to plan properly. The Exchequer would provide finance, but unlike the new towns, implementation would be undertaken by the local authorities and not by a government-appointed body. In this instance Macmillan was less successful in persuading the Chancellor to help the housing drive and although towns such as Swindon,

Bletchley and Daventry were quick off the mark, by the end of 1963 only 13,000 houses had been completed against a target of 62,000. Although only one new town at Cumbernauld in Scotland was commissioned by the Conservative government until the second wave of new town building in the 1960s, Macmillan did manage to keep the programme of existing towns broadly intact and by the end of 1963, 80,000 new dwellings had been completed in the London new towns.

Letchworth Garden City represents for many people the right balance between town and country but it has had few imitators even within the New Towns programme

© Malcolm D. Moor

Property Boom

In his book, Oliver Marriott describes how post-war fortunes were made in property and much of it in London:

As Mr Macmillan lifted the development charge in 1953 and Mr Birch the building controls in 1954, the pace of development hotted up enormously. The

LCC granted planning permission in 1952 for 2.4 million square feet of space; in 1953 this jumped to 3 million, in 1954 to 5.7 million and in 1955 to 5.9 million. Building itself lags behind the granting of planning permission by a year to two years, but it was from around 1955, the peak year for permissions, that property development began to make an impact on the public consciousness. The cranes and the shiny matchbox blocks were there for all to see.

(Marriott, 1967)

The Affluent Society and Concerns

Macmillan's housing programme led the way to the affluent society that would be a feature of England at the end of the decade, but in October 1954 Churchill reshuffled his Cabinet and moved a reluctant Macmillan to the Defence Ministry, with Duncan Sandys becoming the new Housing Minister.

The architect Lionel Esher in his book describing the rebuilding of England between 1940 and 1980 concludes, 'In putting this wily and relaxed politician in charge of planning and housing, Churchill made an uncommonly sensible choice. In the golden glow of the New Elizabethan Age and of the 1953 'bonfire of controls', Macmillan's crusade to get 300,000 houses built in a year was comfortably achieved' (Esher, 1983).

Not everyone has been so euphoric. Alan Clark waspishly concludes in his history of the Conservative Party:

The most tangible remaining monument to the life and work of Harold Macmillan, his enemies can now be heard to argue, is the tower block and the sink estate. He eagerly embraced the Britain of the bulldozer and prefabricated concrete. Housing estates seemingly modelled on the morally debasing aesthetics of the Eastern European Communist bloc, received Macmillan's enthusiastic backing.

(Clark, 1998)

The manufacture and use of prefab concrete units continued apace. Under the Housing Subsidies Act 1956 the allocation of higher subsidies according to storey height started the tower block boom of the 1960s. The rise of the high-rise was destined to end with a bang in 1968, one May morning. Following the collapse of Ronan Point in London's East End, £100 million was spent modifying 400 other blocks after the initial explosion was traced to a faulty nut on a gas cooker. The explosion forced apart the concrete panels which, relying on gravity, were interlocked together.

83

Subtopia: Critical Voices

The car changed the landscape of England. Traffic signs, Belisha beacons, zebra crossings, petrol stations and garages sprang up throughout the towns and countryside, and together with the surviving detritus of the war, vacant airfields and dilapidated defence installations and buildings, England now had a ragged, edgy feel to it. This did not go unnoticed by young architectural critics. The *Architectural Review* in June 1955 published a special edition edited by Ian Nairn, who went on to become architectural correspondent of the *Observer* and a television pundit. Assisted by the illustrator Gordon Cullen, the issue was titled 'Outrage'. Their targets were the spec builders, advertisers, local officials and the visual squalor of the twentieth-century scene. The introductory paragraph gives a flavour:

> In this special issue the *Architectural Review* utters a prophesy of doom – the doom of an England reduced to universal Subtopia, a mean and middle state, neither town nor country, an even spread of abandoned aerodromes and fake rusticity, wire fences, traffic roundabouts, gratuitous notice-boards, car-parks and Things in Fields . . .
>
> (Nairn, 1955)

In the polemic tradition of the critics of suburbia in the 1930s, the authors protested that while planning had started in a mood of idealism, the policy of dispersal was spreading 'subtopia'. 'Outrage' presented a visual record of what Nairn saw on a pilgrimage through England, from Southampton to Carlisle. It showed what was happening to the country as a consequence of the uncoordinated activities of England's myriad post-war agencies for change. Nairn added 'subtopia' as a new word to the language but the feelings expressed in 'Outrage' had a practical outcome in the foundation of the Civic Trust in 1957.

More than a year later in December 1956 the authors published a sequel called 'Counter Attack' which was an attempt to demonstrate best practice, and give examples of how the crime of subtopia – blurring the distinction between places – could be avoided. Some 20 years later the *Architectural Review* asked Nairn, now well entrenched as the first of a long line of television design pundits, to retrace his steps. His conclusions were pessimistic. The only drastic change in 20 years between Southampton and Carlisle were the motorways and their design. The M1 excepted, these were, he concluded, one of the few genuinely collective and hopeful parts of design in the country, not least because the bypassing of the towns and cities was a significant achievement. Reading Nairn's passionate and blustering prose so many years later, there is really no hint of what might be done to overcome his exasperation, but his legacy, like that of Thomas Sharp before him, was to inject into the public consciousness a sense of place and the value of the English countryside, and the towns set within it. Modern-day protestors in the numerous 'planning wars' taking place throughout the country owe much to Sharp and Nairn.

The Civic Trust

In a more practical vein, Duncan Sandys, who had been a vigorous planning minister to whom we will return, set up the Civic Trust. He had been aware of the rapid expansion of local amenity societies (by the mid-1960s there were 700 affiliated societies) and knew the value of a national body that had some clout. His civil servants advised against the initiative, which could be a pressure group against his own department, but the Prime Minister, Sir Anthony Eden, cautiously agreed and Sandys became president. The Civic Trust would win its spurs later in the decade in its campaign against Jack Cotton's naive project for London's Piccadilly Circus named the 'Monico' building, which resembled something imported from Las Vegas. The scheme was called in by the minister who subsequently dismissed it, agreeing with his inspector Mr Colin Buchanan (later famous for the Buchanan Report on traffic in towns). Buchannan. who had written a book entitled *Mixed Blessing: The Motor Car in Britain*, published in 1958, addressed the traffic issues of the scheme and his report came down decisively against the development. In a memorable quote reflecting on the traditional role of Piccadilly as the centre of the Empire he wryly concluded that, 'if a comprehensive development is to take place then it should be to a standard that really justifies a journey from the ends of the earth' (Buchannan, 1972).

Postscript: The Middle Way

It is often asserted that the decision of the Conservative administration in 1952 to dismantle the compensation and betterment provisions of the 1947 Act was an ideological reaction to what was perceived as a socialist land tax.

Looked at from a distance the tax looks even more self-defeating than it may have done at the time, but the Conservative response was more pragmatic than ideological and reflected Macmillan's 'Middle Way'. There was to be no return to the pre-war suspicion of planning and that the Conservatives left the planning system otherwise intact was quite surprising, reflecting back on their pre-war anxieties and uncertainties on land issues.

A Foregone Conclusion

Churchill finally resigned as Prime Minister in April 1955 and on 5 April his successor, Anthony Eden, entered Number 10. He dissolved Parliament on 7 April and an election was held towards the end of May.

> The result was a foregone conclusion in a way in which few British general elections have been. The turnout figures reflected this, dropping from 82.5 per cent to 76.7 per cent. The Conservatives thus emerged with an overall majority of no less than sixty seats and were the first party in a century to increase their majority in Parliament as a result of a general election.
>
> (Sked and Cook, 1979)

Foreign policy was to preoccupy the government, particularly the debacle of Suez, but Duncan Sandys was to have an opportunity to leave a legacy that would survive in planning policy for more than 50 years.

The Green Belts

On 3 August 1955, Sandys addressed a circular to local authorities on the subject of green belts. This was very much a personal initiative, lacking departmental support, but it met with widespread acceptance (Cherry, 1982). The metropolitan green belt around London was conceived in the Abercrombie London Plan in 1944 and became a reality as part of the 1947 Act, but this did not refer to the rest of England. Sandys listed three reasons why green belts were needed. Firstly, to check the growth of large built-up areas, secondly to prevent neighbouring towns from merging into one another, and thirdly to preserve the special character of a town (in 1984 a fourth objective was added to assist in urban regeneration). The need for green belts around towns and cities other than London was pressing. Despite the new towns programme and that of the expanded towns, the majority of new housing was being constructed in privately-built suburban estates. Duncan Sandys made it clear in the circular that whatever the character of the land, if neither green nor particularly attractive, the major function was simply to stop further urban development.

In the following years green belts were established around all the conurbations and around many historic towns such as Oxford, Cambridge, Bath and York. Subsequently there were to be some epic planning battles on the outskirts of cities such as Manchester and Birmingham when attempts were made to export the population to rural areas on their boundaries. The cities lost, and the justification would be the twin arguments of green belt policy and the need to preserve agricultural land. Green belt policy was seen by the government as an essential component of the policy of dispersal implemented through the new towns and expanded towns programmes so as to ensure there was not widespread encroachment into the countryside.

The green belt has always enjoyed much popular support and although people have tended to see its functions and purpose differently, it has turned out to be the most successful of planning concepts, no doubt because of its essential simplicity. Duncan Sandys was a vigorous Planning Minister and had first come to notice in the field of planning in the wartime coalition government. If Lewis Silkin can lay claim to be the soul of Labour's planning ideology then Duncan Sandys can claim a similar role for the Conservatives. Later, in 1967, he was to bring forward a Private Members' Bill which introduced the concept of conservation areas, extending legal protection from individual buildings of quality to whole areas of architectural or historic interest (Cherry, 1982). In relation to green belts and conservation areas, he championed two planning concepts that many Conservatives, ideologically opposed to the spirit of planning controls, were prepared to support.

Clean Air

This was another planning initiative that began life as a Private Members' Bill. In 1952, 4,000 people had died prematurely because of asphyxia, bronchial and heart troubles in the great London smog. Following a report by Sir Hugh Beaver which examined chronic atmospheric pollution, the young, flamboyant MP for Kidderminster, Sir Gerald Nabarro, had introduced a Private Members' Bill called 'Clean Air' to give effect to the principal recommendations of the Beaver Report, and had got it through a second reading in February 1955. The problem with a Private Members' Bill is that it cannot include financial provisions and Sandys persuaded Nabarro to withdraw the Bill against his assurance that a government clean air Bill would be brought in that session. In the event, Parliament was dissolved in the spring of 1955 but the Clean Air Act was passed in 1956, much in the form that Nabarro had originally proposed but supported by all the necessary financial provisions. The Act was a remarkable tribute to the determination of a single backbench member of parliament.

A New Leader

On 7 January 1957, Eden's doctors advised him to give up, and two days later he tendered his resignation and held his last Cabinet. The press were almost unanimous in predicting Butler for Prime Minister but after having been consulted by a number of Conservative politicians including Churchill, the Queen sent for Macmillan and asked him to form a government: 'It was widely assumed that Macmillan's premiership would be a stopgap to tide the Tory Party over the crisis. No one imagined that it would last nearly seven years' (Sampson, 1967). In the new Cabinet, Duncan Sandys moved to become Defence Minister and Henry Brooke moved to Housing. The Rent Act introduced by him in 1957 lifted control over rents on 400,000 houses and was one of the few legislative measures of the 1950s which exposed a clear difference of purpose and ideology. It was a logical step from Macmillan's housing policies but Labour attacked it as a 'landlord's charter' to exploit poor tenants. The minister argued that without rent review landlords could not afford to improve their properties, while Labour asserted that the landlords would pocket the extra money. In the event there was little impact and by the time of the next election in 1959 the issue was spent.

The New Towns Act 1959

This Act repealed the provisions of the 1946 Act for the eventual transfer to the appropriate local authorities of the assets of the new town Development Corporations. The 1959 Act instead set up a New Towns Commission under the central government to take over the Corporations' assets, while delegating responsibility to local communities. It was to signal a new enthusiasm by the Conservatives in new town-building.

Third Parties

The 1959 legislation that we have already looked at also provided that owners of land and agricultural tenants should be formally advised of a planning application when made in respect of their land. Although this procedure was hardly radical and was enacted to rectify abuses by speculators, it was a first step in involving third parties in the planning process by advising them of applications. The change followed the report of the Committee on Administrative Tribunals and Enquiries (the Franks Committee) in 1957.

Never Had it So Good

On 20 July 1957, Macmillan made a speech at Bradford which was to reassert itself through out the rest of his career:

> Indeed let us be frank about it: most of our people have never had it so good. Go round the country, go to the industrial towns, go to the farms and you will see a state of prosperity such as we have never had in my lifetime – nor indeed ever in the history of this country.
>
> (Sampson, 1967)

That rather boastful approach set the tone for the election campaign that finally got underway in the summer of 1959. Macmillan early demonstrated an effortless ease in the new medium of television and the ironical caricature of him as 'Supermac' by the cartoonist Vicky soon rebounded as the Prime Minister adopted it as part of his image: 'It was as the prime minister of affluence that Macmillan established his mass popularity' (Sampson, 1967).

The 1959 election was a decisive blow to Labour. The Conservatives increased their overall majority to 100 seats while the Liberals doubled their share of the vote. Gaitskell, the Labour leader, sought to deal with the reversal and urged the Labour Party conference that October to abandon Clause 4 of the Labour constitution seeking wholesale nationalisation of the country's productive capacity. He was unsuccessful and it remained for Tony Blair to rewrite the constitution more than 30 years later. The election represented a personal triumph for Macmillan.

Population and Traffic Growth

However, prosperity brought its own problems, particularly in planning. The early post-war planning had been on the assumption that the level of population and employment in London would be static and the tremendous growth in offices, service trades and white-collar jobs was not foreseen. By the end of the 1950s the Conservatives knew that they could no longer rely on the Abercrombie Plan, and new planning was required for the whole of the South East region, as the commuting area for central London office workers now stretched as far as Luton, Reading, Southend and the Thanet towns. The increasing importance of planning was recognised in 1959 by the granting of a charter by the Privy Council to the RTPI. Planning was now seen as a separate professional activity, no longer subordinate to the other professional disciplines that had been its genesis.

On 9 November 1959, the first stretch of the M1 was opened. The six lanes of asphalt were viewed as a tourist attraction, and on the Sunday after the opening, crowds of sightseers came to view, some even laying out picnics on the verges of the approach roads. By the early 1960s the sheer scale and pace of urban renewal and the associated transport problems were creating great difficulties. Demand was beginning to outstrip capacity in the construction industry and building costs were rising rapidly. There was a shortage of land for new housing. Land allocations in the development plans, which were supposed to be sufficient for 20 years, had been used up in less than half that time. Shortages of bricks and other materials had fostered a keen interest in 'industrialised building techniques' – factory-built kits for the rapid building of housing, schools and offices.

Two factors proved a powerful boost to continued building at the beginning of the 1960s: population growth and the growth of urban traffic. Population projections were indicating a growth in Britain (but predominantly in England) to a population of between 70 and 80 million by the end of the century. Car ownership had grown to 6 million by 1961 from 2.5 million a decade earlier. Against this background the car ownership projections in the early 1960s were indicating a large and sustained increase in the growth of traffic, with car ownership doubling by 1970 and trebling by 1980 – forecasts which were fulfilled.

The 1961 census had shown that the population growth in the ring of Home Counties around London had amounted to 800,000 people – one third of the net growth of population in Britain. Most of the population was not housed in the planned new or expanded towns but in privately-built suburban estates akin to those built between the wars but now pushed further out by the existence around London of the green belt.

The Conservative government had to act, and in 1961 it reversed its policy and designated the first new town in England for 12 years – Skelmersdale on Merseyside – and the following year initiated a series of regional planning studies which would provide guidelines for the regional planning offices.

After the 1959 election, the pre-election spending spree set off by Heathcoat-Amory's budget of 1959 (nine pence had been taken off income tax) had to be curbed. Profit taxes were raised to 12.5 per cent in the budget of 1960 and a few weeks later credit restrictions and dearer money had to be imposed. The Cabinet lost faith in the Chancellor and he was replaced in 1961 by Selwyn Lloyd, who almost immediately ran into a sterling crisis requiring the bank rate to go up to 7 per cent and large loans from the International Monetary Fund (IMF) and central banks.

The effect of Selwyn Lloyd's deflationary policy and the bad winter of 1962–63 pushed up unemployment to the 800,000 mark. Faced with growing unpopularity, Macmillan appointed Lord Hailsham as Minister with Special Responsibility for the North East in 1963. This resulted in a White Paper on regional programmes for North-East England and also for Central Scotland, both areas being hard hit by unemployment.

Town Centres: A New Brutalism

The early 1960s saw a growing demand from private developers to invest in the redevelopment of town centres, which in many cases had not been the subject of major changes since the 1930s. The government published advice on the redevelopment of town centres in *Planning Bulletin No. 1: Town Centres – Approach to Renewal* (Ministry of Housing and Local Government/Ministry of Transport, 1962). In cities such as Birmingham, Liverpool and Newcastle, engineers and architect-planners seized on the opportunities for major redevelopment ushered in by the advice. Accompanying the document was a practice note which reviewed schemes that had been completed in the past ten years. (Ministry of Housing and Local Government/Ministry of Transport, 1963). Many of these were in the new towns such as Stevenage, Basildon, Harlow and Crawley, and war-damaged Coventry. Two shopping centres under construction at the time at the Elephant and Castle in London and the Bull Ring in Birmingham featured prominently, and subsequently were derided for their crassness and banality. Both were subsequently substantially rebuilt. There were few examples of town centre redevelopment in historic towns, and the overwhelming impression of the document is the brutality of the approach to town centre redevelopment. The redevelopment of Newcastle city centre was one of the most brutal. Promoted by a city council intent that the city would be the 'Capital of the North' and cater fully for the car, an urban expressway was driven through the student suburb of Jesmond and the city centre to link with the Tyne Bridge, effectively cutting the town centre in two. Ten years later the Metro – an urban passenger railway system serving the whole of Tyneside – was opened, rendering the expressway obsolete. The result was 'traffic architecture' (where buildings are stranded by encircling roads and pedestrians are forced onto walkways or into tunnels) of a scale fortunately not seen in many other parts of England. The 1973 oil price crisis saw a marked slowdown in town centre redevelopment and by the 1980s it was overtaken by the out-of-centre superstore boom.

New Planning Methods

As we will see, the Conservatives were willing as a matter of expediency, when economic conditions deteriorated, to experiment with regional initiatives, but were opposed to any permanent regional organisation which would usurp existing central and local government responsibilities. Despite this, the Bow Group had bravely published in 1960 a pamphlet called 'Let Our Cities Live' which included proposals for the establishment of regional area councils composed of delegates from local authorities and ministerially-appointed members.

Planning made a comeback into Tory respectability in 1961 when Peter Thornycroft introduced the new planning machinery of the National Economic Development Council (NEDC) at which government discussed particular economic problems and planned growth with the two sides of industry. The initiative was supported by the Federation of British Industry which had become disillusioned with the impact on investment of stop-go policies and of Keynesian economists who had become convinced of the need for import and wage controls. In opposition, Labour cast doubt over the Conservatives' commitment to planning, suggesting that it was essentially a political stratagem both to reconcile trade unions to wage restraint and to project a failing party in a modern light. However, Anthony Sampson (1967) saw this approach as foreshadowed in Macmillan's book published in 1938 to which I have already referred, which dealt with the economic and social problems during the depression and the case for government intervention.

The Night of the Long Knives

On 13 July 1962, unnerved by by-election losses to the Liberal Party, Macmillan announced a further Cabinet reshuffle, but on a scale unprecedented – seven cabinet members including the Chancellor of the Exchequer were sacked. It became known as 'The night of the long knives' and drew from the Liberal leader Jeremy Thorpe one of the century's wittiest political aphorisms: 'that greater love hath no man than that he lay down his friends for his life' (Clark, 1998). There then followed a long and difficult time for Macmillan before his resignation as leader on grounds of health on the eve of the Conservative Party conference in October 1963. The year had been hell for Macmillan. De Gaulle had vetoed Britain's first application to join the European Economic Community (EEC) in January and Harold Wilson had succeeded to the leadership of the Labour Party on the death of Gaitskell. In June there had been scandals both homosexual and heterosexual involving Vassall, the KGB spy, Steven Ward and Christine Keeler, and the resignation of Profumo, the War Minister. Macmillan conspired to insure that his Foreign Secretary, Sir Alec Douglas-Home, would succeed him and this was announced to the Party conference without a vote. Modernists such as Ian Macleod were aghast and he resigned from office. Much later, in retirement, Macmillan was to reflect ruefully, 'That illness was a sad blow for me. Without being conceited, it was a catastrophe for the Party' (Clark, 1998).

Revolution

Anthony Sampson, in his biography of Macmillan, summing up the man and his era, acutely observes that 'neither Macmillan nor his successor ever managed to establish the sense of confidence in the future, such as Harold Wilson so carefully cultivated' (Sampson, 1967). At the 1962 Labour Party conference that autumn Wilson, in his inaugural speech as leader, brilliantly caught the mood of the country which wished for a political change, a Britain 'that is going to be forged in the white heat of this revolution'. That sentiment was to have enormous implications for both spatial and economic planning but before we consider that, we must deal briefly with what Alan

Clark (1998) has wryly described as 'the short orthodox premiership of Sir Alec Douglas-Home' who was Prime Minister from October 1963 until the election in October the following year. Home ignored Edward Heath's claims to be Foreign Secretary and instead put him in charge of the new enlarged Department of Industry whose responsibilities included regional development. Sir Keith Joseph, who had come into the Cabinet as Housing Minister after Macmillan's purge, remained in the post. One of his key decisions in May, before the 1964 election, was to commission a report from the Planning Advisory Group with a view to reforming and speeding up the planning system. The group was chaired by a civil servant, I.V. Pugh, from the Ministry of Housing and Local Government, but included planning officers from across the country and subsequently reported in 1965 to the new minister, Richard Crossman, about whom we shall hear much more.

London's Government

The last year of the Conservative administration was to prove immensely important for spatial planning because of a number of administrative changes and reports commissioned in this period. The need to reform London's government was keenly felt in the early 1960s. The London County Council had long been overtaken by the outward spread of development and lay embedded in a sea of suburbs administered by neighbouring councils. The London Government Act 1963 provided for a completely new local government structure comprising a new Greater London Council (GLC) and within it a number of large multi-function boroughs. The boundaries of the GLC were very closely defined and some large suburban areas almost totally dependent on the metropolis were excluded because of local opposition to being included in 'London'.

Traffic in Towns

In the autumn of 1963 the Transport Minister, Ernest Marples, received a report, Traffic in Towns, prepared by a working group led by the late Professor Sir Colin Buchanan. He had earlier written an influential book on the planning problems of the motor car and his planning inquiry report on Jack Cotton's Monico scheme had also caught the eye of the Transport Minister. Uniquely qualified in planning, architecture and engineering, Buchannan and his report were to have a decisive influence on urban transportation planning, not only in the UK but throughout the world. As

94

we have seen, Buchannan had been a planning inspector and he knew the value of a clearly written report albeit on a complex and difficult subject. I worked for him on his report on the Greater London Plan published in 1971 and I still remember the prolific use of his blue pencil when editing drafts. He was later to write an eloquent note of dissent as a member of the Roskill Commission to advise on the siting of London's third airport. He could not accept the majority view that the airport should be located north of the Chilterns in the Vale of Aylesbury. His support for an airport off the Essex coast at Maplin Sands would later be championed by Ted Heath as Conservative Prime Minister but scotched by Harold Wilson's government in 1974 as it tried to cope with yet another sterling crisis.

Buchannan's report wrestled with the basic dilemma of how to provide a satisfactory balance between traffic movement and civilised urban life. It advocated two main concepts – primary road networks to cater for the main, longer traffic flows in urban areas where traffic would have precedence, and environmental areas where traffic should be subordinated to the needs of those living and working in them. This should be linked to comprehensive parking and traffic management policies while longer-term integrated land use and transport plans were being prepared and implemented. Throughout his career as a civil servant, consultant or academic, Buchannan did not set a great deal of store by politicians, certainly not local politicians, who he thought unwilling to take the big decisions needed in planning. During a long retirement living on Boars Hill overlooking Oxford's dreaming spires, Buchannan remained disappointed that action in the wake of his report had been inadequate, believing that an opportunity had been squandered. (Buchannan, 2001).

Buchannan's work had been guided by a steering group chaired by Sir Geoffrey Crowther, and in the recommendations of the group there was strong support for the setting up of Regional Development Agencies to oversee the whole programme of urban modernisation in the regions, and through which grants would be channelled and powers of government exercised. It was a radical proposal but was firmly rejected by Ernest Marples who maintained that a programme for local authority reorganisation was already underway: 'If that does not do the trick, we will have to take it a stage further – but we must give then an opportunity first' (Cullingworth, 1964).

Post-war Office Development

London's dominance as a location for office development was already evident during the early post-war years. There was a strong demand for office space in the capital, due partly to the fact that between the wars relatively little office-building had taken place and Victorian offices, many of them obsolete, were ripe for renewal. In addition, in the early 1950s London became increasingly popular as the chosen location for prestige headquarters and cemented its position as an international centre. This, coupled with two crucial political decisions, namely the lifting of the development charge by Macmillan in 1953 and the dropping of building licences by the then Minister of Works in November 1954, led to an unprecedented boom in office development in the capital (Moor, 1979). The scheme of building licences which had restricted most commercial development to the reconstruction of war-damaged offices and factories had been introduced to ration building materials and assist the housing drive. In London, the Victorian regulation that limited the height of new buildings to 25 metres (80 feet) was lifted. The age of the high-rise had begun. In the next ten years an unprecedented building boom completely altered the scale and skylines of Britain's major cities. As Robert Hewison (1987) wryly observed in 1963, the first property developer had been knighted.

During the period from then on until the mid-1960s, London's predominance in terms of office location became increasingly problematic. Policy-makers focused considerable attention on the central area of the city, and in 1957 the *Plan to Combat Congestion in central London* was unveiled. This policy of decentralisation – of attempting to restrain the growth of office employment in central London while encouraging it in outer areas, notably in Middlesex, Kent, Croydon and Essex – was reiterated in the 1960 review of the development plan. At this time voluntary decentralisation was being advocated by the government, which had rejected the idea of office development certificates.

By the early 1960s it was clear that London's enthusiasm for a policy of suburban development was no longer shared by other local authorities. Doubts were soon translated into specific limitations on office development in Middlesex, Kent, Essex, Hertfordshire and Surrey, and in 1963 the government – in response to pressure from local authorities and other bodies such as the TCPA – issued a White Paper entitled *London – Employment: Housing: Land*, in which the problems resulting from the enormous growth of office employment in central London were discussed. Although rejecting the concept of licences, the government did introduce an important adjustment to the Town and Country Planning Act 1962 and advocated the dispersal of civil servants. The Location of Offices Bureau was set up as an agent of this decentralisation policy.

Thirteen Wasted Years?

One of the most comprehensive and readable accounts of the 13 years of Conservative government in the planning field is by J.H. Westergaard and was published in the *Town Planning Review* in October 1964 (Westergaard, 1964). Westergaard divided the period from 1951 into three phases.

During the first – lasting at most a few years – the apparatus of planning control in the 1940s was broadly unchanged. During the next phase, from 1953 to 1961, the scope of physical planning was progressively curtailed through government action by the denationalisation of development values and financial restrictions on local authorities, by an increasing limitation of the role of public development in housing and other fields and a growing reliance by government on the operation of market forces, along with changes in the structure of local government generally, involving a devolution of powers from larger to smaller authorities.

The third phase (1961–64) began tentatively with the Local Employment Act 1960 which introduced much smaller districts for direct government financial assistance. The second report of the NEDC (1963) was implicitly critical of the 1960 Act and suggested that positive incentives to development in the regions of low activity might be improved by increasing the predictability and value of assistance, increasing expenditure on social infrastructure, and on facilities for retraining labour; also by directing aid to larger areas than at present and within those to 'growth points' not necessarily characterised by high rates of unemployment. Many of the recommendations were incorporated in the Finance Act 1963 and the Local Employment Act 1963.

The Town & Country Planning Act 1963 was designed to reduce (and in some circumstances eliminate) the potential liability of planning authorities, under previous legislation, to pay compensation for refusal of applications to extend or rebuild existing buildings. Though of general application, it was directed particularly at office-building in London. As we have seen, in the same year a Location of Offices Bureau was set up under the ministry to encourage and give advice to firms on the decentralisation of office employment from central London.

The South East Study

The first of the regional studies commissioned in the early 1960s was published in February 1964 and known as the South East Study. A further 3.5 million people in the region during the 20-year period was envisaged, necessitating a second round of new towns at a greater distance from London than the first: Milton Keynes, Northampton, Peterborough and Southampton/Portsmouth. The study reiterated the government's emphasis on decentralisation and suburban development, but also included a policy of providing office centres further away from the London conurbation.

The study and the accompanying White Paper caused an enormous amount of interest. The *Guardian* in March ran a four-page supplement and reproduced most of the study. The White Paper (Ministry of Housing and Local Government, 1964) concluded:

> The Government believes that the process of regional planning can contribute greatly to the well-being and prosperity of the country as a whole. They have already published programmes, which are being implemented, for Central Scotland and the North East. Studies of other regions are being prepared. In this way the special needs of individual regions can be identified and a proper national balance achieved and maintained.

There was no intention of departing from green belt policy and the expanded town programme and the new towns were expected to be the means of accommodating the population growth. What was clear was that despite the final acceptance by the Conservative government of the importance of regional planning, no administrative changes were envisaged and local authorities would continue to be in the driving seat for this regional growth.

Westergaard (1964) was critical of the fact that there was no effective relationship between the NEDC and the various departments involved in physical planning and development, and he cited a number of reports such as that into the future of Britain's ports (1962) and the reshaping of British railways (The Beeching Report, 1963) which had been published as if in a vacuum. Writing before the October 1964 election, Westergaard could not have envisaged the extent to which Harold Wilson's government would pick up the scattered fragments of regional planning left by the Conservatives and pull them together into a coherent policy.

Professor Sir Peter Hall (1993) has argued that events forced the Conservative governments of the early 1960s, against their ideological judgement, to embark both on a further new towns programme, but also upon an elaborate series of regional studies and strategic plans. I believe that a close study of the period demonstrates that the Butskellite policies of the time, which were to be so robustly challenged by Margaret Thatcher two decades later, provided the ideological basis for their approach. Hall quotes Macmillan's own aphorism: 'Events, dear boy, events' as the rationale for their actions but as we have seen in Macmillan's housing drive, he pragmatically took those elements that suited his approach. The one area where the Conservatives were not prepared to compromise was on the nationalisation of development value and that can be traced back to the final days of the wartime coalition and Churchill's intervention to prevent this becoming policy. Churchill's opposition was ideological but Macmillan observed that during Labour's 1945–51 administration it simply had not worked. The land market had stalled and so he could easily and pragmatically abolish the development charge.

References

Buchannan, M. (1972) Shop Property, *Goodbye Piccadilly*, June, pp. 14–15.

Buchannan, M (2001) Obituary, the *Independent*, also *The Times* and the *Daily Telegraph*, 10 December..

Cherry, G. (1982) *The Politics of Town Planning*. London: Longman, p. 71.

Clark, A. (1998) *The Tories: Conservatives & The Nation State 1922–1997*. London: BCA, pp. 291, 318, 329.

Cullingworth J.B. (1964) *Town & Country Planning In England & Wales*. London: George Allen & Unwin, p. 270.

Dalton, H. (1961) *High Tide and After*. London: Muller, p. 351.

Esher, L. (1983) *A Broken Wave: The Rebuilding of England 1940–1980*. London: Pelican, p. 51.

Hall, P. (1993) Urban development and urban policy: where have we come from, *RSA Journal*, pp. 511–33.

Hewison, R. (1987) *The Heritage Industry*. London: Methuen, p. 36.

Jenkins, R. (2001) *Churchill*. Basingstoke: Macmillan, p. 827.

Marriott, O. (1967) *The Property Boom*. London: Hamish Hamilton, pp. 4–5, 5–6.

Ministry of Housing and Local Government (1964) *South East England*, White Paper, Cmnd 208, 20 March.

Ministry of Housing and Local Government/Ministry of Transport (1962) *Planning Bulletin No. 1: Town Centres – Approach to renewal*. London: HMSO.

Ministry of Housing and Local Government/Ministry of Transport (1963) *Town Centres: Current Practice*. London: HMSO.

Moor, N. (1979) The contribution and influence of office developers and their companies on the location and growth of office activities, P.W. Daniels (ed.) *Spatial Patterns of Office Growth and Location.* Chicester: John Wiley & Sons.

Nairn, I. (ed.)(1955) Outrage, *Architectural Review,* 117(702).

National Economic Development Council (NEDC) (1963) *Conditions Favourable to Faster Growth,* pp. 14–29.

Sampson, A. (1967) *Macmillan: A Study in Ambiguity.* London: Allen Lane, pp. 47, 125, 157, 158.

Sked, A. and Cook, C. (1979) *Post-War Britain: A Political History.* London: Pelican, pp. 12, 139–40.

Westergaard, J.H. (1964) Land use planning since 1951, *Town Planning Review,* pp. 220–237.

6

Harold Wilson and the Scientific Revolution, 1964–1970

Modernisation

At the end of an energetic and encouraging campaign, Harold Wilson gave his most forceful speech to an eve-of-poll audience at Liverpool's St George's Hall. With Lord Attlee, from whose government Wilson had resigned 13 years before – now an energetic Wilsonite campaigner (Pimlott, 1992) – sitting by him, the Labour leader reiterated his election theme of modernisation with a moral aim, contrasting this with Tory selfishness and amateurism. The final figures gave Labour 317 seats, the Conservatives 304 and the Liberals 9. The effective overall majority was 5, with a gap of only 13 between the major parties. Despite the narrow margin, it was a major political upheaval. The first occasion in peacetime since 1906 that an incumbent Conservative administration had been displaced by a non-Conservative party with an absolute majority (Pimlott, 1992).

On coming into government, Wilson was confronted with information from the Treasury that the predicted balance of payments deficit was double what had been anticipated. Wilson was determined to avoid devaluation of the pound, and chose a temporary import surcharge instead, which chimed with his own views of planned growth, rather than a reliance on monetary adjustments. In the Queen's speech of 3 November 1964, the new programme included a Crown Commission to acquire land for the community, and underpinning the whole economic programme, national and regional plans to promote economic development. At the centre of the programme was the National Plan, a key proposal in opposition, and George Brown became responsible for national economic planning, and threw himself into the project.

The National Plan

The Conservatives had reluctantly turned to planning but Labour were more enthusiastic, 'Rejoicing ideologically in the interventionism of planning, Labour was able to tie it to the socialist objectives of abolishing poverty and creating equality of opportunity' (Pimlott, 1992). But there were opponents. Douglas Jay believed that talk of national economic planning was empty jargon and that 'there was nothing between economic policy and town and country planning' (Pimlott, 1992). A new ministry was created called the Department of Economic Affairs (DEA), with a watchful Treasury reluctantly in cooperation. I still remember the frisson of excitement when the DEA was announced. At last we were using the planning tools that appeared to have enabled European countries such as France to leap ahead of Britain in their economic performance. Change was in the air and the Tories knew it too. Edward Heath, who had led Britain's abortive negotiations to enter the Common Market and was also seen as a moderniser, succeeded Sir Alec Douglas-Home as Conservative leader in July 1965. The National Plan was unveiled on 16 September of that year. It was ambitious and set a target of 25 per cent growth in national output between 1964 and 1970, an average annual rate of 3.8 per cent. The underlying idea was that it was possible to improve economic performance and boost growth over a number of years by the national coordination of resources and investment. This was the distinctive mark of Wilson and the government. Initially, media reaction was encouraging, but ministers and mandarins were less easily won over. Richard Crossman, now Housing Minister, felt marginalised as Wilson and Brown launched their plan and Callaghan as Chancellor thought it too ambitious. Wilson gave it his full backing and at a speech in Lancashire on 17 September 1965 'he presented it as the essence of modern socialism' (Pimlott, 1992).

Despite Wilson's training and expertise as an economist, he failed in the initial stages to appreciate that keeping up the value of the pound required restrictive economic policies that were inimical to the aims of the National Plan. In the summer of 1966 there was a fresh sterling crisis and the government chose deflation rather than devaluation and abandoned the growth objective. Critics argued that the July measures, destroyed not only growth, but also the Plan for growth and the very idea of planning for growth. Ben Pimlott, in his biography of Wilson (1992) was more reflective, arguing that despite the fanfare planning was not really tested:

102

But as an overriding economic strategy it never had a proper chance: the fragile economic conditions which made it an attractive option, combined with the precarious policies of 1965–1966, prevented the subordination of other aims that would have been necessary to make it work.

To provide regional coordination, early in 1965 a series of economic planning councils was set up, based on the old standard regions, which had been used for statistical purposes. Members were appointed representing different groups in each region and there was a counterpart, the economic planning boards comprising civil servants seconded from London. The original National Plan was published before it could contain any contribution from the councils and boards although subsequently the councils did publish their regional studies and plans. The DEA became weaker after the departure of George Brown as its political head, and in 1969 it was formally abolished, its economic planning functions passing to the Treasury and its regional responsibilities to the Ministry of Housing and Local Government.

All sorts of excuses have been offered since for the failure of the National Plan and the DEA: the sterling crisis; interdepartmental rivalries; etc. but New Labour and specifically Gordon Brown as Chancellor learnt an important lesson. The regionalism developed since New Labour's election victory in 1997 has had a major supporter in the form of the Treasury and once in Number 10 as prime minister Brown lost no time in announcing the abolition of the consultative regional assemblies and the primacy of the Economic Development Agencies in regional economic and physical planning, but yet again has failed to stop an economic and financial crisis.

Richard Crossman at Housing and Local Government

As already noted, Wilson in his first Cabinet placed Richard Crossman at Housing and Local Government (planning had long disappeared from the ministerial title). Although only in the post for two years, the diaries kept by Crossman and published a decade later have ensured that the events of those two years have retained a relevance that belies the long interval since then. He was a journalist as well as a politician. After Labour lost office in 1970 and until 1972 when he was succeeded by Anthony Howard, he was editor of the *New Statesman*. His diaries not only give an unprecedented insight into the life of politics at the top but are eminently readable. In the diaries he gives a fascinating account of the decisions he took to allow three housing schemes in the green belt at Chelmsley Wood near Birmingham, Hartley in

Kent (the Span model village later to be called New Ash Green) and at Stannington near Sheffield:

> I'm making these three planning decisions quite deliberately because I've decided, if rigidly interpreted, a green belt can be the strangulation of a city . . . I know this will cause me my first major row but I am pleased about it. I've decided to do it and I think it's good ground on which to fight.
>
> (Crossman, 1975)

Crossman knew that housing figured hugely in the Prime Minister's plans and by May 1965 Wilson had decided that the housing drive must take priority over all the other social services so that housing production could reach 500,000 per annum by 1970. The policy statement, *The Housing Programme 1965–1970* explicitly confirmed the concept of a 'mixed economy' housing market and embraced the pragmatic stance that had been adopted by Macmillan. In that same year Crossman received the report of the Planning Advisory Group (widely known as the PAG Report).

The PAG Report

The PAG report had been commissioned by Sir Keith Joseph and its proposals were enacted in the Town and Country Planning Act 1968. Crossman commented in his diaries that the report was not ideological:

> Of course, the Department would be even happier to put through its own Bills. In my case there was one Bill, the Planning Bill created by PAG. That's the Bill I adopted and I have no doubt we shall see it put through by my successor. But it isn't a Labour Party Bill. It's the kind of Bill which any government will pass in due course.
>
> (Crossman, 1975)

That's as maybe, but PAG was nothing short of revolutionary in its scope and vision and had an enormous impact on planning practice from 1968 onwards. The PAG contained some hugely influential figures in planning, such as Walter Bor, the Liverpool city planning officer, Wilfred Burns, the Newcastle city planning officer and later to become the government's head of planning, Gerald Smart, the Hampshire county planning officer, Peter Stott, the GLC transport director, Hugh Wilson (later knighted) and Jimmy James from the Ministry of Housing and Local Government (later to become professor of planning at Sheffield University). Probably never before or since has a government-appointed panel contained such a dazzling range of talent and ability, although at the time there was criticism that no lawyers featured in the composition of the group (Wooley, 1967).

Under the new system, structure plans were to provide strategic policy guidance and set the relationship between population, employment and communications, with any plans necessary in diagrammatic form. Within their context local plans were to contain more detailed provisions but were not to be like the town map predecessors in defining very specific land use allocations. Action area plans could identify specific locations where comprehensive planning action was needed within a ten-year period. Together with the Buchanan Report on *Traffic in Towns*, the PAG report revolutionised planning, which became in policy terms a specific, discrete activity, separate from architecture and engineering. The recommendations were included in a Town & Country Planning White Paper published in the autumn 1967. This also included clauses that would enable planning inspectors to decide certain planning appeals. There was widespread criticism of the delay obtaining an appeal decision from the minister. The Bill presented to Parliament included for the first time statutory requirements that there should be opportunities for public participation in the formative stages of structure and local plans.

Although not predicted by the authors of the PAG report, the logic of its approach was a powerful incentive to local government reorganisation. As Peter Hall (1992) observed, 'the structure plans could by definition be prepared only for large areas encompassing the whole extended sphere of influence of a city or a conurbation'. In response to concerns about the local government structure necessary to implement these changes, the government proposed to set up a Royal Commission to examine local government in England. But before that there was the matter of another election.

A Convincing Mandate

With Crossman as campaign manager, Wilson called an election for March 1966 and achieved a mandate that none could question. Labour won 363 seats, the Conservatives 253, with 12 Liberals and a single Republican Labour. It was Labour's best ever result at that time other than in 1945. Wilson waited until August before he reshuffled his Cabinet. George Brown left the DEA to become Foreign Secretary, and Richard Crossman became Lord President of the Council and Leader of the House. Anthony Greenwood (the son of Arthur Greenwood, a member of Churchill's first coalition cabinet during the war) moved to the Housing Ministry and James Callaghan remained at the Treasury.

By now Crossman was so much in his stride at housing that he did not want to leave the housing ministry and was even more unhappy when he found out from Wilson who was to succeed him. In his diaries he is very uncomplimentary about Anthony Greenwood and his competence, but this was unlikely to faze the new minister, for after all in his new post he had the room that his father had when he was Minister of Health with many of the same duties. I knew Lord Greenwood, as he became in 1970, very well, as he was subsequently, in 1975, the chairman of a client company. A very different man from Crossman, with great loyalty to his left-wing colleagues, he stood back from the Labour leadership after the death of Gaitskell in order that Harold Wilson would have a clear run. Those who worked with him described his great strength as a facilitator; he allowed things to happen, which is not as easy as it sounds. He was at the ministry for nearly four years. During that time house-building peaked in 1968 when 426,000 houses were built throughout the United Kingdom (352,000 homes were built in England compared with 174,900 in 2007) – a record of which he was immensely proud. Yet because they failed to meet Harold Wilson's ambitious target of half a million houses in a year, the shadow spokesman Geoffrey Rippon and the press were able to portray the figures as being a missed target and a failure. Successive public spending cuts in the following years ensured that the housing figures spiralled downwards. Greenwood, attacked by the left of the party for allegedly not standing up for his department in the face of the severe public expenditure cuts, had to take the blame, and left the Commons at the 1970 election taking a seat in the House of Lords. Other disappointments included being denied the job of Secretary of the Labour Party which Harold Wilson wanted him to have, and his chairmanship of the Commonwealth Development Corporation made by the Labour government in 1970 being rescinded by the incoming Conservative government under Ted Heath. Tony Greenwood was underrated, and the irony is that the 1968 housing figures have never been bettered. Posterity shows that he can claim to have had more impact on the appearance of England than any other minister before or since. When taking account of his housing programme, the number of new towns he designated, including Milton Keynes and his conservation area legislation, it is an impressive record.

New Towns

Not surprisingly, as the pace of new town growth had slowed under the Conservatives, a very modest part of the nation's housing growth was being built in the new towns. In 1966 they accounted for only 160,000 of the houses built with 17,500 under construction (Central Office of Information, 1968). As part of the housing drive a third wave of new towns was to be built, but this time they would be much larger and in some cases form expansions of existing towns. In the three years from January 1967 when he announced the designation of Milton Keynes, which was initially planned for a population of 250,000, to March 1970 just before the election, Anthony Greenwood designated new towns at Peterborough, Northampton, Warrington, Telford and finally the new town centred on Preston, Leyland and Chorley (Greenwood, 1973). This was an enormous programme and the first three projects emanated from the recommendations of the South East Study, which thought that dispersal from Greater London should be at much greater distances than during the first wave of new towns. Research had shown that firms could relocate outside the South East (Moor, 1968).

The Peterborough Effect

This was the strapline for a television advertising campaign that promoted the new town, which featured the comedian Roy Kinnear as a bumbling Roman centurion rediscovering the city. The concept of doubling the population of an existing city to cater for an incoming population from London was a dramatic step change. Tony Greenwood announced that Peterborough was to go ahead at a press conference on 24 May 1967, flanked by his civil servants at a briefing in the great boardroom of the ministry overlooking the bottom of Whitehall. 'New towns are one of our greatest success stories' he told the press. 'The need for more new towns is as urgent as ever. We must keep up the momentum' (Greenwood, 1967). Because of the sheer scale of the new towns being promoted in response to the South East Study, most of the established architects and planners were already busy, and on the recommendation of the Permanent Secretary Dame Evelyn Sharp, a young architect and planner, Tom Hancock, was appointed to advise on the master plan for the new town. Hancock, with his partner John Hawkes, had already done the feasibility study for a new town in mid-Wales, but this was of a quite different scale, and it was an extraordinary break for an up and coming consultant. He repaid the debt. His master plan

107

comprised four district townships, a great country park stretching along the Nene valley, the regeneration of the inner areas of the city, an enlarged city centre, and, holding all these parts together, an armature of parkways. It was generally agreed to be masterly. Although he was subsequently sacked by the first general manager of the new town, Wyndham Thomas, who had been previously been director of the TCPA, Hancock's influence on the final form of the new city could not be denied. The population of the town grew from 85,920 in 1970 to 134,920 by the time the new town corporation was wound up in 1988. Over that period more than 26,000 houses were built in the town by the Development Corporation, local authorities and the private sector. 'The Peterborough effect' proved a good model of how an existing city can almost double its size in less than 20 years in a planned and effective manner.

Milton Keynes

By the time Milton Keynes was designated, Britain had gone as far as any nation in planning new towns (Silver, 1969). The blunders were well apparent: zoning for separation and dullness, arbitrary restrictions on size to ensure tidy final forms, over-management that restricted growth and economic adaptability, over-design that pre-empted change. The team of consultants led by Richard Llewelyn-Davies, a prominent architect who was a Labour peer in the House of Lords, was influenced by Melvin Webber, professor of city planning at the University of California, who worked with them for almost a year. The team rejected the urban village or neighbourhood concept that had dominated new town design. In Milton Keynes a rectangular grid of roads was laid out over the whole urban area, loosely adapted to existing landscape and built-up places, with the roads at one kilometre intervals. The purpose of the grid was to reflect that Milton Keynes would be a car-owning community and be capable of change and growth. It represented a departure from the welfare tradition of the post-war new town and an attempt to plan for a market-orientated society (Cowan, 1969). The new town has attracted plaudits and brickbats in equal measure, but economically it possibly represents one of the most successful examples of public investment in the latter part of the twentieth century.

Milton Keynes New Town. The grid of roads reflected that Milton Keynes would be a car-owning community and be capable of change and growth. It represented a departure from the welfare tradition of the post-war new town and an attempt to plan for a market orientated society.

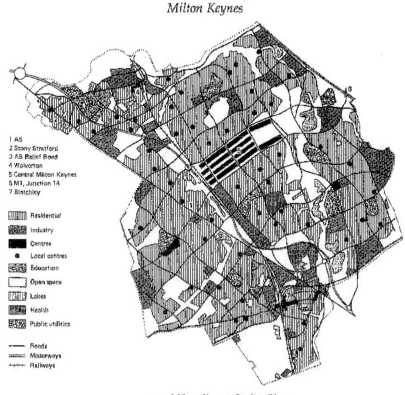

Milton Keynes

1 A5
2 Stony Stratford
3 A5 Relief Road
4 Wolverton
5 Central Milton Keynes
6 M1, Junction 14
7 Bletchley

Residential
Industry
Centres
Local centres
Education
Open space
Lakes
Health
Public utilities

Roads
Motorways
Railways

Milton Keynes Outline Plan.

© New Towns (1977) Osborn, F.J. & Whittick, A. London Leonard Hill

The Civil Service

After Harold Wilson moved him from Housing to Leader of the Commons, Crossman in his diaries reflected on his time at the ministry and in particular on his relationship with civil servants. When he arrived at the ministry, Dame Evelyn Sharp had been Permanent Secretary for almost a decade from 1955 and now, past retirement age, was due to retire soon. A legend in her own lifetime both as a woman at the top of the Civil Service but also for her long-standing connection with town and country planning, after an initial spell at the Treasury she had served in the wartime ministry under Reith, and then Silkin and Macmillan, who she much admired. Crossman thought she ran the ministry as her personal domain and they clashed over the formation of the Land Commission, although Crossman grudgingly admitted that she was right to question its effectiveness. She did retire in 1966 and served as a member of the Royal Commission on Local Government, which we will look at shortly, and was made an Honorary Member of the RTPI.

Crossman's major concern was the low priority given to planning. Understaffing was a perennial problem and as a result planning appeals which at that time had to wait on a ministerial decision would sit around for eight or nine months before they were placed on the minister's desk: 'There was an extraordinary sense of timelessness in that division' he remarked (Crossman, 1975). The influence of the Treasury was all-pervading. Civil servants had a prior loyalty to the Treasury, because for ambitious young people it was the prime source of promotion, and officials would report to the Treasury on what was happening elsewhere. None of this in any way was counteracted by the existence of the DEA. It is all the stuff of *Yes Minister* and Crossman's diaries could have provided the script.

Crossman had some robust views on planning inquiries which still have resonance as the current government aims to overhaul the inquiry system for major infrastructure projects:

> There isn't any planning law, it's all planning lore, particularly planning mythology. Planning inquiries aren't and shouldn't be legal inquiries. They are ad hoc information inquiries which have been turned into pseudo-legal inquiries, just as decisions have been turned into pseudo-judicial decisions based on a mass of lore.
>
> (Crossman, 1975)

Refreshingly, Crossman insisted on writing his own decision letters. After the New Ash Green decision, he had run into a lot of criticism. The letter granting planning permission against the advice of the inspector who had conducted the inquiry had been drafted by a civil servant. According to Crossman his decision appeared to be just arbitrarily imposed on the case with no justification or explanation.

The Land Commission

Labour's second attempt to nationalise development land values had been flagged in the election manifesto in 1964 but did not get onto the statue book until 1967. This delay gave property developers plenty of time to anticipate events and to try and avoid the proposed taxation. Nigel Broakes, the chairman of a major construction and property company, Trafalgar, at that time, described the situation in his autobiography:

> All one could do was to press on as quickly as possible to get planning consents for whatever might be worthwhile in the foreseeable future, and to start work as soon as possible, wherever possible, because either of these events was likely to be a 'chargeable act' under any new legislation.
>
> (Broakes, 1979)

Crossman was opposed as he thought it would frustrate his housing drive in much the same way that Silkin's Act had in 1947. Dame Evelyn vividly remembered that era and was a fierce opponent. Perversely, given its high profile, the minister charged with its implementation, Fred Willey, was not in the Cabinet (but then neither was Silkin in 1947). The money at its disposal was derisory (£100,00 in the first year). The chairman of the Commission, Sir Henry Wells, said at the time that the powers granted by the Act would enable the Commission 'to play a creative and dynamic role in making land available for development' (Wells, 1967). Nothing could have been further from the truth. By the time it was wound up it had sold less than 50 hectares (913 acres). An oft-repeated sentiment is that the failure was not due to any inherent defect but to the ideological bias of the incoming Conservative government in 1970 (as in 1951 and in 1979) which repealed the Act just as it was about to bear fruit. Rodney Lowe, in his book *The Welfare State in Britain Since 1945* gives short shift to this optimistic view: 'Such an argument would, however, be fallacious because within each Labour government there were major obstacles to, and serious reservations about, the full implementation of policy' (Lowe, 1993). He outlined four obstacles which remain today. Economically, each piece of legislation coincided with a sterling crisis which strictly limited the money available for land purchase; politically there were concerns about any policy – whatever its long-term gains – which might in the short term delay the release of land and thus disrupt the housing programme. Administratively officials defended the private market and the Treasury was opposed to the creation of any new body which had the right to raise, and to dispense, the proceeds of taxation. Constitutionally there were serious reservations about an unelected body usurping the power of local government to buy and to plan the development of land: 'Consequently Labour policy ultimately failed because, whilst paying lip-service to manifesto commitments, ministers and their officials remained resolutely opposed to their practical implementation' (Lowe, 1993).

The Brown Ban

Conversely, this ban on office development did achieve many of its objectives, although the consequences were not entirely expected. Developers at the end of the Conservative government expected some measures to encourage office decentralisation but the virtual total ban on office development announced on 4 November 1964 caught them by surprise. The Control of Office and Industrial Development Act 1965 introduced a series of office development permits similar to the IDC system over industry which had been in operation since the war. Every proposed office development (new buildings, re-buildings, extensions and changes of use) involving an increase of 279 sq m or more additional floorspace in the London metropolitan area now had to obtain an ODP (Office Development Permit) from the Board of Trade, as well as planning permission from the local authority. Later, during 1965 and 1966, this stringent control of office-building was extended outside the GLC area to Birmingham, and finally to all of the South East, the East and the West Midlands. The ban had its effect, and new office development in central London slowed down considerably.

But its effect was welcomed (Daniels, 1979) by many developers. By artificially restricting supply, it helped to fill up the unlet blocks, which were becoming more frequent in and around London. It also sent rents soaring, and towards the end of this phase there was acceptance by the government that some relaxation of the policy was necessary in central London. The Location of Offices Bureau during 1967/68 was responsible for moving nearly 14,000 jobs. The property developer Nigel Broakes spoke for many in the property industry when he said at the time: 'I had no doubts at all that Trafalgar could live with Labour, and that we were poised to prosper to a greater extent than could have been anticipated under a continuation of the previous regime' (Broakes, 1979).

Local Government Reform

In 1966, the Labour government decided to set up a Royal Commission on Local Government for England under Sir John Redcliffe (later Lord Redcliffe Maud). In its evidence, the Ministry of Housing and Local Government in 1967 supported the city region concept as the framework for local government reform. The Commission reported in the summer of 1969 and advocated a pattern of unitary authorities capable of running all local services covering all of provincial England, except for the three largest conurbations of Greater Manchester, Greater Liverpool and Greater Birmingham. In these conurbations, as in Greater London, there would be a two-tier structure with a metropolitan authority responsible for strategic transport and planning and metropolitan districts responsible for local services. Dame Evelyn Sharp was a member of the Commission which had rejected the proposals of her former department, although these were supported by a dissenting member, Derek Senior, a journalist from the *Guardian* who specialised in local government. His proposals, which included two tiers across the country, were to prove useful to the future Conservative government which was unhappy with the single-tier solution outside the conurbations.

The Commission also recommended provincial councils, composed chiefly of representatives of the main authorities and partly of co-opted members, which ran into considerable opposition (Sharp, 1969). The Town Planning Institute, 'did not want to see an independent level of government interposed between central government and local authorities and hampering free access between them' (Town Planning Institute, 1969). In 1970, the Labour government accepted with minor modifications the proposals, but the election intervened before it could legislate for the changes, and it was left to the incoming Conservative government to consider how to proceed.

Legislative Measures

Anthony Greenwood addressed the Town Planning Institute in April 1968 and outlined the extensive legislative programme that he and his department were engaged with (Greenwood, 1968). This included the Town and Country Planning Bill, the Civic Amenities Act, a countryside Bill, the Land Commission and the new towns programme. He identified four strands of policy which informed Labour's approach. The first was a major and deliberate devolution of power and responsibility from Whitehall to local government. The second was to create conditions in which local planning could be better directed towards achieving quality and fostering a more creative approach to the problems of the environment. The third was that it was a condition of this new approach that the public must be fully brought into the planning process. Finally, government must use to good advantage the considerable upsurge of public interest in local planning. This was largely associated with the growth of civic and amenity societies. Greenwood paid tribute to the work of the Civic Trust which he considered to be the exemplar of the civic and amenity societies emerging. He mentioned the

Barnsbury Environmental Study in Islington, led by John Hawkes, which had influenced the approach to the designation of conservation areas contained in the Civic Amenities Act. In the wider regional context, the Economic Planning Council and the Standing Conference of Planning Authorities for the South East, together with the Ministry of Housing and Local Government, led by the new chief planner Dr Burns, had decided to initiate a study of the broad pattern of development in the South East.

The Skeffington Report On Public Participation

Arthur Skeffington MP had been invited by Greenwood to be chairman of a new Committee on Public Participation in Planning. Its terms of reference were to 'consider and report on the best methods, including publicity, of securing the participation of the public at the formative stage in the making of development plans in their area'. The report, *People and Planning*, was published towards the end of the Labour government. Looking at it now the report reads somewhat naively: 'We want the paper of the plans to come to life; and to come to life in a way that people want,' but as Professor Gordon Cherry observed (1982), 'in many ways Skeffington hit the right note. Planning was changing, new methods were being adopted and new power structures were evolving'.

The Town Planning Institute was concerned at the changes mooted by Skeffington to then existing power structures (Town Planning Institute, 1970). The Institute believed that increased public participation, as in other local government services, should be sought primarily through the strengthening of the structure and organisation of local government. It was not enamoured of the committee's main recommendation for the setting up of community forums, nor that which recommended that, following the completion of survey, local planning authorities should present the public with the choices which were open to them and invite comment on alternative courses of action. The Institute wanted local authorities to consult but indicating clearly what the preferences were, although allowing for the possibility of subsequent changes in response to consultation. Other concerns were to do with the resource costs to local authorities and that staff and budgets could be siphoned off into consultation at the expense of productive planning work. The Institute took a robust line on Skeffington, and was rewarded in that the consultation practices finally adopted were very much along the lines that it had argued.

Super Ministry

In May 1969, a new 'super ministry' called the Department of Local Government and Regional Planning was set up and this would become the template for all the huge departments that would characterise planning and local government in the succeeding years, with an ever-bewildering and changing range of titles. Tony Crosland was appointed Secretary of State by Wilson with Tony Greenwood, Fred Mulley and Tom Urwin as ministers. Kenneth Robinson was given the planning and land portfolio. The DEA was quietly abolished.

Election Surprise

The 1970 election campaign was highly personalised around Harold Wilson as leader, even more than in 1966. In view of Wilson's recovery in polling surveys and Edward Heath's dismal showing, this seemed an obviously sensible tactic. The Conservatives attacked Labour's record, and unfavourable trade figures published three days before polling day helped their campaign. Many Labour supporters felt that Wilson's campaign had been too relaxed and assured. The election was in June and the Conservatives, although the opinion polls were almost unanimous in forecasting a Labour victory, were surprisingly returned with a majority of 30 seats.

A Confident Profession

During the six years of Harold Wilson's government, as during the six years under Clement Attlee, spatial planning and the planning profession enjoyed a renaissance. Labour politicians supported its interventionist purpose and linked it to their concept of a modern socialism. What was less clear was whether the economy could support the level of public spending necessary to support the legislative programme. Commentators at the time including myself (Moor, 1970) warned that without acceptance of a more market-orientated approach that brought the private sector more fully into play, many of the objectives defined by the administration would not be realised.

One casualty of Labour's loss of office was local autonomy, for Greenwood did passionately believe in a larger role for local government, and wished to see the role of the ministry redefined so that it would concentrate on national and strategic issues, but as we will see the circumstances that might have led to this outcome did not reoccur.

References

Broakes, N. (1979) *A Growing Concern*. London: Weidenfeld & Nichlolson, pp. 96, 102.

Central Office of Information (1968) *Town And Country Planning In Britain*. London: HMSO, p. 15.

Cherry, G. (1982) *The Politics of Town Planning*. London: Longman, pp 121.

Cowan, P. (1969) Milton Keynes: the creation of a city, *New Society*, 13 February, pp. 235–37.

Crossman, R. (1975) *The Diaries of a Cabinet Minister*, Vol. 1, *Minister of Housing 1964–1966*. London: Hamish Hamilton, pp. 87, 621, 623.

Daniels, P.W. (ed.) (1979) *Spatial Patterns of Office Growth and Location*. Chichester: John Wiley & Sons.

Greenwood, A. (1968) Planning policies, *Journal of The Town Planning Institute*, June, pp. 257–59.

Greenwood, A. (1973) New towns, *Journal of The Royal Society of Arts*, CXXI (May), pp. 355–66.

Hall, P. (ed.) (1992) *Urban & Regional Planning*, 3rd edn. London: Routledge, p. 134.

Lowe, R .(1993) *The Welfare State in Britain Since 1945*. London: Macmillan, pp. 241, 242.

Moor. N. (1968) Industrial dispersal – no answers yet? *Journal of The Town Planning Institute*, 54(8), June,pp. 394–96.

Moor, N. (1970) The planner and the market, *Journal of The Town Planning Institute*, January, pp. 9–11.

Pimlott, B. (1992) *Harold Wilson*. London: Harper Collins, pp. 317, 319, 360, 362, 364.

Sharp, E. (1969) The report of the Royal Commission on local government, *Journal of The Town Planning Institute*, July/August, pp. 286–88.

Silver, N. (1969) Milton inspired by angels, *New Statesman*, 28 March, p. 40.

Town Planning Institute (1969) Royal Commission on local government in England, *Journal of The Town Planning Institute*, December, p. 421.

Town Planning Institute (1970) People and planning, *Journal of The Town Planning Institute*, February, pp. 50–51.

Wells, H. (1967) The Land Commission Act 1967, *Journal of The Town Planning Institute*, June, pp. 242–44.

Wooley, D. (1967) The zephyr of change,*Journal of The Town Planning Institute*, September/October, pp. 348–49.

7

Heath, Wilson and Years of Decline, 1970–1979

Selsdon Man

Although different in personality, Edward Heath and Harold Wilson were similar in relation to their education, both being grammar school boys who had gone on to Oxbridge and both had gained their party leadership as modernisers. Each dominated their party. In January 1970, Edward Heath had taken the Shadow Cabinet to the Selsdon Park Hotel in Croydon to begin detailed preparation for the election. The policies that were agreed and the political manifesto that emerged signalled a shift to the Right, and the name of the hotel was often used from then on to identify this shift. Wilson made great play of 'Selsdon Man' – the hard-hearted face of the new Conservatism (Dutton, 1977). A reduction in direct taxation and an Industrial Relations Bill were major items. Heath had ridiculed Wilson's prices and incomes policy as threatening a totalitarian society (Sked and Cook, 1979), and in replacing the liberal Edward Boyle by Margaret Thatcher as Shadow Education minister, he confirmed this shift to the Right. Subsequently, in his opposition to Margaret Thatcher's leadership, Heath stressed his own credentials as a Tory belonging to the traditions of Butler and Macmillan and not those of Mrs Thatcher (Dutton, 1977) but Norman Tebbit, elected to Parliament for the first time in 1970, voiced the views of many in his biography when he said, 'No one should doubt that at the time of the election in 1970 Ted Heath was committed to the end of that corporate consensus and to the new liberal economics' (Tebbit, 1988).

The Department of the Environment

Now in government, in October the Conservatives announced their three major domestic priorities which were to reorganise the machinery of

117

government, to tackle the economy, partly by cuts in public expenditure, and to undertake a major reform of industrial relations. The White Paper entitled *The Reorganisation of Central Government* established a new Central Policy Review Staff and continued Labour's unification of functions within single departments. The White Paper proposed the creation of a new Department of the Environment (DoE) by integrating the Ministry of Housing and Local Government, the Ministry of Transport and the Ministry of Public Buildings and Works. The setting up of the DoE chimed with Heath's belief that fundamental problems could be resolved if the processes and structures of government were right. By the end of 1970 all these changes had been effected and Peter Walker became the Environment Secretary. His was the eponymous surname of Slater Walker, a successful stockbroking and investment firm, and he epitomised the no-nonsense business approach that Ted Heath wanted to bring to government. By a supreme irony, the new environment department was to be housed in a dreadful three-tower speculative block of offices off Victoria Street in London, which had lain empty for some time and many years later – to universal acclaim – was demolished. In an interview that Peter Walker gave in December 1970 (Thorne, 1970) he emphasised his determination to get a system of regional plans in place: 'I'm going ahead as fast as possible at getting each region to agree a regional planning strategy'. He also gave early warning that the Conservatives would pursue a two-tier approach to local government reorganisation as opposed to the single-tier structure advocated in the Maud Report.

Heath's Infamous U-turn

But that year Heath's Cabinet suffered the blow of the death of the Chancellor Iain Macleod, one of the foremost Conservative politicians of his generation, to be succeeded by Anthony Barber, another businessman that Heath brought into the Cabinet and who was relatively new to politics. The first two years of Heath's government were marked by attempts first to reduce direct taxation and public expenditure and then, having underestimated the depth of the recession, to reinflate in March 1972, aiming at an annual growth rate of 5 per cent. However, a whole avalanche of economic problems, decreasing productivity, increased labour costs, an increase in import prices and a deterioration in the balance of payments combined to cause yet another sterling crisis. In June 1972, Barber announced that the pound would 'float' against other currencies, the first time since the 1930s that this had happened. But with world commodity prices, including energy costs, rising, the falling value of the pound brought no immediate help. In a desperate response, the government abandoned many of the policy initiatives it had started in 1970, and now advocated policies similar to those which it had attacked so vehemently in opposition. In addition to a prices and incomes policy, regional policy was dusted off and brought back out of the cupboard, resurrected as a form of the investment grant scheme that had earlier been scrapped.

Planning Policies

In the first few months of the new government there was much unfinished business from the brief sojourn that Anthony Crosland had enjoyed at the Environment Department. The Strategic Plan for the South East was published and Dame Sharp's report *The Men for The Job*. A new *Development Plan Manual* was published in November 1970 giving advice on the changes introduced by the 1968 Town & Country Planning Act. It introduced the diagrammatic plan maps which are now so familiar but which at the time looked awkward and dysfunctional, having lost the authority of an Ordnance Survey base. That summer a controversial planning decision gave the go-ahead for the new National Exhibition Centre buildings on a green belt site outside Birmingham. In July there was a national and regional planning policy statement but the latter part of the year and the early part of 1971, leading to the publication of a new White Paper in February, was dominated by the Local Government Bill in response to the Maud Report.

Local Government Reorganisation

The fundamental reorganisation of local government carried out under the Conservatives had a huge impact on people's lives (Sked and Cook, 1979). The government did not accept the Redcliffe Maud Commission's recommendations, and instead proceeded with its own proposals for reform in England and Wales which received the Royal Assent in October 1972 and came into operation on 1 April 1974, just a month after the general election. The new legislation removed the former dual framework of county councils (and their district councils) and all-purpose county borough councils. They were replaced by a two-tier system which, outside Greater London was based upon 44 counties. In six predominantly urban areas (Greater Manchester, Merseyside, South Yorkshire, Tyne and Wear, the West Midlands and West Yorkshire) new authorities called 'metropolitan counties' were

119

created. Large metropolitan districts with a minimum population size of 200,000 formed the second tier of local government. Former borough councils and district councils were rationalised to form second-tier, non-metropolitan district councils which were to become planning authorities. These changes were accompanied by the loss from local government of personal health services to ad hoc health committees, and water supply and sewage disposal to regional water authorities. In London, the GLC, which had come into being in 1965, remained in place but it lost its water and ambulance services to the new regional authorities. Heath and Walker hoped in this way, particularly at the second-tier level, to preserve Conservative hegemony in local government, but the changes were not popular. One casualty was the historic market towns, which under Victorian legislation had been granted borough council status, and were now demoted to the legal status of parish councils. As a former mayor of one such town, I know that the snub rankled with councillors for many years after.

Bitterly opposed to the Local Government Bill was the RTPI, which thought the two-tier structure probably unworkable. Some 450 local planning authorities were proposed and yet only 4,000 chartered town planners were available (Amos, 1972). Despite these strictures, the system has survived for more than 30 years, but periodically attempts were made to deal with some of the more glaring anomalies.

Land for Housing

Early in 1972, Peter Walker published one of the first circulars from his new department (DoE circular *Land for Housing*), which called on local authorities to release more land for housing and made money available to enable them to acquire land for subsequent disposal to private developers. Local authorities were urged to ensure that they had at least five years' supply of housing land available on their books and, in cases of exceptional shortage, the DoE would support the enforcement of compulsory purchase orders. We have seen how housing production peaked in 1968 while Tony Greenwood was at the helm for housing. From 1972 and for more than 30 years, successive governments have published repeated, and more strident, calls for local authorities to make more land available for housing, in response to criticism from the house-building industry that land shortages were stifling housing production. The conflict between planners and builders on this issue has never been resolved, and in Chapter 13 the continuing relevance of this debate for contemporary times is explored.

Cabinet Reshuffle

In July 1972, Reginald Maudling, who was Home Secretary, resigned from the Cabinet because he would have been responsible for the police investigations into the affairs of the architect John Poulson, who was subsequently convicted of corruption. The reshuffle involved several Cabinet colleagues. Peter Walker, who was only just getting to grips with the enormous new DoE, moved to Trade and Industry and Geoffrey Rippon replaced him.

The Liberal Revival

The Liberals had had a poor election in 1970 having lost seven seats, and been left with only six MPs, but two factors laid the basis for their revival. The first was the acceptance at the Liberal conference in 1970 of a Young Liberal resolution to start campaigning on a community level, and the second was the increasing unpopularity of the Conservative government as unemployment exceeded 1 million in January 1972. This led to a string of by-election victories for the Liberals, and in Liverpool under the leadership of Trevor Jones (known in the city as 'Jones the vote') by 1973 they had become the largest single party on the council. Jones went on to become president of the party. The events of 1972–73 passed judgement on the government as enormous numbers of Conservatives deserted to the Liberals, which was a rehearsal for the 1974 election, but the lasting significance for planning was the new emphasis on community politics.

Community Politics in Action

After it was set up in 1965, one of the first decisions of the GLC was to set up a planning team under the leadership of Ralph Rookwood, later to become head of planning at Westminster City Council, to work on a comprehensive scheme for the Covent Garden area, once the fruit and vegetable market moved away from the piazza designed by Inigo Jones, to a new site south of the River Thames at Nine Elms. The team of architects and planners, of which I was a junior member, was responsible to a steering group that comprised the heads of planning of the three councils concerned, the GLC, Camden Borough and Westminster City, and were heavily influenced by the planning concepts introduced in the Buchanan Report.

The draft plan, when published in 1968, although conserving the historic core of the area, included a widening of The Strand to a dual carriageway and redevelopment for hotels, a conference centre and offices. There was a huge outcry led by the *Evening Standard*, and a young journalist writing for the paper at the time, Simon Jenkins, later to be editor of *The Times*, played a major role in marshalling opposition to the scheme. A group of activists formed the Covent Garden Community Association and campaigned against the scheme, using the public inquiry in 1972 as a forum to present their ideas for preservation and community housing. They succeeded in persuading the Secretary of State Geoffrey Rippon to foil the scheme. By using the powers available under the Civic Amenities Act and powers to spot-list buildings throughout the area, he prevented any prospect of comprehensive redevelopment. That same year Labour won control of the GLC and a very different plan emerged with an emphasis on housing, shops and light industry. The Covent Garden Community Association failed to prevent the gentrification of Covent Garden, which in the last 30 years has proceeded apace, but they set the tone for community action in planning by expertly using the media to present their own narrative.

Community Politics In Action. The plans to redevelop the Covent Garden Market area in London caused great controversy and resulted in one of the first examples of community action in planning.

The Third London Airport and *Concorde*

The Roskill Commission on the Third London Airport had finally recommended that it be built at Maplin Sands on the Essex coast some way from central London. The Conservatives accepted the advice and put in place a development agency to oversee the project. Subsequently, after the 1974 election, it was one of the first acts of the new Wilson government to axe the project, while at the same time continuing with the manufacture of the supersonic passenger plane *Concorde*. How much that had to do with the Bristol constituency, where components of the plane were made, of Tony Wedgewood Benn, who was then Technology Minister, can only be conjecture, but the hindsight of history surely says tells us these two related decisions should have been reversed. *Concorde* was eventually scrapped and London still lacks the airport capacity that Maplin would have given it.

The Three-day Week

January 1973, when the celebrations 'Fanfare for Europe' were held to mark Britain's accession to the Common Market, marked the high watermark of the Heath administration. The miners' strike a year earlier had already unsettled energy prices, and the Arab-Israeli war in October 1973 forced a fundamental reassessment of policy, as oil prices quadrupled and there was an oil embargo on states such as Britain who were perceived by the Middle Eastern oil producers as being too sympathetic to Israel. The Cabinet minister Alan Clark noted in his diary (1998), 'Soon the notion began to spread, in Cabinet as in the press, that the only way "out" for the Government was to dissolve Parliament. A general election would bestow on them the mandate they needed'. By the end of the year, the 'three-day week' to conserve energy had been introduced and a £1.2 million budget cut announced.

The Beginning of the End for Heath

The early months of 1974 saw a succession of disasters for the government. The miners voted to strike from 10 February, while the trade figures published on 24 February were horrific. During the campaign Harold Wilson contrasted the emptiness of Tory negotiating power with his own ability to 'get on with the unions', but the decision of Enoch Powell not to stand as a

Conservative MP at the election (and to have claimed in advance to have cast a postal vote for Labour) along with the revival of the Liberals led by Jeremy Thorpe, were the events that ensured that Heath's campaign as to who should govern Britain (the government or the unions) had backfired and the new Parliament would be hung. For five painful days Heath attempted to form an administration which included the offer of the Home Office to Jeremy Thorpe, but when it was clear that Thorpe could not deliver the Liberal support without the Tories backing proportional representation, Heath had no alternative but to go to the Palace and deliver the seals of office. This he did on 4 March and Harold Wilson became Prime Minister leading a minority Labour government.

Heath's tenure of office is now seen in hindsight as the prelude to the rise of Thatcherism. She certainly saw it so:

> Ted Heath's Government . . . proposed and almost implemented the most radical form of socialism ever contemplated by an elected British Government. It offered state control of prices and dividends, and the joint oversight of economic policy by a tripartite body representing the Trades Union Congress, the Confederation of British Industry and the Government, in return for trade union acquiescence in an incomes policy.
>
> (Thatcher, 1993)

The legacy of Heath and Walker for planning was a system of local government which resulted in too many local planning authorities, many of them very small and poorly staffed, and problems of coordination between county and district which persist to the present day.

Wilson Moves Quickly Forward

After the election, Harold Wilson formed his first Cabinet of the new government. Crosland, with experience at Trade, Education and Local Government and Planning was given the task of looking after the enormous DoE. Wilson moved quickly to settle with the miners, plans for the Channel Tunnel and a new London airport were axed, and repeal of the Industrial Relations Act was promised. Crosland acted to discourage council house sales. The three-day week was soon forgotten. Normally at the onset of a new government, the composition of the Shadow Cabinet would not raise much interest but Heath's appointment of Margaret Thatcher as Shadow Environment Minister was significant. In August of that year, as part of the preparations for the Party manifesto (a further election was anticipated), Margaret Thatcher pledged to abolish domestic rates and to hold down mortgage interest rates to a maximum of 9.5 per cent. In addition she offered council tenants who had been in their homes for three years or more the right to buy them at a price one third below market value, and to claw back only if sold again within five years. For those who cared to look, the early tenets of Thatcherism were being put in place.

A Further Election

On 10 October, Wilson won his fourth election victory, equalling Gladstone's record. He now began to think about retirement. He had been Party leader for 11 years, and had good reason to think about retiring at 60. Despite the fevered speculation at the time, there really was no mystery about Wilson's retirement. He had had enough. On 22 March 1976, the Prime Minister gave a farewell dinner for his colleagues – 'a Cabinet meeting with food' as Barbara Castle called it (Castle, 1970). His recognition honours list became a messy row and clouded his reputation.

Wilson's fourth election victory ensured that Heath's leadership would be challenged openly and on 21 November 1974 Margaret Thatcher announced that she would bid for the leadership. Early in January of the following year Airey Neave MP took on the leadership of her campaign and by 11 February she had won on the second ballot. Following her victory, a perceptive leader in the *Daily Telegraph* observed, 'What Margaret Thatcher ought to be able to offer is the missing moral dimension to the Tory attack on socialism. If she does so, her accession to the leadership could mark a sea-change in the whole character of the party political debate in this country' (Thatcher, 1995).

The Dobry Report

Geoffrey Rippon, when Environment Secretary in the last Conservative government, had appointed an eminent planning silk George Dobry, to review the development control system. The number of appeals had almost doubled and there were persistent criticisms of the delays associated with the system. The report was published in 1975 but practically none of the recommendations were accepted, although the principle of charging for applications, together with a number of other changes, were much later accepted by subsequent governments. Dobry's plan for automatic planning approval after 42 days was quickly binned. The government was much more interested in the new legislation for community land acquisition than development control, and the recession had meant that the number of applications and appeals had slumped, easing pressure on the system. Dobry's report was one of a number of reports that successive governments have commissioned into the inadequacies of the development control system, but rather like housing land shortages, these persistent failures of the system have been extremely resistant to change. Nonetheless, as we shall see, each new government begins its administration determined to make changes.

Dobry's report was one of a number of reports that successive governments have commissioned into the inadequacies of the development control system, and the increasing burden of red tape.

"up to first footings in paper before we get to first footings in bricks"

© Nigel Moor & Robert Langton Planning For New Homes.

The Community Land Act

Where Richard Crossman and Lewis Silkin had failed, his son John Silkin and Tony Crosland were determined to succeed. The attempts of the 1947 Town and Country Planning Act to retrieve 'betterment' for the community struggled with practical problems and political change. The Land Commission Act of 1967 resulted in little more than the purchase of 2,800 acres of land and the sale of 320 acres (White, 1976). Labour was determined to avoid the previous legislative mistakes. Special assistant to the Environment Secretary Tony Crosland was David Lipsey, who in 1973 as a Rowntree Political Fellow had written a Fabian tract entitled 'Land and Labour' in which he opined that there had been previously too much concern with betterment and not enough with the mechanisms for the allocation and development of land. He wanted to see implementation of the legislation as the function of regional land and development corporations set within a framework of elected regional councils. Instead the Community Land Bill, published as a White Paper on 12 September 1974, firmly imposed its obligations on the new local planning authorities. The first step for local authorities was to be the preparation of land acquisition and management schemes (LAMS) and these would have to be in place by the first appointed day in April 1976. It was made clear in the Commons debate that the Environment Secretary would intervene if the LAMS were not prepared to schedule. The Conservative opposition, although not opposed to the notion of taxing betterment, so long as the tax was not at a deterrent rate (Raison, 1976), made it clear that they were completely opposed to the principle enshrined in the Community Land Act – that public ownership of development land is desirable – and therefore if re-elected they would remove the Act from the statue book. Timothy Raison, who in November 1976 was the Conservative spokesman on the Environment, accepted the need for taxing betterment and there was an opportunity for both parties to agree a common approach if the legislation could be revised. As I have explained before, community ownership of development land was like Clause 4 of the Labour Party's constitution, a 'leitmotif' for the party and despite the opportunity in 1976 for a compromise approach to development land acquisition with the Conservatives, the opportunity was lost. In any event, economic difficulties were crowding in on the Labour government and the preoccupation of the Cabinet was not to survive. Public expenditure cuts in November 1976 meant that many local authorities did not even bother to bid for loan sanction, which would have enabled them to acquire development land. In an article in September 1976, I summed up what happened to the Land Act

127

(Moor, 1976) and argued that the public spending costs had ensured that it would go the way of the Land Commission and other attempts before it. I said this not with any pleasure or satisfaction, for we still needed an answer to the problem of land development, but the Land Act was certainly not that.

Power Slipping Away

On 2 March 1976, sterling fell below the $2 mark and the following months saw a succession of events that suggested that Labour were unlikely to survive as a government. Harold Wilson announced his resignation on 16 March and Jim Callaghan was elected Labour leader on 5 April. In his first Cabinet he chose Denis Healey as his Chancellor. On 7 April the government lost its majority whilst on 10 May Jeremy Thorpe resigned as Liberal leader and was succeeded by the more emollient David Steel. That summer sterling was again under pressure and on 28 September Healey was forced to turn back from a plane flight as sterling fell below $1.63 and the government was arguably in the middle of the biggest financial crisis since the war. On 1 November an IMF team arrived in the UK, which was a frank acknowledgement of the dire economic straits that the country had reached, and on 15 December Healey announced his mini-budget which was delivered to obtain an IMF letter of intent which would guarantee a $3 billion loan. The following two years were a dizzying succession of events but the overall conclusion was that the government had lost its way and little legislation would get onto the statute book. Commentators have suggested that both Callaghan and Healey had now converted to a mild version of monetarism and that Keynesian economics was now defunct. Tony Benn, leader of the Labour Left, pithily described the situation: 'The IMF crisis marked the end of social democracy' (Jones, 2004).

Devolution

The dramatic gains of the Scottish National Party (SNP) in October 1974 had thrust devolution forward as an issue to be resolved. Devolution proposals for Scotland and Wales had been published in February 1976, which envisaged the setting up of assemblies in both countries and a major handover of responsibility for internal affairs. A year later, the government was defeated on the Scotland & Wales Bill in Parliament and fearing that the administration would fall, David Steel announced the Lib-Lab Pact' on 23

March 1977, which would shore up the government for a further 12 months. Neither the government or the Liberals wanted an election and for the latter, in a future hung parliament, there was the prospect of electoral reform. With Liberal support, by the end of 1978 the government had at last put devolution onto the statue book, with a referendum scheduled for 1 March 1979.

The Inner Cities

In the Cabinet changes, Peter Shore had become Environment Secretary, and one of his first initiatives was to tackle the problems of inner-city decline. In April 1977 he announced a slowdown in the growth of new town expansion and a new strategy for the inner-city areas based on an annual expenditure of £100 million over the next ten years. *The Sunday Times* and *The Financial Times* described the amounts as 'chicken feed' and 'crumbs' but few at the time seemed to fully appreciate the economic mire into which Britain had fallen. Healey's December 1976 budget had meant a £100 million reduction in the housing programme in 1977/78. The Inner Urban Areas Bill reached Parliament in May 1978 and seven major inner-city areas were proposed: Liverpool, Birmingham, Manchester and Salford, Newcastle

The Inner Cities: Peter Shore tackles the problem of inner city decline.

© Nigel Moor

and Gateshead, and in London, Lambeth, Docklands and Hackney/ Islington, where partnerships were to be established between government, local authorities and other bodies such as the Manpower Services Commission to agree comprehensive inner-area programmes. Against a background of a shortage of funds to implement inner-city programmes, this funding issue was to become one of the major ideological differences between the two major parties in the next decade.

The Winter of Discontent

On 25 March 1978, Liberal leader David Steel announced the end of the 'Lib-Lab Pact' but despite this the government was determined to serve out its full five-year term and at the October 1978 Labour conference, to the surprise of almost everyone, Callaghan announced that there would be no autumn election. During that winter, strikes, particularly among public sector workers – spectacularly the grave-diggers – caused great disruption and hardship to the general public and earned those months the soubriquet 'The Winter of Discontent', originally coined by the journalist Peter Jenkins. By the end of March 1979 the government could no longer hang on – there had been by-election gains by the Conservatives at Ashfield and at Ilford North – and on 28 March, for the first time since 1931, the government lost a vote of confidence in Parliament by 310 votes to 311. The election was held on 3 May. The campaign for Labour went badly and the swing against it was even bigger than in 1970. The 5.1 per cent swing to the Conservatives ensured Margaret Thatcher entered Downing Street as Prime Minister with a majority of 43 seats. Labour's share of the vote fell to its lowest since 1931.

Wilson and his Legacy

Harold Wilson died on 24 May 1995 and his record of winning four of the five general elections he fought is still unbroken. He left office at a time of his choosing and held together a Labour party which, following his departure, almost immediately fell apart. He said that he would want to be remembered for the founding of the Open University, of which he was understandably proud. In planning, he will be remembered for the confidence that planners had during his government but, despite the initial excitement, the deeply misguided notion that a Department of Economic Affairs could plan and regulate the economy better than markets took a generation to repair. As we will see in the next chapter, New Labour not only dropped Clause Four of the constitution concerning nationalisation but, in 1989, their policy statement *Meet the Challenge, Make the Change* committed a future Labour government to work through a successful market. The change of emphasis was marked by the appointment of Gordon Brown as Shadow Industry Secretary in October 1989.

Wilson And His Legacy: Wilson leaves Downing Street March 1976.

THE DAILY TELEGRAPH

© *The Daily Telegraph*

References

Amos, F.J.C. (1972) *The Local Government Bill: Planning Provisions*, RTPI *Journal*, February, pp. 73–74.

Castle, B. (1970) *The Castle Diaries 1964–1970*. London: Weidenfeld & Nicholson, p. 699.

Clark, A. (1998) *The Tories*. London: BCA, p. 350.

Dutton, D. (1977) *British Politics Since 1945*, 2nd edn. London: Blackwell, pp. 93, 94.

Jones, T. (2004) *The Rise and Fall of Ideological Politics in Britain Since 1945*. Oxford: Oxford University.

Moor, N. (1976) The Community Land Act, *Factory & Office Selector,* 8 September, pp. 12–14.

Raison, T. (1976) Planning: some issues at stake, *RTPI Journal,* pp. 195–98.

Sked, A. and Cook, C.(1979) *Post-war Britain.* London: Penguin, pp. 276–77, 306.

Tebbit, N. (1988) *Upwardly Mobile.* London: Widenfeld & Nicholson, p .94.

Thatcher, M. (1993) The *Downing Street Years.* London: Harper Collins, p. 7.

Thatcher, M. (1995) *The Path to Power.* London: Harper Collins, p. 281.

Thorne, V. (1970) *Walker's World* Interview with Peter Walker MP, *Property & Investment Review,* December, p. 29.

White, R. (1976) The Community Land Act, *RTPI Journal,* p. 5.

8

Thatcherism, 1979–1997 and the Loss of Consensus

Introduction

Margaret Thatcher won three successive general elections, and when she entered Downing Street as Prime Minister in May 1979 she was already determined to change the direction of British government. Prime Minister for eleven and a half years, longer than anyone else in Britain in the twentieth century, it was probably inevitable that her period in office would mark the end of the post-war consensus. She nevertheless had a clear conviction that politics could not go on unchanged: 'Change as moral crusade was the leitmotif of her career' (Evans, 2004).

As a minister in Edward Heath's government, she had witnessed the vicissitudes of the three-day working week and, as leader of the opposition, she saw the collapse of incomes policy in the 1978–79 Winter of Discontent. In her memoirs, she observed, 'To cure the British disease with socialism was like trying to cure leukaemia with leeches' (Thatcher, 1993). Thatcher stamped her authority on her three governments to such an extent that in order to appreciate the changes that they introduced to the government of Britain, it is necessary to understand her own personal political convictions.

Robert Leach comments that:

> It was only after Mrs Thatcher emerged as the unlikely winner from the leadership contest in 1975 that her own free-market convictions became manifest in speeches where she extolled Victorian virtues of self-reliance, attacked collectivism, and dismissively referred to bourgeois guilt, a phrase widely interpreted as a criticism of Tory Paternalism as much as socialism.
>
> (Leach, 2002)

In her memoirs (Thatcher, 1993) she summed up her thinking when she took office in 1979:

No theory of government was ever given a fairer test or a more prolonged experiment in a democratic country than democratic socialism received in Britain. Yet it was a miserable failure in every respect. Far from reversing the slow relative decline of Britain vis-à-vis its main industrial competitors, it accelerated it. We fell further behind them, until by 1979, we were widely dismissed as the 'sick man of Europe'.

The Post-war Consensus

What were the commonly held principles that brought about the post-war consensus: principles that were followed by both the major political parties despite their ideological differences? They were essentially Keynesian. David Marquand (Marquand and Seldon, 1996) has identified them as:

a) A belief that the free market could not be relied on. Markets would fail and the failures are systemic, not accidental. They cannot by themselves ensure that social costs are borne by those who incur them and they cannot secure the production of public goods. Because they fail, they have to be regulated and supplemented; and it is the state that has to regulate and supplement them.

b) To make a reality of civil and political rights, social rights had to be guaranteed as well. The post-war welfare state had enshrined the principle of equal social rights in legislation. The implications of this were that citizenship rights are held independently of market power or social status. As a consequence if the domain of citizenship expands, the domain of the market-place contracts.

c) A repudiation of the laws of market economics. It was no longer the invisible hand of free competition but a movement in the opposite direction, from the dispersal to the concentrated, from the individual to the collective. Big firms, big unions and big government were the inescapable hallmarks of the modern age. It is salutary that one of the foremost Conservative supporters of the consensus, Harold Macmillan, should in his book *The Middle Way* published in 1938, comment that he saw existing forms of economic organisation as a 'temporary phase in the onward march of developing social history'.

Roughly from 1945 to 1973, the Keynesian consensus held sway among the political elite in Britain. As we have seen, Margaret Thatcher had her own personal political convictions as to why this should change, but such convictions can count for nothing if the circumstances are not right.

Challenges to the Consensus

Evans (2004) identifies three closely linked factors that enabled Thatcher's great experiment in government to occur:

a)   The first revolves around Britain's growing economic troubles during the post-war period. On the one hand, there was significant social advance, welfare provision, better housing, rising standards of living and consumer booms, but on the other, accelerating relative economic decline. Britain had slipped down the European economic league table. In the decade 1962–72, France sustained an annual growth rate of 4.7 per cent while Britain could only manage 2.2 per cent. Allied to this was poor labour productivity, and right-wing theorists blamed the unions and restrictive practices.

b)   The second was the crisis of confidence caused by the end of the post-war boom in the late 1960s. By the early 1970s international agreements on fixed exchange rates were breaking down, creating a difficult economic climate which was worsened by the oil crisis of 1973–74. Keynesian anti-unemployment policies were pursued but built up inflationary pressures, and a worsening foreign trade deficit put additional pressure on the value of the pound. Evans concludes that 'Keynesianism now appeared to be a busted flush'.

c)   The third factor was the need of Prime Minister Callaghan and his Chancellor Denis Healey in 1976 to negotiate a loan from the IMF which came with deflationary strings attached in the form of additional expenditure cuts. The unions were not prepared to accept these, and their strikes precipitated the Winter of Discontent. Callaghan lost a vote of confidence in the House of Commons by a single vote on 28 March 1979 and defiantly asserted, 'We shall take our case to the country'. It was almost an echo of Edward Heath's call more than a decade earlier as to whether or not the unions ran the country, but Callaghan, as Heath had been, was to be defeated by them.

On taking over the government in 1979, Margaret Thatcher, if not all of her Cabinet, as Leach (2002) has observed, took up the cause of the New Right that Keynesian pump-priming was inherently inflationary, and state planning, even of the modest kind attempted by the governments of the 1960s and 1970s was inherently wasteful. Marquand summarises this approach (Marquand and Seldon, 1996): 'The role of the state was to enforce contracts, to supply sound money and to ensure that market forces were not distorted'.

The Ideological Basis

To trace the ideological basis for this approach, one has to examine the thinkers that influenced Margaret Thatcher. Most commentators are now agreed that she was not an original thinker but action-orientated. A lively academic debate has now ensued as to whether Thatcherism amounts to an ideology, rather than a collection of personal convictions which responded to a particular set of circumstances. What is not in doubt is that she was profoundly influenced by those thinkers that are characterised as constituting the New Right while also endorsing a neo-Conservative strand which emphasised more traditional Conservative themes such as authority, sovereignty, law and order and the national interest.

The two most prominent New Right thinkers were Milton Friedman and Friedrich von Hayek. Friedman reprised the classical liberal economic theory of Adam Smith (that wealth was created by the pursuit by individuals of their own self-interest in the free market – the 'invisible hand') and his influential book *Capitalism and Freedom*, published in 1962, championed the virtues of free markets when Keynesianism was still dominant. Von Hayek published *The Road to Serfdom* in 1944 and argued that all state planning by fascist, communist, moderate social democratic, or even conservative governments involved a loss of rights and was counter-productive. Both authors influenced Sir Keith Joseph, who more than anyone had the ear of Margaret Thatcher, and his central thesis was the need for strict control of the money supply so as to curb inflationary pressures.

Margaret Thatcher's personal economic adviser, who joined her in 1981 from Johns Hopkins University in the United States, was Sir Alan Walters, who died in 2009. Walters was a monetarist and had been a member of Thatcher's circle for some time, and provided the academic justification for her attacks on public spending in the early years of her administration. He had earlier worked in Edward Heath's Cabinet Office but left after Heath's celebrated U-turn. Subsequently, his dispute with the then Chancellor Nigel Lawson over entry into the European Exchange Rate Mechanism (ERM) led to both of them resigning in 1989, and this would prove to be the first intimation of Thatcher's subsequent loss of office.

One other facet of Walters' career is worth mentioning here. This was his work on cost-benefit analysis applied to transport while at Birmingham University. This led to his appointment to the Roskill Commission considering a third London airport, and a celebrated row with one of the other members, the late Sir Colin Buchannan, who could not fathom how cost-benefit analysis could be applied to whether or not a beautiful church in the path of an airport runway could be valued. The answer of course was the insurance value. Sir Colin's minority report advocating an airport at Maplin off the Essex marshes is now being reappraised in the debate over whether or not Heathrow should have a third runway.

The Legacy of Thatcherism

The Thatcher governments did substantially transform Britain, more than any previous administration since Attlee's. Many of the changes, like those of the Attlee government, seem irreversible for the foreseeable future. But Thatcher was never popular, and in three elections she failed to achieve anything approaching the proportion of the popular vote won by either Eden or Macmillan. If not popular, Thatcherism caught the mood for change. The acronym TINA (there is no alternative) was reluctantly conceded by many, even her critics. For the Conservative Party, the enduring legacy, concludes Leach (2002) is that 'the embrace of ideology obstructed the party's former pragmatic flexibility in pursuit of power'. That debate within the Party between ideology and pragmatism continues, and is reviewed in Chapter 9.

How did this mood for change impact on town and country planning, itself a child of the regime of central planning introduced during the Second World War and legislated for by Attlee's cabinet?

There has been an enormous amount written about this period but Mark Tewdwr-Jones (2002) succinctly sums up the changes:

> The effects of Thatcherism on the town and country planning system during the
> 1980s were widespread. The reforms, or deregulation of planning, not only
> affected the local governmental administrative framework and its duties but also
> the planning system itself. Forward planning functions and development control

powers of local authorities were amended significantly following the passing of a number of Acts of Parliament, White Papers and government circulars.

He further adds that the forward planning duties of urban authorities were removed in certain areas as the government introduced a whole range of development initiatives. On the development control side of local authorities' work, the reduction in control was almost as marked and a development boom was sparked off in the mid-1980s with many developers relying on the appeal system to reverse unfavourable decisions of local authorities.

But at the start of the Thatcher era, housing was her pre-eminent concern. From 1980 she pushed though new housing Acts almost on an annual basis in order to force councils to sell houses to their tenants. By the time she stepped down, 1.25 million houses had been sold and house sales were the biggest of Thatcher's privatisations. The £18 billion raised during the 1980s was some 43 per cent of total receipts. Many of these houses must have been Bevan's post-war council homes, for sales proved to have been mostly of houses with gardens on suburban estates. By a supreme political irony, houses intended to be in public ownership in perpetuity became a step on the house-owning democracy ladder for more than a million households. They repaid the debt, for in 1983 homeowners voted Tory by three to one, while council tenants voted Labour by two to one (Jenkins, 2006). The Conservatives were committed to home ownership and by the end of the 1980s local councils were only building some 13,000 houses a year. The Housing Corporation took up some of the building but public house-building was never to reach the levels it had under Housing Minister Tony Greenwood in the mid-1960s.

Deregulation

The defining moment had come in 1979 when the new Prime Minister Mrs Margaret Thatcher announced her intention to 'speed up and simplify the planning process' and set the deregulatory tone which continued through to the 1990s. Her message had been taken up by the new Environment Secretary of State Michael Heseltine who, in a scathing attack on planning procedures delivered to the Institute of Housing Conference in Britain that year, had cautioned that 'I shall not be content until I have satisfied myself that we have got this right'.

Further hints came in the first Budget after the 1979 election in the spring of 1980, when the then Chancellor Sir Geoffrey Howe announced the experimental 'Enterprise Zones' package. The scramble for sites was on. (By 1990, some 25 Enterprise Zones had been designated.) In these areas government advocated the almost total removal of development controls.

No sooner than six months after taking office, Michael Heseltine had designated Urban Development Corporations (UDCs) for Liverpool and London's docklands and more came for Cardiff, Manchester, Salford, Leeds, Sheffield, Tyneside, Teesside, the West Midlands and Bristol. The concept was based on the new town corporations introduced by Lewis Silkin to handle the post-war new towns programme. By yet another political irony this approach was championed by a Conservative minister: 'Free from the inevitable delays of the democratic process' (Heseltine, 1981). Simon Jenkins wryly comments, 'He and Thatcher did not reform local democracy, they dispensed with it' (Jenkins, 2006).

In April 1979, just before the election, the RICS published a report of a working party set up to make recommendations for simplifying and strengthening the planning system. It was titled *Caring for Town and Country*. Considering the composition of the working party, which included many members in private practice, the recommendations were strangely muted. The strongest were for the abolition of ODPs and IDCs (Industrial Development Certificates) and the repeal of the Community Land Act 1975. The Act was repealed in 1980 but the development land tax was initially retained but perceived as a discouragement to development and was finally abolished in 1985. What is so revealing is that reading that document now, it is evident that even chartered surveyors in private practice, often the most vocal in their criticism of planning controls, had no inkling of the deregulation to come.

The powers to declare UDCs came through the Local Government Planning and Land Act 1980 which also ushered in Enterprise Zones. Developers in these zones were promised reduced public involvement in planning decisions and this was later expanded to apply to Simplified Planning Zones (SPZs).

Elsewhere, the Conservative government made it clear that positive attitudes should prevail. Circular 22/80 – *Development Control – Policy in Practice* stated that: 'Development Control must avoid placing unjustified obstacles in the way of any development especially if it is for industry, commerce, housing or any other purpose relevant to the economic regeneration of the country'.

In the summer of 1981, several of Britain's larger cities experienced riots. Mobs of people – mostly young, often unemployed, largely black – vented their anger on property and the police. There was throughout the country a sense of shock and disbelief, although many social commentators had warned for some time that the inner cities could explode. The government appointed a distinguished judge, Lord Scarman, to examine the causes. His recommendations were extensive and included positive discrimination in favour of ethnic minorities and a more integrated approach to inner-city problems. At the time *The Economist*, which had published a series of articles called 'Britain's Urban breakdown' was sceptical of Michael Heseltine's policies for urban renewal. Events since suggest that judgement was harsh.

In 1982, as a contribution to the planning debate, the right-wing Adam Smith Institute published *Town & Country Chaos: A Critical Analysis of Britain's Planning System*. Its author was Robert Jones, a Conservative district councillor who argued for a removal of planning controls other than in areas of green belt and areas of special beauty or historic interest, backed up by land use tribunals and a tough nuisance law. The critique attracted a stinging rebuke in the *Planner* magazine by Alan Hooper of the University of Reading in December 1982. Hooper suggested that the analysis was a chaotic mixture of ideological assertion, gross simplification, distortion and the selective citation of case material. He agreed that an alternative to traditional land use planning from a free market perspective would be welcome but that the publication did not provide that alternative. However, Thatcher and Heseltine did in parts of the country effectively introduce a planning-free zone. Ironically, Robert Jones was later to be elected an MP and become Planning Minister in 1996 in John Gummer's team.

Appeals

Planning consultants and lawyers learnt the paragraph from Circular 22/80 promoting development off by heart and it was chanted like a mantra at countless planning appeal inquiries across the country. Reinforced by Circulars such as 15/84, *Land for Housing* and 16/84 – *Industrial Development*, it created a completely new climate which ushered in an enormous wave of speculative property development.

Local Government

The 1983 White Paper, *Streamlining the Cities* proposed to abolish the metropolitan authorities created by the Heath government in 1974 and restore their city and suburban components, while in London the GLC was to be abolished. Legislation came about through the Local Government Act 1985. But rather than devolve power to local communities, local government functions were more and more assigned to ad hoc quangos and in London to a government office in Whitehall. The suspicion that Thatcher and Heseltine had of local government was almost pathological and it took a Labour government after the 1997 election to restore confidence in its officers and members.

Reviving the Inner Cities

In January 1983, Michael Heseltine left the DoE and was appointed Secretary of State for Defence. In March of that year the Conservative Political Centre published his essay with the above title. It dealt with the development of inner-area policy, UDCs, Enterprise Zones, urban funding, derelict land and housing in the inner cities. It is written in a clear, direct way and was based on his experience at the DoE for three and a half years. Essentially, it was his attempt to ensure that the agenda he had put in place would not be disrupted by his successors. His concluding comments, 'I think we now have answers where formerly there were questions. We now need the energy and time to apply them' are an apt summary of the Conservative approach to urban policy and his agenda survived right through to his return to Marsham Street in 1990.

Draft Circulars on Green Belts and Land for Housing

These circulars provoked concerns that in its enthusiasm to deal with the concerns expressed by the housing lobby, the government would compromise on the tough stance taken to green belt policy by Conservatives ever since that policy was introduced by Duncan Sandys in 1955. The Environment Secretary at the time, Patrick Jenkin, described the opposition to the draft circulars as akin to standing on a garden rake. The House of Commons Environment Committee under the chairmanship of planning lawyer Sir Hugh Rossi was requested to examine the whole subject and to take evidence. It reported in June 1984 and made a series of wide-ranging recommendations, which as far as green belt policy was concerned were incorporated into a new circular. Their effect was to make green belt policy even tougher: boundaries were to be changed only exceptionally and should

141

be maintained as far as could be seen ahead, and when drawing up boundaries no account should be taken of the condition of land. A fourth objective of green belt policy – to assist regeneration – should be put into the circular. The implications were that whatever other changes might be introduced into the planning system, green policy was sacrosanct.

New Settlements

The final version of the housing circular published as DoE Circular 15/84 recognised that 'it may be practicable to consider making provision in structure plans for new settlements', and noted that 'Any such proposals of this kind by private developers must be subject to normal planning procedures'. This provoked an avalanche of schemes from house-builders. The volume builders formed a consortium that submitted planning applications across the country and the RTPI had given a cautious welcome to their first scheme near Thurrock in Essex (RTPI, 1985). The speculation only ceased in October 1989 when Chris Patten rejected the scheme at Foxley Wood in Hampshire.

Lifting the Burden

More was to come. In 1984, Margaret Thatcher had put into the Lords, and into her Cabinet, David Young, a highly successful businessman. First as Minister Without Portfolio and the following year as Secretary of State for Employment, he began a crusade against controls and regulations. He set up a committee on deregulation and was determined that this approach would spread to all government departments. He began with planning and employment. On Thursday 16 July 1985, he introduced to the House of Lords the White Paper *Lifting the Burden*. He comments in his biography, *The Enterprise Years* (Young, 1990):

> We had a competition in the unit for the name for the paper. I won with my suggestion 'Lifting the Burden' which was hardly surprising, as I was the sole judge. In the first paragraph of the paper I wrote: 'It is the growth of enterprise, the efforts of millions of our people engaged in the creation and development of businesses large and small that is the real driving force of the economy.'

Nicholas Ridley, now at Environment, arranged that he would synchronise his circular to local authorities with the White Paper which would again stress the existing presumption in favour of development. The accompanying circular asserted that 'There is always a presumption in favour of allowing applications for development unless . . . [it] would cause demonstrable harm to interests of acknowledged importance'.

David Young, in his memoirs (1990), rather uncharacteristically undersold the impact of the circular: 'This was a very important circular and would have considerable effect on planning decisions in the future' (Young, 1990). It did more than that. It ushered in the property boom that throughout the length and breath of the country is the lasting legacy of Thatcherism. Margaret Thatcher was impressed:

> David Young did not claim to understand politics but he understood how to make things happen . . . And he had that sureness of touch in devising practical projects which make sense in the marketplace that few but successful businessmen ever acquire.
>
> (Thatcher, 1993)

Property Boom

So far as the development plan system was concerned, development plans were to be treated as 'One, but only one, of the material considerations that must be taken into account in dealing with planning applications' (Circular 22/80). Everything was now in place. The White Paper was an essential component of the property boom that took place in the late 1980s. The transformation of the British landscape was massive. Out-of-town shopping, retail parks, business parks, motorways and new housing villages. At planning appeal inquiry, the odds on success at times exceeded 50 per cent.

A year later, in May 1986, a further White Paper was published: *Building Businesses, Not Barriers* which contained a review of the deregulation measures across the whole of Whitehall. Chapter 5 dealt with planning and the environment and several measures were trailed in the document. These included Simplified Planning Zones, changes to the Use Class Order to simplify the different categories, enabling redundant agricultural buildings to be converted to other uses to help the rural economy, and changes to the content and procedures of development plans. All of these changes were predicated on a single maxim: the need to create jobs. The Conservatives were in mid-term and Margaret Thatcher, as David Young describes, was worried:

Development: the New Cash Crop: The future of the countryside will become a dominant issue of the next decade

© *Building Magazine*

Parliament rose for the vacation and I had my last meeting with the Prime Minister. I found her tired and worried about unemployment. She thought that we were losing the battle for people's hearts and minds on the issue. We were halfway through the term and she knew that the changes she would have to make this time would take us through to the election.

(Young, 1990)

Abolition of Structure Plans

This suspicion of development plans continued with the publication of a government Green Paper in 1986, *The Future of Development Plans*, by the Secretary of State at the time, Nicholas Ridley. On earlier becoming Secretary of State for Trade and Industry, the chain-smoking minister had surprised his civil servants when he announced that he needed neither an in-tray nor an out-tray but what he did want was an ashtray. A clever but unguarded Etonian right-winger, he was a key supporter of Margaret Thatcher's New Right agenda. The paper advocated the abolition of structure plans and their replacement with county planning statements. Also proposed were district-wide unitary development plans, as had recently been introduced in the metropolitan areas, following the abolition of the metropolitan counties. These proposals caused much criticism and disillusionment among the planning profession and local authority associations. As we have seen, traditionally the planning profession was strongest in the counties and the proposals by Nicholas Ridley were seen as an attack on this professionalism and local autonomy. They were carried forward to a White Paper published in January 1989 but change was in prospect.

In 1988 the government decided to draw together many of its ad hoc circulars into a document setting out the government's general position. 'PPG1' was the first of this series of advisory notes. It contained the iconic statement that summed up the Thatcher approach to planning: 'Moreover the plan is only one of the material considerations which must be taken into account'. At paragraph 15, it clearly placed the burden of proof on the local planning authorities: 'the onus is on them to demonstrate clearly why the development cannot be permitted'.

Roads for Prosperity

In May of that year, a White Paper was published by the government which was to have enormous consequences and was eventually to act as a huge spur to the environmental lobby. *Roads for Prosperity* and the companion document which was a consultation paper on bringing in private finance, *New Roads by New Means* which featured on its front cover an artist's impression of the proposed new Thames bridge crossing at Dartford, were presented to Parliament by the Secretary of State for Transport Paul Channon. In line with Margaret Thatcher's enthusiasm for road transport, the White Paper announced a greatly expanded motorway and trunk road programme. The companion document set out ideas for privately financed tolled roads. The programme was immediately controversial. It included the bypasses to Winchester and Newbury which were to be the scene of intense skirmishes and obstruction by the anti-road protestors and would launch the career of the environmental activist, 'Swampy' who would come before David Cameron's mother sitting as a magistrate at Newbury's Criminal Court for his refusal to obey court orders obtained by the road-builders. The force and media attention of these campaigners persuaded New Labour when they came to power in 1997 to abandon most if not all of the expanded trunk road programmes.

Retailing

On 3 September 1987, planning permission was granted on appeal for the development of an out-of-town retail development at Lakeside, near Grays in Thurrock. The centre was colossal – some 1.65 million square feet of shopping and leisure floorspace. The decision was made possible because towards the end of his two-year term as Environment Secretary in July 1985 Patrick Jenkin had outlined the government's planning policy on large new retail developments:

> It is not the function of the planning system to inhibit competition among retailers or among methods of retailing, nor to preserve existing commercial interests as such; it must take into account the benefits to the public which flow from new developments in the distributive and retailing fields.
>
> (DoE, 1985)

Jenkin had previously been Industry Secretary and was sympathetic to the economic case put by Tesco, Asda, Sainsbury's and the other superstore operators. That policy changed the face of England as the rival superstores vied with each other to erect new centres on the edge of towns and was not challenged until John Gummer became Environment Secretary in 1993.

A Summer of Discontent

The summer of 1988 saw an open split between the Thatcherites in the Cabinet and Conservative backbenchers. Nicholas Ridley published a discussion paper on new villages which suggested that well located and well planned new villages warranted careful consideration, while Lord Young at the Department of Trade and Industry (DTI) had backed the scheme by Consortium Developments to build a new town in North Hampshire (Foxley Wood). Opposing them were the Sane Planning Group which included 90 Conservative MPs including Michael Heseltine, now a back-bencher after his resignation from the Cabinet in the wake of the Westland helicopter argument, who was facing a plan in his own constituency by Consortium Developments to build a new town to the east of Oxford close to the M40 which they charmingly called 'Stone Bassett'. The discontent continued into the following year but by then the Thatcherites had begun to lose their momentum.

Green Belt Policy

One area where the Conservatives were not prepared to allow a more market-driven approach was green belt policy. Since Duncan Sandys had encouraged the designation of green belts around cities and towns outside Greater London in 1955, the Conservatives had been very supportive of the policy and there was deep-rooted public support. In January 1988, advice on green belts was consolidated in the advice document 'PPG2' which set out five main purposes including the policy that had been introduced in 1984 that green belts would assist in urban regeneration.

There were some Conservatives who felt that competition and deregulation had implications for green belt policy and wanted to see a more flexible approach. The Centre for Policy Studies in October 1988 published a policy document *Planning Planning: Clearer Strategies and Environmental Controls* which advocated less local detailed planning and an opportunity for landowners to bid for development permits, while in October 1989 The Phoenix Group published a pamphlet *Green Belt or Green Gardens?* The Phoenix Group was a group of councillors representing metropolitan boroughs who were frustrated by planning policies that encouraged town-cramming within cities and wanted to see development diverted into the green belts. Whether consciously or not, these Conservatives realised that there was an ideological gap between support for green belts and the deregulation that had been applied to the rest of the planning system. But the Party leaders positioning to replace Margaret Thatcher were moving away from them and within the Parliamentary Party there was little support for such neo-Conservative views towards planning and the land market.

The Erosion of Planning

In his book *Radical Planning Initiatives*, published in 1990 but written before the resignation of Margaret Thatcher, Andy Thornley, one of the two editors and a planning academic (Montgomery and Thornley, 1990) summarised the changes introduced during the Thatcher era in an interesting way. His conclusion was that the principle of a universal planning system covering most of the country had been abandoned:

> As a result there are those areas where strict controls still exist and in which administrative discretion still operates. These are the national parks, areas of outstanding natural beauty, conservation areas and green belts, all of which have been exempted from the relaxations to the planning legislation. Then there is the much relaxed 'normal planning system' in which there has been a shift to a much greater acceptance of market criteria and a downgrading of development plans and policies. There is considerable evidence to suggest that this shift will be extended with a greater degree of central control. Third there is the preconceived planning framework approach of the simplified regimes which introduces an alternative approach to that of development control and administrative discretion.

Backbench Revolt

Not all Conservative politicians were happy. Backbench Tory MPs in the shires began to get a highly critical postbag from their constituents angered at the pace of building. Having played a key role in the 1987 election, Lord Young resigned in 1989 to resume his business career and the pressure for deregulation began to slacken. The dominance of Margaret Thatcher was also waning in the debacle of the introduction of the Poll Tax. Nicholas Ridley was replaced by Chris Patten as Environment Secretary in July 1989. Patten knew he had a poisoned chalice and described his promotion as a 'hospital pass'.

The Prince's Vision: Poundbury

There was also an intervention from an unexpected quarter. Following the success of his television programme *A Vision of Britain* in October 1988, the Prince of Wales published a book of the same title in 1989 in which he expanded on his theme, set out his ten principles and reiterated his despair of regulations. In many ways his themes were those of Thomas Sharp and Iain Nairn, but with his publishers Doubleday he presented these in a visually attractive form suitable to a contemporary audience, and they had an enormous impact. He asserted, 'At present, under the existing planning and highways regulations, it is next to impossible to achieve the kind of changes I have been suggesting' (HRH The Prince of Wales, 1989). The Prince, together with master planner Leon Krier, sought to implement the principles expounded in his book in the Poundbury community, which is an urban extension of Dorchester in Dorset. Expected to be fully complete by 2025, with a population of 5,000 and some 2,000 jobs, the design of the community reflects traditional Dorchester vernacular. Residential densities are

Poundbury has determined to demonstrate a sense of place and not just appear as another housing estate and now attracts thousands of visitors each year.

© Malcolm D. Moor

149

high, and the highway layout is constrained, deliberately inconvenient for cars, so that the main streets are left for pedestrians and visitor parking.

Later that year the youthful, popular president of the RTPI, Frances Tibbalds, who was to die an untimely death only four years later, responded to Prince Charles with his 'Ten Commandments of Good Urban Design'. The critical and professional climate was changing and, as we shall see, Chris Patten made sure that the government responded to these new concerns.

A Change of Direction

In her memoirs, Margaret Thatcher described the 1989 reshuffle in this way:

> In moving Nick Ridley to the DTI, I was generally seen to be responding to the criticisms of him by the environmental lobby. This was not so. I knew he wanted a change. I was, of course, quite aware of the fact that the romantics and cranks of the movement did not like it when he insisted on basing policy on science rather than prejudice. I also suspected that from Chris Patten they would get a more emollient approach. Certainly, I subsequently found myself repeatedly at odds with Chris, for with him presentation on environmental matters always seemed to be at the expense of substance . . .
>
> (Thatcher, 1993)

Whatever the criticism of him by Margaret Thatcher, Chris Patten was determined to move the government's planning policies away from the free market approach of Young and Ridley. In the autumn he announced that the proposal to abolish structure plans was withdrawn. He indicated a change of direction. A White Paper entitled *The Future of Development Plans* earlier that year had recognised that local plans were required for comprehensive development control. A new system consisting of comprehensive district development plans with mandatory preparation was put in place across the whole of the country. I can recall attending a press conference at Marsham Street in October 1989 when Chris Patten introduced his discussion paper *Local Choice*, which proposed a series of changes to the planning system. A key sentence was: 'If the planning system works properly at the local level, there is less need for central government decision-taking – by me or by my inspectors – which can so easily appear to the local community to attach too little weight to their views' (Patten, 1989). It was clear that there was to be a break with the free market approach encouraged by Lord Young and Nicholas Ridley. As if to demonstrate this in the firmest possible way, Chris

Patten also announced that he was going to accept the inspector's recommendation to dismiss the appeal by Consortium Developments, which was promoting a new settlement at Foxley Wood in Hampshire, which Nicholas Ridley in an interim announcement had indicated he was minded to approve.

Chris Patten was to become Chairman of the Conservative Party and against all the odds steered the Party under John Major to an election victory, although his time spent in the national election campaign cost him his Bath constituency seat. Patten settled the Conservative backbenchers by setting his face against the Ridley changes and this was an important step towards election victory. By July 1990, Ridley was gone from the Cabinet having declared in an interview with Dominic Lawson, published in the *Spectator* magazine, his concerns about giving up sovereignty to a German-led federalist European Community: 'You might just as well give it to Adolf Hitler, frankly'. This was strong meat even for Margaret Thatcher and his resignation was inevitable.

Environmentalism

In that same year, Chris Patten introduced The Environmental Protection Act and already by the time Margaret Thatcher was deposed as leader of the Conservative Party following the leadership election of November 1990, a new approach to planning had emerged. Patten was alert to the international changes taking place in environmental policy. The Greens had done particularly well in the 1989 European elections, winning 15 per cent of the vote. Again that year, Patten introduced the 1990 Planning Act which consolidated the many amendments made to the original 1971 Act in three separate pieces of legislation, which were again to be revised by the Planning & Compensation Act the following year. This received Royal Assent in July 1991. Some elements of the 1989 White Paper did survive. The need for a central government minister to approve structure plans was removed, the requirement to prepare district-wide local plans became mandatory and the weight to be afforded to development plans in the decision-making process was considerably strengthened. The role of the country councils in the development plan system was consolidated.

Plan-led System

The final parliamentary approval to the changes introduced in 1990 was not to take place until 1991, after Chris Patten had relinquished the environment portfolio, but it is helpful to consider these now as he was so much involved. The introduction of a plan-led system was made even more important by Section 54a of the 1990 Act introduced in 1991. The introduction of this section during the passage of the Bill in 1990 was prompted by a Labour opposition question. Back in 1989, the Labour Planning Group had resolved that Labour would abolish the presumption in favour of development and would remove the automatic right of appeal against the refusal of planning permission. Probably to many people's surprise, the revised section, introduced in response to the Labour intervention, significantly increased the importance of the development plan. But Chris Patten had intended to move away from the deregulatory planning regime that characterised the 1980s and this Labour intervention provided him with the means to do this.

Centralism

The removal of the necessity for a planning minister to approve submitted structure plans did not in practice or intention signify more independence for local planning authorities. The introduction of Planning Policy Guidance Notes (PPGs) and Regional Planning Guidance Notes (RPGs) had begun in January 1989 and the 1991 Act made it clear that these documents established a new planning framework by which central government could ensure that its planning policies and objectives were carried forward in the new wave of mandatory district-wide local plans. Independent planning inspectors from the Planning Inspectorate who carried out local public inquiries into the plans would be on notice from the regional offices of the DoE to ensure that the plans reflected current national planning advice. In many ways it is extraordinary that this degree of centralism should be introduced by a Conservative government, but the Tory backbenchers had made it clear that they did not like a deregulated planning regime. House-building and commercial property lobbies could and did petition government ministers to speed up plan-making and release greater amounts of land for development, but ministers knew where their votes came from.

Until 1988, central government planning statements in England had been released through a series of advisory departmental circulars concentrating on a mixture of policy, procedural and legal issues. From 1991 the approach was to become more directive.

In May 1990, Labour published its plans to reform local government. Powers would be transferred from central government and quangos to elected assemblies in Scotland, Wales and England, and the shire counties would be abolished. There would be a new elected body for London. As we will see, John Prescott trialled these proposals to the RTPI in 1983.

At a time when Margaret Thatcher's political powers were waning, Chris Patten had succeeded in responding to the concerns of Tory backbenchers by ditching the free market approach to planning that had characterised most of the 1980s and introducing a formal plan-led system as well as retaining the influence in planning issues of the shire counties. Ironically, days before he moved at the end of November 1990 from the Marsham Street headquarters of the DoE, the massive out-of-town Lakeside shopping centre in Essex opened. Costing some £350 million and within one hour's drive of 20 per cent of the UK population, it was a monument to the deregulatory planning system that Patten had inherited. However, earlier in September he had published the White Paper *This Common Inheritance* which was the first comprehensive statement of government policy on the environment ranging from the street corner to the stratosphere. It addressed issues such as greenhouse gases, waste and recycling, and the use of private motor vehicles, and was yet another pointer to the changes he had introduced.

The publication of the White Paper stimulated an interesting contribution to the debate from TCPA which in 1991 published a paper by Ray Green and John Holliday, both members of the TCPA council, which took Ebenezer Howard's concept of the social city and applied it on a much larger scale to south Devon, showing how sustainable principles could be applied at this scale. The paper had some effect, for a new settlement in south Devon has now emerged as an approved policy.

Housing

One area that Patten had little or no impact on was housing policy. On gaining office Margaret Thatcher and Michael Heseltine had lost no time in dismantling Labour's housing programme. In February 1980 the new government cut Labour's planned Housing Investment Programme for 1980–81 by some 40 per cent. In October, believing that this much-reduced total might be overspent, it imposed a complete moratorium on all new commitments in England. In December 1980 it announced a further cut of at least 15 per cent in permitted capital spending for the following year. Although the main target of those cuts was council-house building, then at its lowest level since 1925, the cuts also affected improvements in the private sector, through mortgages and improvement grants.

The cuts were truly staggering. Government expenditure on housing was to be reduced by 47.6 per cent over the period 1981 to 1984 and, as a proportion of the planned total public expenditure, housing would drop from 5.4 to only 2.9 per cent. The government's policy towards public housing is summed up by the reply of the Secretary of State Michael Heseltine in response to questioning from the House of Commons Environment Committee. His reply to the question, 'Does it concern you that we have estimated a shortfall in our first report of something in the region of half a million dwellings?' was:

> obviously anyone who is interested in the problems of housing needs is entitled to my attention. But I am pursuing, I would argue, within the constraints of an economy in decline, the housing policies most fitted to a situation where we have the largest crude surplus ever and where the essential challenge now is to make better use of the existing stock.
>
> (Heseltine, 1980)

The year 1979 was the post-war high watermark for housing completions, not the highest – that had been in 1968 under Anthony Greenwood as Housing Minister, but after 1979 public housing was never to reach the levels it had enjoyed under Labour. Mortgage tax relief however was still sacrosanct and even the Green Paper on housing produced by the previous Labour government had warned of 'the shock to the market and household budget' which removing the subsidy would bring.

Coupled with the cuts in public housing expenditure was 'the right to buy'. The 1980 Housing Act compelled local authorities, new towns and non-charitable housing associations to sell their housing stock to sitting tenants, irrespective of the scale of local demand for rented houses. Local authorities in England received some 300,000 applications to exercise the 'right to buy' in the first year of the operation of the Act. Politically successful though the initiative was, Conservative strategists did not appear to think through the long-term consequences of the massive cut in council-house building. At the time, the average sale produced about £1,755 for a local authority while it cost them about £22,250 to build a new council house. Following these dramatic changes, for the rest of the decade new house-building was principally the responsibility of the private sector. Since that time, millions of words have been written on the subject of 'affordable' housing but no Party has been prepared to sanction the resumption of the levels of housing grant paid to local authorities before 1979. This enormous transfer of house ownership from the public sector to individual households has been one of the most enduring legacies of the Thatcher revolution. During the lifetime of the Thatcher government as a whole, housing accounted for about 40 per cent of the total proceeds of government sales. (Dutton, 1997).

Thatcherism: A Synthesis of Two Ideologies

Thatcherism was essentially a synthesis of two ideologies, economic liberalism and authoritarian conservatism. Neither sat well with a planning system that had been promoted by the Attlee welfare agenda and had been sustained by the political consensus that had survived the three post-war decades to the mid 1970s. Thatcherism was the ideology of free-market globalisation. Its power was to recognise the way in which the world – and not only Britain – was changing and thereby also to help shape these changes. The towers of Canary Wharf silhouetted against the flat Thames landscape will stand as an icon to Margaret Thatcher's policies, but deregulation and privatisation also changed the face of England. In the next chapter we follow the intriguing story of how during the mayhem of John Major's government, the reforms initiated by Chris Patten at the end of Margaret Thatcher's term as Prime Minister not only survived but were pushed forward by John Gummer as Environment Secretary and one of the survivors in John Major's Cabinet, which was beset with sackings and resignations.

References

DoE (1985) *Government Policy On Planning and Large Stores*. London: DoE.
Dutton, D. (1997) *British Politics Since 1945*, 2nd edn. Oxford: Blackwell, p. 127.
Evans, E. (2004) *Thatcher and Thatcherism*, 2nd edn. London: Routledge, pp. 1, 9.
Heseltine, M. (1980) Answer to a question from the House of Commons Environment Committee. Report of the House of Commons Environment Committee. London: HMSO.
Heseltine, M. (1981) Evidence to House of Lords Select Committee on the

Environment. Report of the House of Lords Select Committee on the Environment. London: HMSO.

HRH The Prince of Wales (1989) *A Vision of Britain*. London: Doubleday, p. 15.

Jenkins, S. (2006) Thatcher & Sons. London: Allen Lane, pp. 125, 126, 127, 130.

Leach, R. (2002) *Political Ideology in Britain*. London: Palgrave, pp. 193, 194, 202.

Marquand, D. and Seldon, A. (1996) *The Ideas that Shaped Post-War Britain*. London: Fontana, pp. 11, 15.

Montgomery, J. and Thornley, A. (1990) *Radical Planning Initiatives*, Aldershot: Gower, p. 46.

Patten, C. (1989) *Planning and Local Choice*. London: DoE.

RTPI (1985) *New Country Towns Proposal*. London: RTPI press release 8 May.

Tewdwr-Jones, M. (2002) *The Planning Polity*, London: Routledge, pp. 10–11.

Thatcher, M. (1993) *The Downing Street Years*. London: Harper, pp. 7, 8, 421, 758.

Young, D. (1990) *The Enterprise Years*. London: Headline, pp. 146, 147, 149.

9

The Major Years: The Revolution Continues, 1990–1997

The Revolution Continues

Margaret Thatcher was determined that her revolution would continue under John Major. As Andrew Marr observed, 'When Margaret Thatcher left Downing Street for the last time in tears, she already knew that she had successfully completed a final political campaign which was to ensure she was replaced as Prime Minister by John Major, rather than Michael Heseltine' (Marr, 2007). But one of John Major's earliest moves was to bring Michael Heseltine back into the Cabinet as Environment Secretary. It is unusual for a politician to head a department twice, but as Heseltine himself observed, 'I was pleased by the opportunity and I could not deny there was a certain justice in it – from the beginning I had campaigned for the leadership on the platform that the Poll Tax had to go' (Heseltine, 2000).

So, on 30 November 1990, Michael Heseltine was back at the ugly Marsham Street headquarters of the DoE until the election of 1992 when in the new Cabinet he took the DTI portfolio. During his time at the DoE he built on the new policies that Chris Patten had introduced: 'Chris Patten, whom I succeeded at the DoE, had been an extremely effective Secretary of State and I was particularly enthusiastic to build on the environmental policies he had been pursuing' (Heseltine, 2000). He had a strong team, with Michael Portillo, David Trippier and Sir George Young as junior ministers in the department.

City Challenge

Two significant initiatives were to make the regional offices of government that had been set up more effective and more multi-disciplinary, and this came fully into effect in 1994. But Heseltine began the change which was to signal a more regionalised approach to local government and to set up 'City Challenge'. Local authorities in deprived areas were invited to submit competitive bids as to how they would invest the £37.5 million over five years on offer from central government. This scheme was launched in July 1991. A bitter critic of the scheme was Sir Jeremy Beecham, former leader of Newcastle City Council, who commented: 'Thus in my own authority within the five-year period of City Challenge we will have received £37.5 million and reduced our main line services by £150 million to meet the Government's capping targets. The contrast apparently does not strike the Government as incongruous' (Beecham, 1993).

Canary Wharf

At Marsham Street, Michael Heseltine was again responsible for the London Docklands Corporation. The Canadian developer Paul Reichmann saw the need for the great trading floors now required by the financial world in their new offices and not available in the traditional areas of the City. Canary Wharf in London's Docklands was the logical choice and there was the attraction of the financial incentives of the Enterprise Zone introduced by Geoffrey Howe when Chancellor. Enterprise Zones were introduced in the 1980 Local Government and Planning Act and although they were now finished, planning permissions for developments already begun could continue indefinitely under Sections 88 and 89 of the Town and Country Planning Act 1990. What that meant for Canary Wharf was that 1.15 million square metres of office floorspace could be built without further approvals. In my *Building* column in 1995 I wrote, 'In years to come, commentators might be perplexed to learn that the blueprint for the massive group of towers at Canary Wharf never went near a democratically elected planning committee. The towers, silhouetted against the flat Thames landscape, will be remembered as Margaret Thatcher's final political statement' (Moor, 1995). But the property industry was far from buoyant and Reichmann persuaded the government to first extend the Docklands Light Railway (DLR) and ultimately the Jubilee Line to Canary Wharf so that it became much more accessible to office workers living in the rest of London. To do this, control of the DLR was taken from London Transport.

London Docklands

The London Docklands is the planning paradigm for the Thatcher age. I worked on the original Docklands study and wrote an article for *Built Environment* in 1971 outlining the scope for major development in the area (Moor, 1971) but the area had to wait for ten years before regeneration finally took hold. This distinctive approach to urban regeneration has had many critics. Dr Brian Edwards, writing in the *Planner* in February 1993, pithily described it as 'The manifestation of a distinctive political will [that] has resulted in the Isle of Dogs [the commercial core of London Docklands] resembling not mainstream European urbanism but the unplanned cityscapes of North America and the Pacific rim'. The irony is that the Isle of Dogs has become the template for much more urban development in London, predicated on London's emergence as the world's leading financial centre in the wake of the 'Big Bang' which freed the London Stock Exchange from a restrictive share dealing system. Another perspective on the approach to design in the Docklands comes from the architect Piers Gough. In an interview in *Building* magazine he describes working in the area at that time:

> Things really picked up in the eighties with the Docklands. Planning there was much easier than anywhere else because it wasn't democratic. There were four men who sort of ruled and if they liked your building, you got to do it. That was exhilarating because you could design what you wanted rather than just what was acceptable, nice or friendly.
>
> (Boyd, 2007)

Over 20 years on from 1988, Canary Wharf had become London's Manhattan, so that by 2008 the highest tower, One Canada Square (235 metres) was surrounded by other towers, and these soaring skyscrapers were occupied by some 100,000 workers.

Another person who influenced Michael Heseltine at this time was Professor Peter Hall (later knighted by Tony Blair), a left-of-centre academic and a leading planning expert. He impressed Heseltine with his stimulating grasp of the issues, and the basis was laid for the growth strategy that emerged of channelling development from Docklands into the East Thames Corridor on either side of the river. The project had originally emerged in an agenda paper written for a 1987 meeting of the now defunct regional planning body Serplan by its planning adviser, Martin Simmons. Heseltine uncharacteristically continued with the loose federation of central government and local authorities as the delivery mechanism. This was a model he had spurned for London Docklands, relying instead on the Docklands Development Corporation, but the Thames-side local authorities were determined that this time they would not lose control and Heseltine was not able to devote the level of energy and commitment he had previously done. He did however secure the commitment of the government that the planned Channel Tunnel rail link would be re-routed through the Corridor. The Thames Corridor concept was subsequently enthusiastically taken up by John Prescott when he took on the environment portfolio, but progress was pitifully slow and the scheme began to look less convincing after the severe summer floods of 2007 and an investment in flood defences that could exceed £1 billion. Most of the scheduled growth areas were in the Thames flood plain.

In the run up to the 1992 election, the changes introduced by Chris Patten were firmly consolidated by Michael Heseltine. The Planning and Compensation Billl was published in November 1990 and received Royal Assent in July 1991. Earlier in July, Heseltine had announced that the present two-tier system of counties and districts introduced by Heath and Walker in 1974 would become a single tier in some areas. In November of that year, a new Local Government Bill was published which proposed the establishment of a new Local Government Commission to review the local government structure.

Election Victory, 1992

John Major's election victory was indeed impressive. More people (some 14.1 million) voted for the Conservatives than had voted for Thatcher in any of her three elections. No leader has ever won a larger number of votes than Major achieved in this election. The lead over Labour at the election was 2 million votes and was some half a million more votes than Blair received in 1997. But Britain's electoral arithmetic, with its bias towards small urban constituencies which were safe Labour seats, meant that this enormous victory actually secured a parliamentary majority of little more than 20 seats.

John Major, in his autobiography, was stoic about this:

> Above all, our victory in 1992 killed off socialism in Britain. It also, I must conclude, made the world safe for Tony Blair. Our win meant that between 1992 and 1997 Labour had to change. No longer is Britain trapped in the old two-party tango, with one government neatly undoing everything its predecessor has created.
>
> (Major, 1999)

Black Wednesday

The authority that Major gained at the election was short-lived. 'Black Wednesday', which saw Britain forced out of the ERM, disastrous poll ratings and party splits soon characterised a government that seemed to drift from crisis to crisis. Although the Major administration involved a marked change in political style, were there significant changes in political ideas? The Poll Tax was an early casualty but that had long been a political necessity. The Major government energetically pursued the changes in education and health begun under Margaret Thatcher, and extended competition in public services. There was no slackening of the privatisation programme and the politically contentious break-up of British Rail was forced through.

Seismic Shift

The loss of Chris Patten from the Cabinet was a blow. He said in an interview that it had knocked the stuffing out of him and thought it was the worst thing that could have happened to him, but three months after losing Bath he was on his way to Hong Kong as governor: 'Out of the wreckage came what were to be the most wonderful five years of my life (Patten, 2007). But on planning Patten had, before the election, already shifted the Conservative Party back into a protectionist stance that was altogether more popular with backbenchers and party activists. Gone was the pro-market and development stance of Lord Young, Thatcher and Ridley. This was a seismic shift which is still in evidence and became more marked as Gordon Brown, first as Chancellor and then as Prime Minister, picked up the pro-market planning agenda discarded by the Tories.

Inner Cities

In local government and planning, under John Major the centralism that we have observed continued. According to Simon Jenkins (2006), 'The answer is that centralism was the only vehicle Major found in the Downing Street garage on arrival'. As we have seen, following Major's appointment as Prime Minister, Michael Heseltine was reappointed Secretary of State for the Environment, in November 1990, having been previously Secretary of State from 1979 to 1983. The Thatcherite approach continued but principally in urban regeneration. Three Enterprise Zones and one Urban Development

8

Corporation were designated between 1990 and 1997. Competitiveness in urban funding was encouraged through City Challenge, Single Regeneration Budgets, the National Lottery (introduced by John Major in 1994) and the Millennium Commission.

The period after Major's accession to the premiership was characterised by this changed climate for the planning system. The introduction of a plan-led planning process, the incorporation of the environmental agenda and a balance between environmental and market concerns was in marked contrast with Thatcherism, but Major did not challenge the centralism that had developed during Thatcher's premiership.

The Greening of the Conservatives

One change for which John Major is given little credit is the greening of the Conservative party. David Cameron now takes the accolade for this but John Major was the first head of a G7 government to announce that he would attend the Rio Earth Summit held in June 1992. At the summit two important conventions were agreed. One, on climate change, which committed the UK government to cut the emission of 'greenhouse gasses' to 1990 levels by 2000, and the other on biodiversity. On the latter, John Major was much influenced by Sir Crispin Tickell who was not only an expert on environmental policy, but also Britain's ambassador to the United Nations. He subsequently helped set up a Panel on Sustainable Development. The Earth Summit drew up a plan called Agenda 21, for addressing the environmental, economic and social problems facing the world, and this stressed the role of local authorities in implementing the aims of the Declaration.

Sustainable Development

Michael Howard was briefly Environment Secretary for a little over a year but in the May 1993 Cabinet reshuffle, John Gummer succeeded him. During that year Howard sanctioned the enormous Trafford Centre regional shopping centre (1.3 million sq ft) outside Manchester promoted by Peel Holdings. Objectors tried to block it by legal challenge but Gummer was persuaded to finally allow it to go ahead. In his defence he pointed out that it was a collective Cabinet decision and that to allow planning decisions to be reopened by the courts would create a situation where there was no conclusion to the planning process. In July that year the CPRE published a document entitled *The Lost Land* which contained a new study of regional land use statistics between 1945 and 1990. It pointed out that in the South East the urban area had grown by almost twice as much as any other region – 188,000 hectares – and the largest area of farmland had been lost. Gummer was sympathetic – after all, the CPRE had 45,000 vocal members – and he pledged to increase the amount of development occurring on brownfield land.

He introduced The Environment Act 1995 and the setting up of the Environment Agency. This was to be the lead agency to procure sustainable construction and the principal environmental adviser to the government. Startlingly, the energy used in constructing, occupying and operating buildings represents 50 per cent of greenhouse gas emissions in the UK. In his memoirs, John Major describes John Gummer's time as Environment Secretary:

> John never holds any views half-heartedly, and was passionate about the environment . . . He built up an excellent reputation amongst lobby groups, and unfailingly challenged policies that had an environmental cost. He was the guiding force behind the White Paper on Sustainable Development we launched in January 1994 and lobbied energetically for me to include the subject in every speech I could to give it profile.
>
> (Major, 1999)

Gummer was one of the longest-lasting environment ministers, serving for four years from May 1993 to the May election in 1997, and was to emerge again in opposition as the co-author with Zac Goldsmith of the environmental policy report presented to David Cameron in August 2007.

Regionalism

One nettle left by Michael Heseltine was how strategic planning would fit into a reorganised local government structure. When pressed on the subject in October 1993, John Gummer refused to give any indication other than to announce a speeding up of the then current local government review. Just over a month later, in November, he announced that from April 1994 there would be ten regional offices throughout the country combining the work of the four ministries: environment, transport, industry and employment. The establishment of the regional offices was widely interpreted as an attempt by John Major's government to slow down the almost irresistible pressure for regionalism that emanated from the EU in Brussels. The intention was that the government offices for the regions would devise regional strategies subject to advice from local authorities, but regional guidance evolved towards a system where it reflected conversely the regional view on how development should be distributed throughout the region. We will see how New Labour was to employ the nascent structure left by the Conservatives to erect a much stronger regional framework for local government.

A year later the government bowed to a report from the Local Government Commission that dealt a severe blow to its plan to replace county councils with more unitary authorities as the commission recommended no change to the majority of councils it had examined. In November 1994, John Gummer, who was no fan of the local government reforms that he had inherited from Michael Heseltine, announced that he wanted to keep the two-tier councils and that England should have a 'variable' local government structure. Regionalism has proved to be one of the great ideological differences between the Conservatives and Labour.

Town Centres

In that first year in office, Gummer and his team, which included David Curry, Tim Yeo and Tony Baldry, were as busy if not busier than Michael Heseltine had been, with a flurry of initiatives which included the first guidance on the environmental appraisal of development plans required by EU directives. One initiative that was to really signal a change came in January 1993 when Gummer warned the TCPA: 'I have decided to take a closer interest in retail proposals outside the main shopping centres of towns and cities'. He subsequently dismissed a sub-regional shopping centre at Duxford near Cambridge. The document *PPG6* was the first major government guidance on town centre planning and was published in August 1993, introducing a sequential test favouring town centres for new retail development. Gummer put his own personal gloss on the advice that he wanted a return to traditional town centres. Subsequently, the House of Commons Select Committee on the Environment published in 1994 a report dealing with shopping centres and a further report on the same subject in 1996. Both unequivocally supported Gummer's tough stance on shopping developments. Gummer was much influenced by a report commissioned from the research group URBED, which reported in 1994 on the future of town centres. Its findings convinced him of the need not only to encourage new shopping development to locations where it could reinforce the town centre, but to discourage development on greenfield sites on the edge of centres, where it would result in an unacceptable impact on a town.

During 1994 the pace continued. A more sustainable approach to transport was broached in the document *PPG13*, and curbs were to be introduced on trunk-road building. The DoE offices at Marsham Street were to be demolished and the document *Quality in Town and Country*, aimed at promoting high-quality design, was published.

Thames Gateway

In September 1994, Gummer left David Curry to launch a revamped version of Heseltine's East Thames Corridor as the Thames Gateway. The Channel Tunnel rail link, the backbone of the project, was emphasised but there was no indication of government funding other than for a series of transport projects. Curry defended the approach, which Heseltine had perpetuated, that rejected a Development Corporation and instead relied on a partnership with local authorities. In November, the final recommendation of the Local Government Commission dealt a severe blow to government plans to replace county councils with more unitary authorities and most of the counties were to keep their two-tier structure.

Labour Advances

As the government's popularity continued to decline, Labour had made big advances starting under John Smith, who had been elected Party leader in July 1992 after Neil Kinnock's resignation, and from Labour's old Right had unified the party. Smith's death in May 1994 transformed the political scene. Tony Blair emerged as the favourite to carry forward the modernisation of Labour. He convincingly defeated John Prescott after Gordon Brown had agreed to step aside, but Prescott went onto become his deputy after playing a crucial role in securing the rewriting of Clause Four at a special conference in April 1995.

Two months later, John Major resigned the leadership of the Conservative Party and sought re-election, subsequently defeating John Redwood. A key factor was the support of Michael Heseltine, then President of the Board of Trade, who became Deputy Prime Minister.

During this time, Labour gave notice of its draft agenda. In September 1994, Shadow Environment Secretary Chris Smith pledged to introduce a 'right to roam' in what would be known as the John Smith Memorial Act. In March 1995, a consultation document was published, *Renewing Democracy, Rebuilding Communities*, with a foreword from Tony Blair pledging that Labour would give local communities more say in local government. In July, MP Keith Vaz announced the setting up of a top-level review of planning law to sweep away 'a jungle of anomalies' (Moor, 1995). Subsequently, in April 1996, ten years after Margaret Thatcher had abolished the GLC, Frank Dobson proposed a new city-wide authority for London – the Greater London Authority.

Ironically, that same month the government sidelined CrossRail – the cross-London rail line that would link the western suburbs with Docklands – in favour of the Jubilee Line extension and the Channnel Tunnel rail link. It would be more than ten years before Gordon Brown as Prime Minister, in advance of the mayoral contest between incumbent Ken Livingstone and contender Boris Johnson, could announce the financial support of the City of London that would kick-start the project.

Regional Strategies

In June 1996, John Prescott launched a report which promised that when in power Labour would overhaul regional strategies and in particular disband the Rural Development Commission (RDC) and English Partnerships, which would be subsumed by the Regional Development Authorities. Prescott had a particular aversion to the RDC of which I was for a time a committee chairman, seeing it as a club for Tory landowners. In truth, it was a very successful hands-on agency promoting best practice in rural areas and the successor to the council for small industries in rural areas originally promoted by Lloyd George. Prescott was true to his word when in government and the RDC was absorbed into the Countryside Commission but dispensed with its national network of voluntary committees.

Brownfield Land

Earlier, in April, John Gummer had published a White Paper that encouraged more small businesses in rural areas but during the last year of the Conservative government the principal themes were opposition to out-of-town shopping and leisure developments, the need to push up the target for new housing on brownfield land from 50 to 60 per cent and, in February

166

1997, the publication of a *Planning Policy Guidance Note* which introduced a much more sustainable approach to planning and development control. Gummer made it clear that he was not proposing any new taxes on greenfield sites but would use the planning system to provide the clear and unambiguous framework that was needed. Labour was strangely ambivalent about the need to push up the amount of recycled land for housing and Shadow Housing Minister Nick Raynsford, in March 1997, promised to scrap the housing paper that promoted the higher figure. In November 1996, the White Paper *Household Growth: Where Shall We Live?* had been published which reported a need for 4.4 million new homes by 2016. As we will see, New Labour courted controversy early in office by backing major new housing schemes in Hertfordshire and Newcastle which were in the green belt.

Government is faced with housing projections that require a doubling of the current rate of house building but previous attempts to push up the rate of house building have had disastrous results. Many of these estates now require significant refurbishment.

© Malcolm D. Moor

Speeding Up Plans

Concerned that a survey conducted in September 1996 showed that complete local plan coverage of England might not be achieved until after 2000, the DoE published, in January 1997, a consultation paper, *Speeding Up the Delivery of Local Plans and UDPs.* The suggestions in the paper were timid and tentative, but the government was on the horns of a dilemma. Through the introduction of Section 54A, the Conservatives had emphatically supported the preparation of district-wide local plans mandatory for all areas, and had anticipated substantially complete coverage by the end of 1996. That expectation now looked wildly optimistic and the development industry, recovering from the recession of the first part of the decade, was incessant in its criticism of the slow adoption of local plans. The election in May 1997 would overtake the consultation on the document but New Labour would need to overhaul the local plan process.

Election Campaign

During the election campaign of spring 1997 environmental issues featured highly. The Liberal Democrats promised to change the basis of planning and remove the presumption in favour of development (although it could be argued that in practice the Tories had dropped that in 1990), and pressed for a development tax on greenfield development. John Major claimed that the future of cities and the regeneration of depressed areas would be important planks of the Tory manifesto. Labour leader Tony Blair pledged to put the environment at the heart of policy-making.

A Kinder Verdict

As Environment Secretary, John Gummer pretty much reinvented his political career. He had been a very unpopular Minister of Agriculture and his public relations stunt during the BSE crisis to persuade people to eat beef by involving his daughter backfired spectacularly. Yet, as Environment Secretary, he achieved three important objectives which survive today. He put sustainability at the heart of planning policy, he raised genuine concerns about the long-term viability of our town centres and he promoted the reuse of brownfield land, particularly for housing, and the need for a sequential test to prioritise the release of this land.

Milton Keynes has arguably demonstrated that New Town Development Corporations are the most effective means to plan for and deliver major growth.

© Malcolm D. Moor

In a perceptive piece written in *Planning* in March 1997, the magazine's columnist Anthony Fyson observed:

> From the 'Bonfire of Regulations' sought by Lord Young to the current 'plan led' system championed by Mr Gummer, the conversion appears complete. No previous regime ever awarded development plans such status. Even the cherished 'presumption in favour of development' – an open-ended commitment – has finally been transmogrified into a blunt 'presumption in favour of the plan . . .' So planning has enjoyed an unexpected, if partial, apotheosis. The change of direction, forced on the Government as much by its shire county supporters as by any coherent arguments from its opponents, has reasserted the value of public control over development. The right to develop remains, in effect, nationalised as it has been for half a century.
>
> (Fyson, 1997)

169

Critics have savaged John Major's five years as Tory leader, concentrating on his struggle, after an unexpected victory which confounded the pollsters, to hold the Party together. But now, after ten years, the verdict may be kinder. Even at the time, Peter Riddell (1997) could conclude that, 'Despite the steady erosion – and, in February 1997, final disappearance – of his Commons majority, Mr Major succeeded in keeping his Government in place for its whole five-year term and enacting almost all its 1992 manifesto pledges'.

Simon Jenkins (1997) has argued that, 'History will treat the Thatcher–Major years as a political unity', but on environmental issues and planning policy, that verdict is not convincing. John Major, Chris Patten and John Gummer laid the foundations for the green politics that David Cameron was to champion. The fascination of the Blair years to come was how he and John Prescott championed the pro-development policies of Thatcher, Young and Ridley and ushered in, during the first decade of the new century, what was to become an even greater property boom than anything experienced in the previous century.

References

Beecham, J. (1993) Urban change: the local perspective, *RSA Journal*, July, pp. 534–45.

Boyd, O. (2007) Interview with Piers Gough CBE, *Building*, 19 October, pp. 66–67.

Edwards, B. (1993) Deconstructing the city: the experience of London Docklands, *The Planner*, February: pp 16–18.

Fyson, A. (1997) The Fyson agenda, *Planning*, 21 March, p. 17.

Heseltine, M. (2000) *Life in The Jungle*. London: Hodder & Stoughton, pp. 379, 380.

Jenkins, S. (2006) *Thatcher & Son*. London: Macmillan, p. 191.

Major, J. (1999) *The Autobiography*. London: Harper Collins, pp. 311, 511.

Marr, A. (2007) *A History of Modern Britain*. London: Macmillan, p. 474.

Moor, N. (1993) Gummer puts brakes on superstore gravy train, *Building*, 25 February , p. 28.

Moor, N.. (1995) Towering imbroglio, *Building*, 20 October, p. 34.

Moor, N. (1971) Docklands: transport links, *Built Environment*, August, 34, pp. 582–85.

Moor, N. (1995) All change, says Labour, *Building*, 28 July, p. 34.

Patten, C. (2007) Interview with Chris Patten by Elizabeth Grice, *Daily Telegraph*, 25 June.

10

New Labour's First Term, 1997–2001

The Third Way

With their enormous House of Commons majority, New Labour did not have to worry about the backbench revolts which had so paralysed the Major government, and was in a unique position to implement its manifesto and develop a momentum of its own, rather than be tossed around by events. New Labour's manifesto was about 25,000 words in length. It covered a huge range of subjects, and the authors claimed that more detailed policy had been produced by New Labour than by any opposition in history. In economic management, it accepted the global economy as a reality and rejected the isolationism and 'go it alone' policies of the extreme Right or Left. Concern for the environment was at the heart of policy-making, informing the whole of government from housing and energy policy through to global warming and international agreements.

Tony Bair was much influenced by the book written by Anthony Giddens and published in 1994, *Beyond Left and Right: The Future of Radical Politics*. Subsequently, in 1998, following Labour's election victory, Giddens published a second book, *The Third Way: The Renewal of Social Democracy*, which can be viewed as the ideological basis for New Labour. Rydin (2003) has identified three key elements that can be deducted within the Third Way. The first is the emphasis on community, understood in terms of a set of reciprocal rights and duties: government should encourage the creation and recognition of these rights. The second is that government policy should have a strong social dimension in recognition of its own duty to society, and encourage a more open partnership of all stakeholders, including community groups. The third is that the state should be open and transparent in its activities, to enhance accountability to society.

Will Hutton (1995), in his critique of Thatcherism, refers to the work of Giddens, who argued critically that the free play of market forces had unleashed fundamental de-traditionalising forces which had undermined the institutions which were essential to the social stability of conservative England. Nonetheless, despite this paradox, in Blair's first term, the market-orientated policies of the Conservatives were maintained. For the first two years, the new government continued the Tory freeze on public spending, and a pledge not to increase income tax. However, The Budget and Comprehensive Spending Review of 2002, which heralded a significant increase in public spending on key public services, indicated a change in this approach, and a gradual move to the Keynesian economics advocated by Hutton.

Rydin (2003) points out that the Third Way is not without its vociferous critics on grounds of intellectual rigour as much as political direction. Simon Jenkins (2006) mounts a characteristic critique of the Third Way in his book *Thatcher & Sons*, referring to Giddens' 1994 book, and Tony Blair taking up the term in a 1995 article in the *Daily Mail*, promising a health service that would be neither private nor centralised but locally based and patient-led. Jenkins describes Giddens as becoming the:

> arch-purveyor of clichés to the Blair court, conjuring a locust swarm of abstract nouns, consuming all meaning in their path. Old-style socialism he condemned as fundamentalist, as was a harsh, uncaring Thatcherism (unlike the other sort). Elevated in their place were community, responsibility, opportunity, inclusion, and traditional values in a changed world.

Giddens answered his critics in a further book, *The Third Way and Its Critics*, published in 2000, and in an interview with the BBC in 1999 he provided a succinct definition of the term:

> something different and distinct from liberal capitalism with its unswerving belief in the merits of the free market and democratic socialism with its demand management and obsession with the state. The Third Way is in favour of growth, entrepreneurship, enterprise and wealth creation but it is also in favour of greater social justice and it sees the state playing a major role in bringing this about.

(Giddens, 1999)

Collaborative Planning

Giddens' earlier work, *The Constitution of Society* (1984), has influenced a recent development in the theory of spatial planning: collaborative planning. Healey (1997), in her book *Collaborative Planning: Shaping Places in Fragmented*

Societies, has proposed that planners should manage a process that becomes more inclusive and concerned with power-sharing. Five tasks are identified: identifying and bringing together stakeholders; designing and using arenas for communication and collaboration; trying and using different routines and styles of communication; making the discourses of policy; and maintaining consensus. Collaborative planning implicitly rejects the procedural approach of post-war planning with its emphasis on the plan being produced by means of a set of procedures proscribed by statute. It seeks a role for professional planners which, on the one hand, is sensitive to people but on the other addresses social, economic and environmental issues. It has proved attractive to many in the planning profession but still to be resolved is how it would relate to local politicians and their responsibilities, particularly at a time when New Labour's modernising agenda in local government is perceived as marginalising the role of the local councillor.

The New Labour Manifesto

The detailed policies of the manifesto were to reflect this approach. One-stop regional development agencies to coordinate regional economic development would be set up. Housing was a priority, and capital receipts from the sale of council houses would be reinvested in building new homes and rehabilitating old ones. An overall strategic review of the roads programme was promised. The manifesto promised to place on councils a new duty to promote the economic, social and environmental well-being of their area. Every council would be requested to publish a local performance plan with targets for service improvement. The Audit Commission would be given additional powers to monitor performance and promote efficiency.

London, following a referendum to confirm popular demand, would have a strategic authority and a mayor, each directly elected, and taking responsibility for London-wide issues such as economic regeneration, planning, policing, transport and environmental protection. Regional chambers would be established to coordinate transport, planning, economic development, bids for European funds and land-use planning. Legislation would be introduced to allow people, region by region, to decide in a referendum whether they wanted directly elected regional government. As soon as possible after the election, legislation would be enacted to allow the people of Scotland and Wales to vote in separate referendums for a Scottish Parliament and a Welsh Assembly (Austin, 1997).

On Friday 2 May 1997, a day after the election, Tony Blair began to appoint his Cabinet. First to see him was the Deputy Prime Minister, John Prescott, who was given a vast Whitehall empire and appointed Secretary of State for the Environment, Transport and the Regions. As Alistair Campbell notes in his diary, 'John Prescott came in first and was really happy with his lot' (Campbell and Stott, 2007).

Peter Riddell (2001) has observed that Tony Blair took office in May 1997 with an overriding objective – to be the first Labour Prime Minister to win a second full term. Both he and Gordon Brown were preoccupied with avoiding the economic mistakes of the Labour governments of the 1960s and 1970s and determined to prove that Labour could be competent in office, particularly managing the economy. This meant that despite its enormous majority in the Commons, the government wanted to avoid any risks, but the exception was constitutional reform. After referendums in Scotland and Wales in September 1997, legislation led to the creation of a Parliament in Edinburgh and a National Assembly in Cardiff, with elections in May 1999 under a system of proportional representation. London gained an elected mayor and assembly from the summer of 2000, also following a referendum. The rest of England was to all intents and purposes under the stewardship of the Deputy Prime Minister. Simon Jenkins (2006) viewed this with great concern. His view was that Prescott shared Blair's belief that local democracy should have no part in planning land use, and Prescott was determined to remove that power from city and county authorities and vest it in his own office. That was to come in the second term with the passing of the Planning and Compulsory Purchase Act 2004 but the basis was laid from 1997.

Housing and the Green Belt

Both the opposition parties had extensive manifestos, and initially planning and environmental policies did not appear to be issues that would divide the parties. All the parties appeared to agree on the importance of sustainable planning objectives, although there were major differences on the future structure of local government. But the debate began to change after the election. One of the last policy documents to emanate from the DoE with John Gummer at the helm dealt with the latest household projections. The document's title asked a question, *Where Shall We Live?* Figures published by the government showed that by 2016 the number of households in England could be up to 4.4 million higher than in 1991. The projections were higher than previous ones, predicting a rate of household formation some 10 per cent higher than the planning system was then catering for. The issues raised in the document could not be ignored or sidelined. John Prescott had two rising stars as ministers in his huge empire, Nick Rainsford and Richard Caborn, who were tasked to deal with the issues raised by the projections.

Conservative backbenchers, urged on by the CPRE, were vociferous in their opposition, no doubt grateful that they no longer bore the responsibility for talking the decisions about growth. Labour was accused of being 'consistently contemptuous' of country dwellers as the Tories mounted a fierce Commons attack on Labour's planning policy in January 1998. The arguments had been fuelled by decisions to permit the building of 10,000 new houses in the green belt near Stevenage in Hertfordshire, and more than 2,000 new homes in countryside outside Newcastle. In their manifesto, the Tories had pledged to continue to protect the green belt from development and to make sure that derelict and under-used land was developed in preference to greenfield sites. New Labour, however, saw housing as a pressing issue.

New Labour had changed policy on defence, the unions and privatisation, and gained office. The New Labour government adopted many of the policies of the New Right in addressing planning policy matters, but with a greater emphasis on a regional agenda. For a system that was under a perceived threat of virtual abolition by the Thatcher governments in the 1980s, notes Mark Tewdwr-Jones in his book *The Planning Polity* (2002), planning as a government activity received a renaissance in the 1990s under the New Labour government which saw planning as a way of encompassing a range of political aims and objectives and as a form of state coordination.

Regional Planning

During 1998, draft guidance on the strategies to be pursued by the new Regional Development Agencies (RDAs) was published and subsequently, on 1 April 1999, the government set up eight RDAs covering the whole of England. They were part of the government's response to criticism that Scotland and Wales had more autonomy, and the English regions had no comparable voice. Despite their economic remit, unlike the UDCs innovated by Michael Heseltine, the RDAs had no planning powers. How their economic strategies would fit into the regional planning guidance produced by the regional planning conferences was unclear, and this tension has persisted throughout New Labour's terms in office. However, despite strong lobbying that these unelected bodies should not have such powers, it is as we will see when dealing with Gordon Brown's housing agenda, anticipated that they will have planning responsibilities and evolve into Regional Boards to replace the Regional Assemblies originally set up in 2000.

John Prescott was to fail in his attempt to introduce elected Regional Assemblies but the RDAs which Gordon Brown favoured as the vehicles for regional planning were flagged by Prescott as long ago as September 1983 when he addressed the Town & Country Planning Summer School at the University of St Andrews as the Labour Party's Shadow Spokesman on Regional Affairs and Devolution (Town & Country Planning School, 1983). In a barnstorming speech that autumn evening he laid out to an appreciative audience of professional town planners Labour's devolution agenda. I was in the audience and on the receiving end of his criticism, for earlier that day I had given one of the main papers on the role of the private sector in the urban regeneration of the inner cities. I highlighted the growth of the Urban Programme which was specially for the inner cities, and noted that the Conservative government had staked a great deal politically on making progress in these areas. John Prescott was having none of this but little did I apprehend at a time when Labour was literally on the ropes politically, that subsequently, as deputy Prime Minister, he would assume such a significance in the country's planning system. That is the fascination of politics. The slippery pole is to be climbed or slid down depending on circumstances.

Modernising Planning

On 15 January 1998, Planning Minister Richard Caborn announced a far-reaching reform of planning regulations. Everything from housing policy to the use of green belt land and from public inquiries to transport policy and industrial development would be under review. One of the most controversial elements of the package was a set of proposals for changes to the planning procedures for major projects. The lengthy inquiry over BAA's aim for a fifth terminal at Heathrow had convinced everyone, other than perhaps the lawyers, that there had to be an end to expensive and time-consuming inquiries. The system had become sclerotic.

Caborn also announced, under the UK presidency of the EU, that he would reverse the previous government's opposition and draw up a draft version of the *European Spatial Development Perspective*, a non-binding document intended to promote an integrated approach to development across the EU.

The Housing Battle

The pace of change was urgent. In February of that same year, John Prescott published a comprehensive document, *Planning for the Communities of the Future*, a response to criticism from the Tories and the CPRE, and he pledged to ensure that the best use was made of previously developed land. There would be a sequential approach, using brownfield land first. He proposed to ask the Regional Planning Conference to draw up estimates of housing need, and to get away from the discredited top-down 'predict and provide' approach to estimating housing needs. Also announced was the setting up of an Urban Task Force to be led by the architect Lord Richard Rogers.

Controversy over housing numbers and where to locate the development continued apace and Boris Johnson, writing in the *Daily Telegraph* on 21 January 1998, coined a particularly pithy aphorism, 'As Mr Prescott said this week: the green belt is a Labour achievement – and we mean to build on it'. Later that year, the late Professor Crow, as chair of the panel that had examined the government's draft regional planning guidance for the South East, recommended that unless 55,000 new homes were built in the region annually, democratic and economic changes would lead to spiralling house prices. Much of the new housing was to be built in four massive new settlements at Ashford in Kent, Stansted in Essex, Milton Keynes in Buckinghamshire and Crawley in Sussex. In November of that year, he told a Commons committee that the growth of the South East was largely unstoppable. In the shires, the Conservatives were able to mine the opposition to this growth, which provided a subsequent platform for local government election success. After repeated government retreats, the target that finally emerged was 39,000 completions a year. In the event, completions never got remotely near that figure in the region.

Later that year in December, the Agriculture Ministry announced that it would give up its veto on building on prime farm land, announcing that this policy, introduced 50 years before, was no longer relevant. Yet this battle of words between John Prescott and the Conservatives was a phoney war. The houses were not being built in sufficient numbers, and in the next parliamentary term an exasperated Chancellor Brown was to wrest control over housing policy from Prescott, and to orchestrate a much more centrally-driven housing agenda.

The Retail Revolution

The houses may not have been being built, but the enormous regional shopping centres were. Bluewater Park, Europe's largest retail and leisure centre, opened in February 1999. Built on a former chalk quarry, the figures were compelling. Over a 100-hectare site were laid three malls containing 154,000 square metres of floorspace accommodating 330 outlets accompanied by 13,000 car parking spaces. Some 80,000 shoppers a day were anticipated. Reluctantly granted planning permission by John Gummer when Environment Secretary in the Major government (and who promptly then shut the policy window), the centre was the seventh of the enormous shopping centres opened in England. These were the Gateshead Metro, the Meadowhall at Sheffield, Merry Hill at Dudley, Cripps Causeway at Bristol, the Trafford Centre at Manchester and Lakeside across the Thames at Thurrock. Shoppers might feel that they should shop locally to keep their towns alive, but the attraction of the 'megamalls' seemed irresistible. These shopping cathedrals are likely to prove a lasting legacy of Thatcherism. Ironically, they proved to be the driving force of the retail-led Brown consumer boom, and in harsher economic times are proving more resistant than the high streets, which for many shoppers they have replaced.

This rejection of the high street has subsequently culminated in the invasion of city centres by the out-of-town centre, bringing about a reversal of policy not anticipated by the policy-makers. In Shepherd's Bush, the Australian developer Westfield, in December 2008, opened an enormous multi-billion shopping centre named eponymously, Westfield London, which contains 280 shops and 47 restaurants and is spread over a 17-hectare brownfield site previously occupied by redundant industrial buildings. The centre has a floor area of 150,000 square metres which makes it the largest in-town centre in Europe. In England, only the out-of-town Metro Centre and Bluewater are larger, and the opening of the centre poses a threat to the traditional high streets of Ealing and Hammersmith nearby.

The Urban Task Force

Lord Rogers reported in June 1999 to a great fanfare of publicity. His committee made a list of 105 recommendations which included the anticipated 60 per cent of housing completions on brownfield sites, a national urban design framework, urban neighbourhoods managed according to principles of sustainable development, and over a 20-year period to plan for the migration from the cities to be reversed. Urban regeneration companies were to be set up which would concentrate on physical regeneration, while the RDAs would concentrate on job creation. The urban neighbourhoods echoed the 'urban villages' concept that had been trialled in the latter part of John Gummer's time and signalled the end of the car-led approach to neighbourhood design that had been a feature of the later phases of new town development such as Milton Keynes, and Washington in the North East. Perhaps mercifully, much of the new bureaucracy advocated by the Task Force did not materialise, but the real value of the report was to change perceptions, and to particularly make more acceptable the higher residential densities that building on brownfield sites entailed.

Regional Government

John Prescott was determined to force the pace on regional government. Interviewed in the *Observer* on Sunday 29 August 1999, he said that he was 'adamant that the county/district system will have to be scrapped as elected regional government comes to England'. In addition 'it will have to be brought in with a synchronised uniformity over the whole country – in contrast to those who have suggested it should be introduced first in the North, where it is popular, and postponed in the South, where it isn't'. The RDAs and Regional Chapters were seen as a part of an emerging network of regional governance. Directly elected Regional Assemblies were to be the basis of this new governance. John Prescott announced this vision in a triumphant speech to the Labour Party conference at Bournemouth on 29 September, quoting from Nye Bevan: 'The language of politics is the religion of socialism'. In the right-wing press the speech received less coverage than his taking the 30-metre trip from his hotel to the conference centre in a chauffeur-driven limousine. When questioned he retorted, 'My wife does not like to have her hair blown about'.

In response, the new Shadow Environment Spokesman, John Redwood, promised that the Conservatives would abolish the 'regional bureaucracy', give stronger protection to the green belt and support a more 'localist' approach to planning decisions. These commitments were contained in a document *Common Sense for Environment, Town and Country* published by the Conservative Party in November 1999. Undaunted, John Prescott was at the height of his political powers, and the Conservatives did not help their case by periodically changing their team at environment. Gillian Shephard had left in a Shadow Cabinet reshuffle in May to be replaced as spokesperson on planning by Shaun Woodward, the MP for Witney, who was subsequently to cross over to the Labour Party. Later that year the Labour team also reshuffled, with Richard Caborn moving to the DTI and Nick Raynsford, who had a strong housing background having been a director of the housing lobby Shelter before becoming an MP, being appointed Planning Minister. In the following year, John Prescott, with a new team in place, took the opportunity of a major parliamentary debate on planning policy to push forward his agenda.

Parliamentary Debate on Planning Policy

Nearly three years in office, John Prescott set out his planning policy in a debate in the House of Commons on 7 March 2000 (Prescott, 2000). Opening the debate, he put away the old 'predict and provide' approach to housing needs, championed the sequential approach to brownfield development and promised a more flexible approach to planning for housing. These measures would be introduced in a new policy document aimed at local planning authorities: *PPS3 (Housing)* which would replace existing advice. He took the opportunity to emphasise that the Thames Gateway would be a main focus for development, and that the other two main growth areas in the South East would be Milton Keynes and Ashford. In the longer term, there was the possibility of growth in the M11 corridor, including Stansted. On housing numbers he steered a middle course between Professor Crow's 1.1 million and the lower Serplan figure with a proposal to build 43,000 additional houses a year in the region, some 10,000 dwellings a year higher than the Regional Assembly had advocated. This figure would be subject to regular five-yearly reviews. The government was moving away from a 20-year time plan. 'No one can with any certainty predict how many extra households will exist in 20 years time' he concluded.

Prescott's speech was an attempt to take the initiative away from the Conservatives, who over the previous three years had continually harried the government over its housing programme for the South East, where many Tory MPs had their constituencies. There was a lively debate and a leading Labour MP, who chaired the House of Commons Environment Committee, Andrew Bennett, concluded, 'Will my right honourable friend accept the congratulations of Labour Members on a very skilful performance on the tightrope'.

The subsequent failure of the Blair government to reach its housing targets was to prove the futility of this debate about numbers. John Prescott, in his autobiography, assisted by Hunter Davies (Prescott and Davies, 2008), provides a convincing account of his negotiations at the 1997 Kyoto conference to persuade the major countries to agree a stabilisation of their carbon emissions. He also explains how the Cabinet, chaired by him, after Tony Blair had found an excuse to absent himself from the debate about the future of the Millennium Dome, bequeathed to New Labour by Michael Heseltine, agreed to continue with funding the venture. Prescott remembered his visit to the Festival of Britain and thought the Dome and the Millennium Village alongside, could have a similar role in the regeneration of the Greenwich peninsula as the Festival had had for the South Bank. But nowhere in the autobiography is there any account of the debates and controversies about housing and green belt policy. It is as if this all passed over his head. It was left to Gordon Brown as Chancellor in the second Blair government to try and extricate housing policy from the impasse that had emerged under Prescott.

In August, the Joseph Rowntree Foundation published a research report that examined the impact of migration on housing requirements. In the South East the report identified natural increase – net migration out of London and net inward migration from outside the country – as the factor determining housing needs. In the subsequent second and third terms of Labour's administration, net inward migration was to become the dominant population issue.

New Conservative Policy to Strengthen the Role of Local Communities

Sensing that John Prescott's hold on his vast ministerial empire might be slackening, the Conservatives brought in the ex-head of the supermarket group Asda, Andy Norman, now an MP, to shadow him. Norman's opening salvo was: 'John Prescott is a series of embarrassments and failures. He's a character, but he's not an asset. He knows he's in the last year of being in charge of a sizeable department' (Norman, 2000).

The Conservative Leader William Hague's speech to the 2000 Local Government conference in Bournemouth ushered in this new policy of localism, devolving the power to set future house-building to local authorities, abolishing 'regional diktats' and giving a right of appeal to local residents where there was a breach of due process or a development disregarded a development plan. Finally, he announced that future secretaries of state would be prevented from intervening in planning appeals. The Tories clearly

181

had to pay attention to the concerns of those in seats that they had to win back from Labour where urban building was an issue, but many back-benchers, including the former Environment Secretary John Gummer and Sir Paul Beresford, a planning minister in John Major's government, publicly aired concerns that the measures were impractical and would require a sharp U-turn in government. Similarly acknowledging the power of constituency support, the Liberal Democrats at their Party conference in September voted to back third-party appeals against planning decisions.

Cabinet Office Concerns

Earlier in the year, Lord Falconer, Cabinet Office minister and close friend of the Prime Minister, had been appointed head of a new Regional Coordination Unit (RCU). Its formation followed a damning report from the Cabinet Office's Performance and Innovation Unit (PIU) which argued that current government action on the regions was incoherent and had become hamstrung by the need to negotiate the system rather than concentrating on delivery (Cabinet Office Performance and Innovation Unit, 2000). One of the aspects that the RCU intended to examine was the relationship between regional planning guidance and the RDAs. At the time, this initiative was perceived as the Prime Minister reminding John Prescott that his hold on his vast government department was not guaranteed, and delivery must now be the focus.

Local Government

One of the key areas for reform in New Labour's election manifesto had been that of local government. It was no exaggeration to say that at the end of Margaret Thatcher's administration local government in England was demoralised and uncertain of its role. The renewal of local democracy had the personal backing of the Prime Minister. He had stressed the need to separate the executive from the representative role and while both had an important part to play in community leadership, this must be in different and complementary ways (Blair, 1998). The Local Government Act 2000 was an attempt to give local authorities a new leadership role in their communities and to encourage new forms of governance. The duty to produce a Community Strategy, combined with the establishment of local strategic partnerships, provided a vehicle for establishing and delivering a shared vision for local areas (Moor, 2004). The Local Government Act also introduced a new ethical framework aimed at ensuring high standards of conduct in local government, and required all authorities to adopt a Members' Code of Conduct based on a national model, which councillors must sign up to. The Act gave local authorities the opportunity to develop new approaches to community leadership, but subsequently those who have been successful will look at central government to see whether this success is rewarded by more financial freedom.

Green Paper on Planning Reform

Linked with local government changes was the subject of reform of the planning system. The Green Paper, *Planning: Delivering a Fundamental Change*, published in 2001, comprised a critique of the whole spatial planning system. This included that the speed of decision-making for councils was often failing to meet targets, planning committees resisted the opportunity for applicants or objectors to present their case, elected councillors on committees were sometimes insufficiently trained, and in order to achieve the targets set in the Best Value regime instituted by the Local Government Act, there needed to be more delegation to officers in terms of decision-making. The changes sought in the Green Paper were to be subsequently introduced by the Planning & Compulsory Purchase Act 2004, legislated for in New Labour's second term. What had begun as an attempt to iron out some of the bottle-necks in the planning system was to turn into a complete overhaul of the plan-making apparatus, causing yet further delays and confusion. No sooner was the ink dry on this legislation then there came further calls for change and modernisation. Each decade since the advent of the 1947 Act has seen governments of all persuasions at the outset seemingly promising to themselves that they would simplify the system, but in the event adding yet further to the complexity, so that by the end of the decade there emerged a recognition that the only answer may be to remove entirely a whole raft of decision-making from the system.

Transport 2010 – the 10-year Plan

Late in July 2000 the government announced its ten-year transport plan. Transport had been included in the enormous ministerial department led by the Deputy Prime Minister in order that an integrated approach to investment could be pursued, and the intention was that transport planning would be developed at regional level by regional transport strategies as an integral part of regional planning guidance. The plan was predicated on a £180 billion investment package designed to modernise the country's transport system and cut congestion. The programme covered both public and private investment and the total figure was split evenly between railways, strategic roads and local transport including London. The combined level would be an increase of almost 75 per cent compared with the last ten years. Objectives for the programme included a 50 per cent increase in railway passenger journeys, a significant increase in rail's share of the freight market to around 10 per cent and congestion in larger urban areas reduced from a forecast growth of 15 per cent to 8 per cent. No decisions on the role of charging in reducing inter-urban congestion would be taken until solutions had been found to the problems of diversion. The plan set out the broad strategies for improving the transport system rather than decisions on individual projects, and marked a significant step forward in terms of an integrated approach to road and rail infrastructure planning.

The Urban White Paper

Towards the end of the year, in November, the Urban White Paper, which was a response to the Urban Task Force's recommendations, was published. The government wanted to see taxation changes which would encourage urban regeneration, but the Chancellor insisted that John Prescott make do with marginal easements in tax. The White Paper was denounced by Lord Rogers as missing crucial ingredients, and Prescott hinted that he too was disappointed. The key elements were a £1 billion programme over five years to encourage property conversions and the cleaning of contaminated land. Twelve urban regeneration companies were to be set up, and five more millennium villages. There was to be an initiative to improve urban parks and open spaces. The importance of better design standards to achieve urban revival was to be promoted and a new Cabinet committee on urban affairs was to be set up. The disappointing response to the recommendations of the Urban Task Force yet again demonstrated the reluctance of the Treasury to secede power over taxation to an urban ministry, and the omens were that after the 2001 election there would be a break-up of John Prescott's unwieldy empire.

The Alconbury Judgement

In May 2001, a month before the June election, the House of Lords delivered an important judgement interpreting the Human Rights Act. The Lords dismissed the judgement of the divisional court brought in respect of a proposed development at Alconbury, near Cambridge, where the court held that the current planning system denied protestors the right to have their objections heard by an independent and important tribunal, as required by Article 6 of the Human Rights Act. The Law Lords reasserted that the British planning system is a process of political decision-making. The judgement marked the end of a campaign that had begun with the passing of the Human Rights Act in 1998 for the introduction of an Environmental Court that included Lord Woolf and Professor Malcolm Grant among its supporters.

Election Campaign

Early in May 2001, the Prime Minister announced that the general election would take place on 7 June, the same day as the local elections. Labour, the previous month, had pledged that it would introduce legislation to set up elected Regional Assemblies if it won the election. Another straw in the wind was the recommendation of the think-tank the Institute for Public Policy Research to break up John Prescott's department and the remit for the regions to be transferred to a new department for nations and regions, and the remaining environment and transport departments to be strengthened, taking over regulatory responsibilities for power stations and farming.

The Conservatives aimed to make planning a central issue in the election as their leader William Hague launched his party's local government manifesto *Time for Common Sense*, which focused on community, environment and property policies. Despite some backbench reservations, the Party's new planning spokesman Damien Green argued that their policy to allow local authorities to decide their own house-building targets was popular with the party (Green, 2001). His own constituency, Ashford in Kent, was one of the growth areas identified by the government. The Conservative's high-profile 'Save Our Greenfields' campaign lay at the heart of their environmental policy.

Labour's manifesto, *Ambitions for Britain*, pledged to continue the modernisation of the planning system, and to introduce fast-track procedures for projects of 'national significance', such as the Terminal 5 scheme at

Heathrow Airport. The document also contained a commitment to create a new department for rural affairs, which would lead renewal efforts in rural areas alongside RDAs. These agencies were to intervene directly to tackle the economic disparities between the regions, because – cautioned the authors – sitting back and leaving regional problems to the market was not acceptable.

The Liberal Democrats were equally as enthusiastic as the Tories to take a stand on greenfield development, proposing a greenfield development levy and changes to VAT on repairs and renovation so as to help bring back into use an estimated 750,000 empty dwellings. Their policy on setting house-building figures was that this should be made at the local level rather than being imposed by central government. Each local authority would get the opportunity to set its policy on housing levels in the context of a regionally agreed plan. This would be agreed by the elected Regional Assemblies that the Liberal Democrats proposed to introduce.

Postscript

During New Labour's first term there was real progress on the modernisation programme, both in respect of local government and planning, and the new regional planning framework was set in place, as was the integration of transport and land-use planning. The target of securing 60 per cent of new housing development on brownfield sites was helping the drive for urban renaissance. New Labour's enormous majority in the House of Commons had enabled them to push forward a raft of legislation, including devolution for Scotland and Wales. In opposition, the Conservatives had adopted a policy of localism, which sat oddly with the deregulatory policies pursued under Margaret Thatcher and John Major, and chimed more with the grass-roots approach of the Liberal Democrats. It was no coincidence that in the South East the Tories and the Liberal Democrats were more often fighting each other than Labour for the shire constituency parliamentary seats. The question-mark for New Labour was whether, in the next term, it would focus on the delivery of additional houses and urban renewal or whether the prospect of a yet fuller agenda for modernisation might prove too tempting.

References

Austin, T. (ed.) (1997) *Guide To The House Of Commons*. London: Times Books, pp. 307–83.

Blair, A. (1998) Interview, *Planning* 20 March, p. 11.

Cabinet Office Performance and Innovation Unit (2000) Interview, *Planning*, 18 February, p.1.

Campbell, A. and Stott, R. (2007) *The Blair Years*. London: Hutchinson, p. 199.

Giddens, A. (1984) *The Constitution of Society*. Cambridge: Polity Press.

Giddens, A. (1994) *Beyond Left and Right: The Future of Radical Politics*. Cambridge: Polity Press.

Giddens, A. (1998) *The Third Way: The Renewal of Social Democracy*. Cambridge: Polity Press.

Giddens, A. (1999) What is the Third Way? Interview with the BBC, Monday 27 September.

Giddens, A. (2000) *The Third Way and its Critics*. Oxford: Blackwell.

Green, D. (2001) Interview, *Planning*,11 May p. 21.

Hutton, W. (1995) *The State We're In*. London: Jonathan Cape, p. 29.

Jenkins, S. (2006) *Thatcher & Sons*. London: Allen Lane, pp. 227–28, 296.

Moor, N. (2004) *Delivering the Community Vision*, paper delivered to the Planning Summer School, University of Reading 3–6 September.

Norman, A. (2000) Interview, *Building*, 28 July, pp. 20–22.

Prescott, J. (2000) National planning guidance for housing, regional planning guidance for the South East, speech to the House of Commons, 7 March, Hansard columns 863–78.

Prescott, J. and Davies, H. (2008) *Prezza, My Story: Pulling No Punches*. London: Headline, pp. 222–26, 235–37.

Riddell, P. (2001) Blair's date with history kept him clear of pitfalls, in T. Austin and T. Homes (eds) (2001) *The Times Guide to The House Of Commons*. London: Times Books, pp. 19–21.

Rydin, Y. (2003) *Urban and Environmental Planning in the UK*. London: Palgrave Macmillan, pp. 69–70.

Tewdwr-Jones, M. (2002) *The Planning Polity*. London: Palgrave, pp. 10–11.

Town & Country Planning School (1983) *Report of Proceedings, University of St Andrews 3–14 September*. London: RTPI, pp. 11–14.

11

The Blair Project Continues, 2001–2007

Election Victory

Tony Blair was returned to office on 7 June 2001. He had gambled by going to the country a year early, and then had to postpone the election by a month because of the outbreak of foot and mouth disease in parts of the country's rural areas. His majority was barely reduced but the turnout was very low, down to 59.4 per cent as compared to 71.4 per cent in 1997; the lowest turnout since the end of the First World War in 1918. For the Conservatives it was a second massive setback with only one more MP than the 1997 debacle. William Hague resigned as Tory leader on the morning of the election result, and was succeeded by Iain Duncan Smith. If the electorate had not given Tony Blair a ringing endorsement, he nonetheless had the confidence that came from being the first Labour leader to be re-elected to a second successive term of office.

Cabinet Changes

Tony Blair moved quickly to put together his new cabinet, and he was determined to learn from the mistakes of his first administration. He abolished the Department of the Environment, Transport and the Regions (DETR) and Stephen Byers was placed in charge of the new Department of Transport, Local Government and the Regions (DTLGR) which would have responsibility for planning. Lord Falconer was appointed as the new Minister for Planning and Housing, and also took over the regeneration portfolio, with responsibility for urban policy and neighbourhood renewal. Nick Raynsford was moved sideways to become Minister for Local Government and London. A second new ministry – the Department for the Environment, Food and Rural Affairs (DEFRA) was headed by Margaret Beckett.

Michael Meacher retained his post of Environment Minister and Alun Michael became Minister of Rural Affairs. John Prescott retained the office of Deputy Prime Minister and a seat in the Cabinet but his responsibilities were reduced to cross-departmental issues, including social cohesion, the regional coordination unit and government offices in the regions. In his autobiography he explains that it was always his wish to be in the Cabinet Office, close to the centre of government, but adds ruefully that he was never consulted by Tony Blair on the break-up of the DETR (Prescott and Davies, 2008).

Tony Blair was aware of the Chancellor Gordon Brown's Treasury investigation into the planning system and its delays, and wanted to ensure that the legislative changes to the system trialled by the DETR before the election were in the hands of a trusted Blairite, and Lord Falconer had the legal background to see the legislation through Parliament. Although there was almost universal agreement that the DETR had been too big and unwieldy, the new structure attracted criticism from the outset. The former Conservative Environment Secretary, John Gummer (2001), criticised the divorce of environment from planning, and pointed out that ever since Ted Heath had created the DoE in 1970 it was the envy of other European nations whose environment ministries tended to be weak and small.

Environmental policy, the countryside, wildlife protection and sustainable development were all now contained within a single department, and the driver for this had been – following the BSE and foot and mouth crises – a determination to be rid of the Ministry of Agriculture, Fisheries and Food (MAFF), which was held responsible for not dealing with this crisis in farming quickly enough. Another important change was to bring the regional development agencies within the ambit of the DTI.

Conservatives Advance in the Shires

Although still firmly in opposition in Parliament, the Conservatives' grass-roots election campaign in the shires reaped rewards, and they took control of Norfolk, East Sussex, Essex, Dorset, Cheshire and Lancashire, and made significant gains in counties that had opposed house-building figures in regional guidance in Kent, Surrey and West Sussex. Shadow Environment Secretary Archie Norman welcomed the results, pointing out that the Conservatives were now the largest party of local government in county and district councils. Rebuilding their local government base would provide the Conservatives with a foundation for recovery in national government, he claimed (Norman, 2001). Later in the year, following the resignation of William Hague as leader, the two contenders for the leadership, Iain Duncan Smith and Kenneth Clarke, pledged to fight greenfield housing as major parts of their campaigns.

Terminal 5 to Go Ahead

In November, the Transport Secretary Stephen Byers announced to no one's surprise that Terminal 5 at Heathrow was to go ahead. Its journey through the planning system had taken eight years, and it was no coincidence that the decision to go ahead was only weeks in advance of the publication of the planning Green Paper. The delays associated with Terminal 5 had been seized on by bodies such as the Confederation of British Industry (CBI) to demonstrate that the planning system was now a brake on business growth in the country. Lord Digby Jones, then director of the CBI, and subsequently for a short time a minister in Gordon Brown's cabinet argued that 'The biggest driver for change is the need for clarity and transparency in the decision-making process and then speed' (Winkley, 2001a). Not since Lord David Young had been a minister in Margaret Thatcher's Cabinet had the planning system faced such a challenge from business interests.

More Change for the Planning System

Early on in the new term, Lord Falconer gave an indication of the pressure that government intended to put on local planning authorities in terms of their performance in determining planning applications within eight weeks. He pointed out that only 30 councils had managed to meet the government target of deciding 80 per cent of applications within that time and asserted that the performance of local authorities must be improved (Winkley, 2001b).

In December, the DTLGR published the long-awaited planning Green Paper entitled *Planning: Delivering a Fundamental Change*. County structure plans were to be abolished and strategic policy would be set at the regional level through regional spatial strategies. A new type of plan was to be established at district and borough level, named Local Development Frameworks (LDFs). These would comprise criteria-based core policies. Site-specific policies would be contained in allocation documents and action area plans. Proposals to establish business Planning Zones where no consent would be necessary for development in accordance with 'tightly defined parameters' were also proposed. The planning Green Paper also dealt a body blow to the advocates of third-party rights of appeal, favouring instead a more self-regulatory approach in which local planning authorities would have to give reasons for approving applications as well as for refusing them. Also proposed was a reform of the planning obligations process, to make it more transparent by introducing standardised tariffs for different types of development through the plan-making process.

Optimistically, the authors claimed that the new plans would take less time to prepare. The proposals were welcomed by professional and business interests, but the environmental lobby and the Conservatives expressed concern that community involvement in planning could be diminished by the focus on strategic issues. The new Shadow Secretary of State for Transport, Local Government and the Regions, Theresa May, expressed her concerns thus:

> People's confidence in the planning system will be damaged if their voice cannot be heard, and the government's proposals threaten to strip local communities of their involvement in local planning decisions. The voice of local communities should not be silenced.
>
> (May, 2001)

The Millennium Dome

Early in 2002, Planning Minister Lord Falconer brokered a controversial deal handing the debt-ridden Millennium Dome to a consortium of property developers for free. He would not reveal whether the government would be financially responsible if the scheme flopped. Critics quickly condemned the proposed deal, under which there was no up-front payment to the government.

Probity for Councillors

Revised guidance on probity for councillors involved in the planning system was published by the LGA. The guide outlined codes of conduct for councillors and officers to ensure that their participation in the planning system was fair and transparent. The revised guidance took account of the ethical framework for local government outlined in the Local Government

The Millenium Dome. Now one of the world's most popular music venues.

© Creative Commons Attribution 2.0 Licence. Taken by zakgollop

Act 2000, and covered lobbying, declaration of personal interests, development proposals from councillors and conduct during pre-application discussions. The introduction of the advice caused considerable anxiety among councils, and ward members were discouraged from voting on proposals within their wards for fear of bias. As we will see, by the end of the decade there was mounting concern that councillors were being isolated from discussions on planning applications and development proposals.

London's Congestion Charge

London Mayor, Ken Livingstone, confirmed that his congestion charge proposals for central London would go ahead the following year. From February 2003, drivers were to be charged £5 by Transport for London to enter the zone during weekdays until 6.30 p.m. The Conservatives urged Transport Secretary Stephen Byers to block Livingstone's plans, after research revealed that the Mayor could be forced to change his proposals if they were considered to be 'inconsistent with national policy'.

More Delegation to Officers

In March, the government pressed ahead with its controversial target for local planning authorities to delegate 90 per cent of planning decisions to officers. The move was first floated in a consultation paper in November

2001. Lord Falconer urged councils to 'embrace' delegation. Tory planning spokesman, Geoffrey Clifton-Brown, accused the government of 'control freakery', saying that there was real anger among councillors that they were being prevented from scrutinising applications on behalf of their constituents (Clifton-Brown, 2002).

The government's drive towards directly elected Regional Assemblies with overall responsibility for regional planning and economic development moved closer with the publication in May of the regional governance White Paper, *Your Region, Your Choice*. The proposals were to hold referenda in each of the eight regions. Regions which voted for devolution would be forced to scrap county councils in favour of a single layer of unitary or district councils. Deputy Prime Minister, John Prescott, said: 'This will be the conclusion of a political dream I have held for decades' (Prescott, 2002a). Theresa May said that county structure plans were being sacrificed to Whitehall's new agenda for regional government and that the proposal to abolish the planning role of county councils was motivated by the government's commitment to regional government rather than a desire to streamline the planning system.

Break-up of The DTLGR

Stephen Byers' sudden resignation from the Cabinet at the end of May 2002 signalled the break-up of the DTLGR, and the end of the link between planning and transport in Whitehall. Tony Blair put Deputy Prime Minister John Prescott in charge of a revamped Cabinet Office which would take on responsibility for local government, regeneration and the regions. Byers had only been in the job since the previous year's general election and during his time as Secretary of State he had presided over the review of the planning system and the publication of the planning Green Paper in December 2001. He also granted planning permission for Heathrow's Terminal 5, but he had been plagued by rows over spin and by continuing criticism over Britain's creaking transport system. Announcing his resignation, Byers said that he thought it would be the 'right thing to do for the government and the Labour Party' (Byers, 2002). Now Alistair Darling was to be transport secretary; Lord Rooker was Planning Minister and Lord Falconer moved to the Home Office as Minister for Criminal Justice. The break-up of Byers' former department prompted the question as to whether Labour's much-vaunted 'joined-up government' policy had fallen by the wayside. Having originally been part of the Ministry of Housing and Local Government, planning has gone on a long journey via the Environment (1970–97), Environment, Transport and the Regions (1997–2001) and Transport, Local Government and the Regions (2001–02), before ending up as one function within the newly created central department of the Office of the Deputy Prime Minister (ODPM). Ironically, the housing, local government, planning and regions brief of the new department bore a striking resemblance to that held by the pre-1970 Ministry of Housing and Local Government (MoHLG), so it had been on a 30-year long return trip. In July, John Prescott presented to Parliament a statement on sustainable communities, housing and planning (Prescott, 2002b). Asserting that all governments had failed to meet the housing needs of the country and that 150,000 fewer houses were being built than 30 years previously, he nonetheless vowed to plough on with the Sustainable Communities Programme.

Opposition Mounts to Planning Reforms

In July, the select committee report on the planning Green Paper called for delay to system reform, and criticised the government for adopting a 'business agenda'. The report severely criticised the proposal to replace the development plan system with LDFs and area action plans, and said that the planning system 'is the key bulwark in preventing urban sprawl and restraining unsustainable development. It should not be subservient to business requirements'. The report also said that the government's theory that the planning system inhibited economic growth was based on 'anecdote and prejudice'. The Tories promised to fight government proposals for planning and regional reforms, and to oppose the removal of planning powers from district and county councils, also to fight the plan for regional government in England. In the same month, Chancellor Gordon Brown announced that extra money would be given to planning departments, but only on condition that performance against Best Value targets improved. Later that year, he announced who would get what and gave an early boost to many district councils, but a cold shoulder to the counties. The £350 million Planning Delivery Grant budget would be distributed over the next three financial years. All district councils, and the Greater London Authority, would receive a guaranteed basic payment of £75,000, and extra payments would be made to authorities with a strong planning track record and those in housing demand hot-spots and designated growth zones. Many councils in southern England were set to receive six-figure payments, with Barnet and Westminster the biggest beneficiaries. Councils receiving dividends as part of the government's growth strategy included Milton Keynes (£348,120). The announcement of the planning incentive grant followed widespread calls for the government to allocate more money to planning departments. In September, a report by the Commons Transport, Local Government and the Regions select committee raised concerns that new Cabinet and scrutiny committee constitutions in local government were excluding many councillors from the decision-making process. In addition, the overall quality and credibility of local government was at an all-time low, the report claimed. The committee asked whether councils were drowning under a glut of red tape and regulation and whether they had been bullied into adopting the mayoral and Cabinet system at a local level, thus cutting normal councillors out of the loop. None of this deflected the government and, urged on by the Chancellor, now determined to focus the planning system on a 'business first' agenda.

Planning and Compulsory Purchase Bill

This Bill was unveiled in November in the Queen's Speech in Parliament and was the first piece of major planning legislation since the Planning and Compensation Act 1991, and likely to be fast-tracked through Parliament. The legislation would usher in the reforms announced by John Prescott in July. Fears persisted over the Bill but Lord Rooker said that the planning process would be 'clearer, faster and more certain', and 'focused on getting the community meaningfully involved in decisions and in creating the right environment for business'. Critics feared that the Local Development Documents (LDDs) (previously known as LDFs) would be too complex and alienate many local people and that the government's approach would lead to chaos and a 'planning black hole for at least five years'. Sceptics remained concerned about the centralising tone of the Bill. Conservative Eric Pickles attacked the Bill for diminishing the role of local people in planning decisions, and predicted 'an explosion' of appeals (Pickles, 2003). Liberal Democrat Edward Davey said it was 'wrong to give strategic planning powers to unelected regional bodies'. Simon Jenkins wrote a powerful critique of the Act arguing that its purpose was to nationalise planning, and that, in future, regional and national officers of Prescott's own department would decide where and in what form development should occur. If they consulted it would be with the regional development agencies that they had appointed. Britain, he asserted, would became the only free country in the world where the planning of the use of land was removed form local government determination (Jenkins, 2006).

Electoral Reverse

The government was determined to maintain the pace of its reforms, but the mid-term local government elections held in May 2003 saw the Tories gain more than 500 seats and win control of 27 extra councils. The Liberal Democrats picked up 200 additional seats. Labour fell victim to a large-scale protest vote, losing more than 800 councillors and control of more than 30 councils. Despite the reverses, John Prescott unveiled plans for three regions to vote on whether to have regional assemblies (the North East, North West and Yorkshire and the Humber), but they were to face a shake-up of their two-tier council structures before devolution could take place. Over the next 12 months, the Boundary Committee for England was to carry out a local government review in each of the regions and to recommend at least two options for unitary structures in the six shire counties in the North. The ODPM said it was an 'absolute must' for regional assemblies to be accompanied by a unitary structure (ODPM, 2003).

Kate Barker's Report

Now preoccupied with regional assemblies, John Prescott had lost responsibility for housing, and in December of that year the interim *Barker Review of Housing Supply: Securing our Future Housing Needs* was published by the Treasury. Kate Barker had been a member of the Bank of England Monetary Policy Committee, and had been picked by the Chancellor to lead this investigation. The report highlighted the housing shortfall, then an annual figure in England of 39,000 homes per year. The blame was partly apportioned to the planning system, and also to house-builders. The report found that in the South East more than 40,000 homes had planning permission, but were being held up by lack of infrastructure. Meanwhile, late that year and through into the spring of 2004, skirmishes continued in the House of Commons and then in the Lords as the combined Conservative and Liberal Democrat opposition tried to amend and delay the planning bill. The Planning and Compulsory Purchase Act was finally passed by Parliament in May 2004, almost 18 months after the Bill was unveiled in the Queen's Speech of November 2002. The Bill could be regarded as the most

197

significant piece of planning legislation for more than a decade and would also pave the way for reforms to development plans, development control, planning obligations and CPOs (Compulsory Purchase Orders). It would also free up extra cash for planning aid services, enable greater community involvement in the planning process and end Crown immunity from planning control.

Tory Gains

The focus by the Tories on Labour's housing plans, despite the fact that nothing like the forecast targets was being built, was paying off and further local elections in the middle of 2004 resulted in heavy losses for the Labour Party, which lost overall control of several councils, including Birmingham, Newcastle, Leeds, Cardiff and Swansea. Conservative gains included Peterborough, Trafford and Dudley. In Newcastle City, the Liberal Democrats gained control from Labour. In August, the Tories pledged to scale back the growth areas and overhaul the government's sustainable communities plan. Bedfordshire, Cambridge, Northampton and Kent were cited as areas where a Conservative administration would block or scale back housing development, but not the Thames Gateway. The Tories also promised to re-establish the original purpose of green belts as narrow belts of land around towns and villages under pressure from development, especially in the South East, South West and the East of England. The Tory spokeswoman, Caroline Spelman, said that the Labour government's claims that the area of green belt had been increased by 19,000 hectares since 1997 were misleading. Almost all the increase had been in the Blyth Valley, Tynedale, Bolsover and Blackburn areas; hardly the areas facing the greatest development pressures, she asserted.

The North East Rejects Regional Assembly

In November, the North East rejected the idea of an elected Regional Assembly. The government bid to devolve more power to the region was rejected by 78 per cent of voters in the referendum. Some 696,519 people voted against the proposal, and only 197,310 in favour. Following the result, John Prescott abandoned plans for referenda in the North West and Yorkshire and Humber regions. The law precluded any further votes on a Regional Assembly in the North East for at least seven years. In his autobiography, Prescott admits that his biggest disappointment was regional government but asserts that Regional Assemblies are a good idea and would be introduced one day, while also maintaining that all parties were committed to retaining the RDAs (Prescott and Davies, 2008). Simon Jenkins rebuked Prescott for his reaction to the vote in the North East (Jenkins, 2006). Undaunted, Prescott forged ahead and expanded the RDAs, originally set up in 1999, with a cross-departmental budget of £1.8 billion. In January of the following year, the Tories revealed their plan to scrap the ODPM and Regional Assemblies, thus saving taxpayers £255 million. The Party's ideas on government structure followed the report of the James Review, which it commissioned to look into the issue. The review suggested that the ODPM should be replaced with a slimmed-down department of local government. There were now only five months before the general election in May, but the pace of change did not slacken.

The Election Beckons but no Slackening of Pace

The latest plans to redevelop the Millennium Dome looked set to meet government objectives for the Greenwich peninsula as developers set out a plan for the whole peninsula over a 20-year period, including using the Dome as a sports and entertainment arena. The end of January saw the official launch of *The South East Plan*, the draft regional planning document which set out three options for housing growth from 2001 to 2021 – either a further 25,000, 28,000 or 32,000 new homes per year. *Delivering Sustainable Development* (PPS1) was unveiled in February and enshrined the duty of the planning system to promote sustainable development and design quality. In that same month, the House of Commons Environmental Audit Committee launched a stinging attack on ODPM proposals for growth in the South East, saying that John Prescott's proposal to build more than 1 million homes over the next 20 years was a 'predict and provide' approach that would undermine other regions' prosperity. Ahead of the election, the latest Planning Delivery Grant was announced. For 2005–06 it would be the largest to date: £170 million, and took the total awarded to £350 million since 2003. Designed to reward good performance and recognise council work in creating sustainable communities, the grant was used as both carrot and stick. The biggest winners that year were in London, with four boroughs receiving more than £1 million each: Newham, Tower Hamlets, Enfield and Greenwich. But the grant was cut by 20 per cent in the case of 26 local planning authorities with poor performance in defending appeals. In March,

Kate Barker published her final report on her review of the housing supply (ODPM, 2004). There were a significant number of recommendations, but distilled to their essence they included a greater use of market information to identify where, when and how additional housing should be supplied, a greater allocation of land to increase supply and competition, and a more flexible response to changing market conditions. Landowners were to be taxed on windfall gains on increases in land values as a result of development, and a development gains tax (called a Planning Gain Supplement) based on local land values ran the least risk of reducing supply. The tax would run alongside a restricted form of Section 106 with a tariff which could only include mitigation measures and affordable housing contributions. Gordon Brown subsequently responded in a pre-budget report after the 2005 election.

Delivering Sustainable Development

It was a decade since the Environment Act had been passed in 1995, and although John Prescott had attended the Kyoto conference in December 1997, there had been little new advice. Government now saw the planning system as an effective way of implementing sustainable policies, and published, in February 2005, a paper that set a framework for incorporating sustainable development within the planning system. (PPS1, *Delivering Sustainable Development*.) This was followed in March by a policy document *Securing the Future* which promised an integrated approach to protect and enhance the physical and natural environment, and to use resources and energy as effectively as possible.

Party Manifestos for the May 2005 Elections

Tony Blair announced in the autumn of 2004 that the next election would be his last, and the election campaign was a joint promotion of him and Gordon Brown with Blair going as far as he could to identify Mr Brown as his eventual successor. The divisions between the parties were clear and the manifestos contained no surprises. For New Labour, continued housing growth and renewal, and more responsibility for Regional Assemblies were the key issues. The Conservatives pledged to abolish the Regional Assemblies, and to return powers to the councils, to replace the ODPM by a local government department, and to scrap the sustainable communities plan. The

Liberal Democrats would introduce a community planning system, cut government departments and return power to councils as well as transferring strategic planning to the county level. Milton Keynes was to prove an election battleground with considerable opposition to government proposals under the sustainable communities agenda which were to double the size of the new town to 400,000, which would make it the largest city in southern England outside London and Bristol. The Conservatives gained a seat there and, in all of the 47 Labour losses, 12 were in the growth areas designated under the sustainable communities plan. The Green Party was also a beneficiary of the opposition vote in growth areas such as Ashford and Hertford and Stortford.

Blair's Third Term

Tony Blair was fortunate in that although New Labour's share of the popular vote was now down to 35.2 per cent – barely a percentage point higher than that won by Neil Kinnock in his unsuccessful campaign against John Major in 1992, a strong showing by the Liberal Democrats of 22 per cent of the popular vote pinned the Conservatives down, and they only increased their number of seats by 31 to a total of 198. For a third term, New Labour enjoyed a strong working majority against all the other parties, and yet within hours of the election victory there was backbench pressure on Blair to announce when he intended to step down. On the Friday morning after the campaign, the Conservative leader Michael Howard repeated the action of his predecessors as Tory leaders at elections in 1997 and 2001 and announced his resignation. At local government level, however, the Conservatives and Liberal Democrats made significant gains, which would mean a limited New Labour presence on the regional planning bodies. In Greater London, the Conservatives gained control of seven London boroughs and Labour lost control of the majority of the London boroughs for the first time in almost a generation.

In the campaign, for the first time since 1970, immigration became an election issue. In 2004, immigration reached its highest ever level with a net inflow of 223,000, largely as a result of the expansion of the EU. Forecasts for 2005 predicted a net migration figure of 255,000 which compared with a net figure of 50,000 a year when Labour took office. Population projections of an increase of 7 million people in the next 25 years reflected this scale of immigration, and in many communities the strain on public services produced cultural tensions which surfaced in the election campaign.

In shaping his Cabinet for a third term in office, Tony Blair attempted to reconcile the impossible, and while keeping John Prescott as Deputy Prime Minister and head of the ODPM, he handed David Milliband and Yvette Cooper key positions – he as Minister for Communities and Local Government, she as Minister for Housing and Planning. Planning and the sustainable communities agenda stayed under the remit of the ODPM and John Prescott but the original objective of combining all those functions to do with planning, transport, housing and the environment was now abandoned. Ruth Kelly became Secretary of State for the new Department of Communities and Local Government but transport was under Douglas Alexander.

Tall Buildings in London

Over the next few months, a whole phalanx of tall buildings, principally in and around the City of London, were either approved or proposed. In July, plans for one of London's tallest skyscrapers – Bishopsgate Tower – were submitted to the Corporation of London. The tower would dwarf the Swiss Re tower (the Gherkin) nearby, and be slightly shorter than the Shard of Glass at London Bridge. A fortnight later, two office towers with 28 and 34 floors, designed by Richard Rogers, along the River Thames were granted planning consent. Before the end of the month, the Vauxhall Tower was given the go-ahead by John Prescott and in the following year he overturned the inspector's refusal and allowed the building of 25- and 37-storey towers at the disused Lots Road power station site in Chelsea. On the Isle of Dogs, four towers for a mixed-use development between 8 and 40 storeys were permitted, eight towers at the Elephant and Castle as part of a £1.5 billion renewal, and finally the Bishopsgate Tower – the tallest in the City of London with 60 storeys – was given the go-ahead. Not since Harold Macmillan's dash for housing in the 1960s had so many tall buildings been approved.

2012 Olympic Bid Successful

In July, one of the defining moments of the Blair premiership took place when London was chosen for the 2012 Olympics, paving the way for the Olympic Delivery Authority to drive the regeneration of former industrial sites in the Lower Lea Valley. The Olympic zone falls within the boundaries

The Heron Tower, one of the few new office buildings under construction in the City of London and due for completion in 2011.

of the London Thames Gateway UDC, established to revive the area. At least £2.3 billion in funding was initially promised from central government and Council Tax payers in London. The need to regenerate the Lower Lea Valley was recognised in London's Olympic bid, and this legacy was a compelling feature of the choice of London for the Games.

Local Government White Paper

At the end of October 2006, the government published its local government White Paper *Strong and Prosperous Communities*. The principal themes were local leadership, the value of local strategic partnerships, cutting back on performance targets, an increased regional basis for public services, and stronger political leadership by requiring all councils to opt for a directly-elected mayor for a four-year term. The proposals were quickly transformed into a local government Bill, which was included in the Queen's Speech in November.

Planning Gain Supplement

By means of a pre-budget statement in Parliament on 9 December, Chancellor Gordon Brown announced planning reforms designed to tackle the shortfall in housing supply and improve affordability, in a long-awaited response to the Barker housing review. Over the next decade, the government pledged to increase the rate of house-building from the current level of 150,000 per year to 200,000, and a package of funding and support for local communities who wished to pursue large-scale growth through the New Growth Points initiative was announced. Also introduced were proposals for a planning gain supplement (PGS) to fund infrastructure, which would capture a portion of the increase in land values when planning permission was granted, while in tandem scaling back the current planning obligations system. This met with a mainly hostile reception from private sector and professional bodies. The RTPI criticised the folly of introducing a land tax but the TCPA was more welcoming of an updated tax system. Lawyers, developers and the RICS were united in their opposition to a further land tax.

David Cameron Elected New Tory Leader

Before the end of the year, David Cameron had been elected the new leader of the Conservatives, and he quickly set up two new key policy groups – social justice and quality of life. The former was to be chaired by Iain Duncan Smith, and the latter by John Gummer. Cameron reappointed Caroline Spelman as Shadow Secretary of State for the ODPM. A parliamentary answer from the ODPM in December on the amount of house-building on land allocated as green belt was a boon to the Tories. It showed that the figure had increased from 4,456 hectares in 1997 to 5,521 hectares in 2003, and included the 'Newcastle Great Park' consisting of 2,700 houses approved by John Prescott in June 2000.

Prior to his election as Conservative leader, David Cameron, writing in *The Times* in September (Cameron, 2005) outlined a Conservative response to the urban pressures on the countryside. Referencing back to the Conservative heritage and civic leadership of Joseph Chamberlain, Cameron saw urban renaissance as the answer, but to achieve this Labour's top-down approach specifying the number of houses to be built in each region had to be replaced by a transfer of power and control to the local level, with a new generation of visionary local leaders including more elected mayors. During the year, writing in the *Guardian*, Simon Jenkins (2005) had taken Yvette Cooper to task over the consultation paper *Planning for Housing Provision* which saw the effective supply of land through the planning system as fundamental to the successful delivery of its housing policies, and the emphasis of planning as a system that replaces the market to one that works with the market to reconcile interests and facilitate development to meet social objectives. Jenkins criticised the analysis arguing that planning has always reflected market pressure because that is all it can do, and the document offered no guidance to planners, for instance on respecting the green belt or countryside. The intention was that wherever a developer wanted to build houses, planning permission must be given. This was 'anti-planning' he concluded.

Natural England and the Countryside

In October, a new integrated agency, Natural England, responsible for countryside and land management in England, was set up and brought together English Nature, the Countryside Agency's Landscape, Access and Recreation division, and the Rural Development Service's environmental land management functions but there were concerns about possible spending cuts despite the huge size of the new agency. In the same month, the government's rural advocate reported that rural communities and business people felt disconnected from the decisions taken by policy-makers and officials. The planning system was seen as over-complicated and tending to stifle rather than encourage business growth.

More Legislation

In November, Tony Blair promised to overhaul the planning system in respect of major infrastructure and investment projects – ministers would set down planning policy, leaving an independent commission to decide nationally important energy, transport and housing schemes. It was inevitable in the light of the Baker and Eddington reports that the government would feel compelled to simplify the planning system in terms of delivering the infrastructure that the country required to maintain its economic competitiveness in a global economy. The need to secure stable power generation, and the building of airports and motorways necessary to improve long-term economic growth, would come before the IPC (Infrastructure Planning Commission) which was an attempt to 'de-politicise' these issues. Other changes mooted were to replace the soundness test in Statements of Community Involvement produced under the new LDF system. The move came after most of the first wave of SCIs (Statements of Community Involvement) failed procedural tests. The SCI would be integrated into a wider strategy for community engagement put together by local strategic partnerships and local authorities. Other key proposals included options for councils to collaborate in city regions and apply for unitary status. On 17 November, the Queen's speech announced the overhaul of the planning system, following the Prime Minister's pledge to legislate.

A New Regeneration Agency

At the beginning of January 2007, Communities Secretary Ruth Kelly announced a new national housing and regeneration agency which would bring together the functions of English Partnerships, the Housing Corporation and a range of work carried out by DCLG including housing market renewal, housing growth and urban regeneration. It would have an annual budget of £5 billion, and be expected to be operational around 2009.

Later that month, the House of Commons Culture, Media and Sport Committee warned that detailed planning for the 2012 Olympic Games must start and it also expressed concerns that the original estimates were already outdated just 18 months after London had won the bid, and greater clarity was needed on the £2 billion budget for the London Organising Committee of the Olympic Games. That same week the Olympic Delivery Authority was launched.

Eco Towns

In March, Yvette Cooper endorsed the eco town concept and announced a £2 million funding to develop the eco town plans. The settlements of homes would have strong public transport links and could be built on surplus public sector land such as former NHS sites. This was the opening salvo in a long drawn-out struggle between the eco town promoters and objectors, reminiscent of Nicholas Ridley's new villages campaign 20 years before.

Energy White Paper

The government reiterated its support for building nuclear power stations in an Energy White Paper and, at the same time, a planning White Paper proposing an Infrastructure Planning Commission (IPC) was published to deal with nationally significant utilities projects under a unified consent regime (as mooted in the Barker review). The proposed axing of the right to be heard at inquiry was condemned by Friends of the Earth.

Blair Leaves Downing Street

Gordon Brown's final performance as Chancellor at the dispatch box in Parliament was in March 2007, and included the mantra 'we will never return to the old boom and bust', and he predicted that Britain's economy would grow between 2.5 and 3 per cent in 2009. Three months later, on 27 June 2007, which now looks like the most incredible foresight, Tony Blair left Downing Street, ahead of the impending financial collapse. Preoccupied with foreign policy and the Iraq war, and with the taunt of David Cameron in the House of Commons, 'You were the future once' still reverberating, the Prime Minister had allowed the Chancellor to increasingly set the agenda for housing policy, and begin to shape the planning system to a business agenda. This meant that when the economic crisis overwhelmed the country in 2008, the future of the planning system, and the delays and obfuscation which many in the business community associated with it, came to the fore in the debate as to how the country could build its way out of recession.

Blair's England

How much had England's appearance changed during the terms of Blair's government? The answer is not as much as under Thatcher. There were few new, large, out-of-town shopping centres as most had either been built or were permitted under Thatcher and Major. Although housing completions by 2007 had risen above the low figures reached in the mid-1990s, these were still below the rates experienced in the 1980s. Much of the housing that was built occurred on brownfield sites, and in city centres; the amount of housing being built on greenfield land had dropped significantly. John Prescott's planning policies had had an effect, although the amount of housing built was substantially below requirements. The amount of housing built on brownfield land had grown from a figure of 47 per cent in 1997 to 69 per cent by 2007. In the South East, despite the acres of newsprint devoted to the green belt battles, housing completions were well below the target figures.

The most dramatic changes were in the City of London and in the provincial cities. During the Docklands boom of the Thatcher period, financial services had migrated to the new office buildings at Canary Wharf in London's East End, which had large floor plans suitable for the open plan offices required for the financial dealing rooms. Alarmed by this, and encouraged by the Mayor of London, Ken Livingstone, the City Corporation changed its policy, and began to encourage new tall buildings in the historic, tightly laid-out streets of the City. Granted planning permission in August 2000 by John Prescott, the Gherkin was completed in December 2003. Some 40 floors high, its construction symbolised the start of a new high-rise construction boom in London. It was followed by the Willis building in 2007 and the Broadgate Tower in 2008. Other buildings were planned, or under construction: the Heron Tower, the Leadenhall Building, the 'Walkie-Talkie Tower' and the Pinnacle, which on completion would be the City's tallest building. Even taller buildings were planned including the glass tower, the Shard, and a cluster of office towers around London Bridge station, but the economic downturn of 2008–09 raised doubts about both the need for and the financing of these buildings. In a short period of time, the City of London had acquired its 'Grand Projects' which would provide a permanent reminder of the financial boom of the new millennium engineered by Blair and Brown's deregulation of the banks.

The Channel Tunnel rail link opened in 2007 and Britain's first high-speed rail line reached the brilliantly refurbished St Pancras station. The link would provide a boost to the redevelopment of King's Cross, the largest redevelopment site in the country, and the Stratford International Railway station area, the gateway to the Olympics site.

The Cultural Boom

During the Blair era, the the Heritage Lottery Fund contributed more than a billion pounds to arts and cultural projects throughout the country. The result was a cluster of iconic buildings in the provincial cities unmatched since Victorian times, and an enormous boost to young aspiring architects. In Newcastle-Gateshead, there was the Millennium Bridge across the Tyne, the Baltic Centre for contemporary art and the Sage music centre by Foster & Partners. At Salford Quays, there was the Lowry Centre by Michael Wilford and Daniel Libeskind's Imperial War Museum. In the Midlands, there was Will Alsop's Public Arts building in West Bromwich and the New Art Gallery by Adam Caruso and Peter St John in Walsall. In London, the Royal Opera House, RADA, Sadler's Wells, the Royal Albert Hall, Tate Modern and the Royal Court Theatre all benefited from the largesse available.

In an interview in *Building* magazine published on 18 May 2007, in one of his last engagements before travelling to Sedgefield to announce his resignation, the Prime Minister was asked what were the physical changes to the country that he would look back on (Blair, 2007). He picked out the regeneration in Manchester, Birmingham, Leeds, Newcastle and Liverpool, and Stratford City on the edge of the Olympics site as well as King's Cross in London. Throughout the country, he referred to the new schools and hospitals. Few were larger than the Birmingham New Hospitals project which was the first new general hospital to be built in the city for 70 years. Once complete in 2012, the new 'super' hospital will have over 1,200 beds and 30 operating theatres. Clad entirely in steel, the design consists of three truncated pods, connected by walkways and set on a three-storey rectangular podium block. The striking architectural design will be a legacy of New

The Culture Boom. The Baltic Centre for contemporary art. The conversion of the derelict Baltic Flour Mills into an international centre for contemporary art is one of the highlights of Gateshead's arts-led regeneration scheme. The architects were Ellis Williams.

© Nigel Moor

Labour's commitment to the NHS. Tony Blair also had high hopes for Thames Gateway, as an example of meeting housing demands in a sustainable way.

Looking Back

Any review of this period must focus on Blair's appointment of John Pre-scott as Planning, Local Government and Environment minister from 1997 to 2006, a length of time in this office unequalled by anyone. By common consent, this was to do with party politics and keeping the Labour Party together, and Blair's indulgence to his deputy carried a high price in terms of a dismal housing performance that caused anguish to the Treasury and Chancellor Gordon Brown. The irony is that John Prescott not only kept the Labour Party together, but performed the same role for the Conservatives. The controversy in the shires he caused over the Sustainable Communities Programme, and which he appeared to relish, helped the Conservatives,

New schools and hospitals have been built in the Blair era. Few are larger than the Birmingham New Hospitals project, the first new general hospital to be built in the city for 70 years.

© Nigel Moor

close to oblivion in 1997, to rebuild at the grass roots level, and contemplate a return to power in 2010.

The political historian David Marquand delivered a withering verdict on Tony Blair's premiership (Marquand, 2008). He picked out 'sofa government', Cabinet irrelevance and managed populism as Blair's trademarks, and at a deeper level, Blair exacerbated Thatcherism's worst excesses, a culture of targets, audits, centralisation and authoritarianism. Marquand wanted to see a revival of popular participation in politics.

References

Blair, A. (2007) Interview, *Building* Magazine, 18 May, pp. 30–31.

Byers, S. (2002) Interview, *Planning*, 31 May, p 1.

Cameron, D. (2005) Where is the most civilised place on earth? *The Times*, 1 September.

Clifton-Brown, G. (2002) Interview, *Planning*, 15 March, p. 1.

Donati, M. (2003) Interview with Lord Rooker, *Planning*, 24 January , p. 13.

Gummer, J. (2001) Afterthought: new departments bolster prejudices, *Planning*, 22 June, p. 5.

Jenkins, S. (2005) The verbal smokescreen that hides dangerous government, *Guardian*, 14 October.

Jenkins, S. (2006) *Thatcher & Sons*. London: Allen Lane, pp. 298, 312.

Marquand, D. (2008) *Britain Since 1918: The Strange Career of British Democracy*. London: Wendenfeld & Nicholson.

May, T. (2001) Interview, *Planning*, 14 Ddecember, p. 2.

Norman, A. (2001) Interview, *Planning*, 15 June, p. 2.

ODPM (2003) Interview, *Planning*, 20 June.

ODPM (2004) *The Barker Review of Land Use Planning*. London: ODPM.

Pickles, E. (2003) Interview, *Planning*, 10 January, p 1.

Prescott, J. (2002a) Interview, *Planning*, 17 May, p. 8.

Prescott, J. (2002b) Sustainable communities, housing and planning, *House of Commons Hansard Debates*, Columns 438–42, 18 July.

Prescott, J. and Davies, H. (2008) *Prezza, My Story: Pulling No Punches*. London: Headline, pp. 212, 254, 331.

Winkley, R. (2001a) Agent for inclusion, *Planning*, 7 December, p. 13.

Winkley, R. (2001b) Falconer launches first speed attack, *Planning*, 6 July, p. 1.

12

Gordon Brown Takes Over, 2007: The Credit Crunch and the Return of Keynesianism

The Departure of Blair

In June 2007, not long after Gordon Brown had been selected unopposed as leader of the Labour Party and Britain's new Prime Minister, Anthony Giddens, now a Labour peer, writing in the *Independent* (Giddens, 2007) asked whether the departure of Tony Blair would also mean the disappearance of his distinctive political philosophy 'the Third Way'? He answered his own question in the following way. Some have seen the Third Way as a sound bite, empty PR – a political outlook devoid of significant policy content. This view underestimates the significance of Labour winning three successive elections for the first time in its history, and it could well win a fourth because the Third Way is policy rich. Gordon Brown was unlikely to use the term but he would not revert to Old Labour, and would further develop the main framework of Third Way political thinking.

This would involve a number of policy principles. The first was to hold the political centre ground. The second was to ensure the economy was strong, for social justice depended upon a robust economy. The third was to invest in public services but coupled with reform. The fourth was to create a new contract between state and citizens based upon responsibilities as well as rights, and finally not to allow any issues to be monopolised by the political Right. All these policy principles would have an influence on the government's thinking about planning and local government in Gordon Brown's premiership, and as we will see the crisis in banking and liquidity that emerged in the summer of 2008 gave him the opportunity to try and occupy the political centre ground.

Cabinet Changes

On 29 June, Gordon Brown took over as Prime Minister and pledged to give the Housing Minister more clout, including attendance at Cabinet meetings and lead the debate on vital new homes. In July, he launched his Green Paper on constitutional reform, *The Governance of Britain*, which suggested that regional, spatial and economic strategies could be merged. He reshuffled his Cabinet, and Hazel Blears became head of the DCLG; Hilary Benn became Environment Secretary, and James Purnell took the culture brief from Tessa Jowell who was made Olympics Minister. Yvette Cooper moved to housing, and John Healey was given the local government portfolio.

More High Buildings in London

London's high buildings boom continued. London's tallest block of flats, the 50-storey Vauxhall Tower, was granted planning permission by John Prescott despite warnings from his officials that the tower would fail to offer adequate affordable housing. Another controversial skyscraper planned for the City was the 'Walkie-Talkie' tower, on the site of 20 Fenchurch Street, which had been called in after opposition from English Heritage, concerned at skyline views on Waterloo Bridge.

Policy Changes

In July, Gordon Brown delivered a statement ahead of the Queen's Speech to Parliament which covered a wide variety of planning and housing issues. The government's U-turn on the PGS was widely welcomed. The U-turn came as Gordon Brown unveiled a programme of draft legislation, saying the government would defer the PGS Bill if a better option could be found before the pre-budget report. Plans were published to hand over power to the RDAs (Regional Development Agencies), scrapping Regional Assemblies and giving RDAs executive responsibility for planning and housing, as outlined in the *Review of Sub-National Economic Development and Regeneration* published that same month. The RDAs would be responsible for planning, transport and housing functions and produce new Single Regional Strategies incorporating spatial and economic policy. The DCLG urged local authorities to embrace eco town growth and reaffirmed government plans to build five eco towns, which would feature 5,000–20,000 homes of which no less than 30 per cent would be affordable. There would also be an area-wide transport plan to increase journeys by public transport, walking and cycling. Housing targets were yet again revised with an increase for the whole of Britain from 200,000 to 240,000 a year after 2016, which would mean an extra 250,000 houses by 2020.

Soon after assuming the leadership of the Labour Party, Gordon Brown made it clear that housing supply was now the priority in domestic politics, and he wanted to recover the dynamism of the inter-war years and the 1950s in getting houses built. His minister, Hazel Blears, reflecting her background as a solicitor in Manchester's local government, was perhaps more aware of the tensions this would introduce in the relations between central and local government. In oral evidence to the House of Commons Communities & Local Government Select Committee in July 2007, she told the Committee that the priority to build houses meant getting local authorities to recognise their responsibility, and for her to be able to take forward the agenda was going to be quite challenging.

A new parliamentary bill was announced to set up the new super-agency, Communities England, which would be the successor to English Partnerships. This had relied for most of its funding on land sales, and had proved vulnerable to the economic downturn. The new agency would rely on the Exchequer for its annual £5 billion expenditure. It would be charged with delivering the Thames Gateway regeneration, bringing social housing up to the decent homes standard, delivering 240,000 homes each year, and promoting housing market renewal in areas of low demand in northern England.

By October proposals for a PGS were dropped in favour of a tariff-based system. First mooted more than three years before, the PGS had attracted brickbats from across the planning and property sectors. Yvette Cooper outlined how local authorities would be given powers to incorporate tariffs into LDFs. Planning charges would work alongside S.106 agreements to bring forward infrastructure to support housing growth, but the government had yet to clarify how charges would be set, how high they might be and what mechanisms would be available for people to appeal against them. There were also new initiatives to speed up housing supply delivery with incentives worth £500 million to be channelled through the new Housing & Planning Delivery Grant (HPDG), which would supersede the former Planning Delivery Grant. This initiative was directed at the expansion areas which included the four growth areas, and the nearly 50 cities and towns that had proposed extensive housing growth in their areas.

Major Population Growth

At the end of November, the Office for National Statistics predicted that the current population of Britain of 60.6 million would increase to 75.4 million by 2031, and to 91 million by mid-century, and pass 100 million by the late 2060s if levels of immigration, fertility and life expectancy remained at existing levels. Some 70 per cent of the population rise over the next 20 years would be attributable directly to immigration. Ordinarily, the scale of these projections would have raised a storm in the press, but because of the overriding preoccupation with the latest fallout from the recession, reaction was muted. There was also the suspicion that high levels of immigration might be stalled by the wave of redundancies and job losses taking place.

More prominence for Eco Towns

In February 2008, Caroline Flint, previously Minister for Employment and Welfare Reform, took over the planning and housing brief from Yvette Cooper in the latest cabinet reshuffle following Peter Hain's resignation as Work and Pensions Minister. Cooper became Chief Secretary to the Treasury where she had always wanted to be. The new minister embarked on an energetic campaign to try and win more support for the eco towns, and insisted that the government would shortlist eco towns that focused on quality of life not quantity of homes. Between 30 and 50 per cent of the homes would be affordable, and there would be an acre of green space for every 100 homes. Subsequently, 15 of the 57 schemes submitted were shortlisted, the majority in Conservative controlled areas, and proposals at Pennsbury in Leicestershire, Middle Quinton in Warwickshire, where lawyers acting for the objectors were pressing for a judicial review, and Marston Vale in Bedfordshire were already arousing vehement local opposition.

Yet More Reform

At the end of March, a press conference was held to launch yet another 'red tape-busting review' of the planning system (Blears, 2008). Attended by Communities Secretary Hazel Blears, Business Secretary John Hutton and Housing and Planning Minister Caroline Flint, it was announced that Joanna Killian, chief executive of Essex County Council, and David Pretty, former group chief executive of Barratt Developments Plc would review how

216

planning applications were dealt with, and make recommendations for improving the process. The report had been prompted by a World Bank report published earlier that year which ranked Britain's planning system as 61st in the world in terms of delays to major development. One item singled out in the briefing was unnecessary duplication of paperwork in the process. Yet, just a week later, new regulations were introduced requiring a whole suite of documents to be submitted with a planning application before that application could be accepted as valid. Originally, the objective of the new regulations was to introduce a national standard planning application form, which was certainly long overdue, but the opportunity was taken to add yet another raft of paperwork. It was a graphic example of how out of touch ministers were with the actual workings of the planning system, and how much they relied on the briefings they were provided with, which contained the same platitudes about reforming the planning system that had been drafted by civil servants 30 years before.

London Mayoral Campaign

In March, the London mayoral campaign began in earnest, as Ken Living-stone and Boris Johnson went head to head over affordable housing. Both pledged to provide 50,000 affordable homes, but by different delivery methods. Johnson promised to relax Livingstone's policy of demanding 50 per cent affordable housing in new developments, and instead would use £130 million from the regional housing pot to launch a first-time buyers' scheme as well as investing £60 million in renovating London's 84,205 empty properties. Johnson also pledged to reinstate planning rules protecting views of St Paul's and the Palace of Westminster, set new viewing corridors and protect the green belt. In May, Johnson won the election, and made fellow conservative Sir Simon Milton, former Westminster City Council leader, his chief planning adviser. He promised less major intervention in borough decisions. The London Assembly now comprised 11 Tory members, 8 Labour, 3 Liberal Democrats, 2 Greens and 1 BNP member. The electoral humiliation for the government was very evident in London, but also reverberated across the country.

The new London Mayor would allow London boroughs to set their own affordable housing target. Johnson scrapped proposals for a carbon charge that would have seen owners of large family cars pay a £25 congestion charge. Ken Livingstone had launched the plan earlier that year, and it was due to come into force in October. In July, London's Crossrail received approval following nearly 20 years of false starts, after the Bill confirming planning permission for the link won Royal Assent. Despite electoral pledges, the new London Mayor announced that he intended to retain transport power and take control of Transport for London, rather than delegating his powers, following his similar U-turn on retaining powers over planning decisions. Johnson said his personal involvement was crucial to ensure democratic accountability.

Tory Opposition

In October, at the Tory Party conference, pledges were made to give communities more say in planning decisions – one of a series of decentralising measures proposed by the Party. The Conservatives also pledged to scrap density targets, RSSs and regional and national housing targets, and the 'top-down approach' whereby 'the Housing Minister is saying we must build lots of homes, but people are saying no'.

Eco Towns Advance

That same month, there was a further government reshuffle prompting calls for continuity as Margaret Beckett became Labour's eighth Housing and Planning Minister since 1997, replacing Caroline Flint, and Geoff Hoon its seventh Transport Secretary. In November, the government issued its draft eco town PPS (Planning Policy Statement) and sustainability appraisal, although it ran the risk of it being found unlawful. The DCLG issued the documents before the date set for the judicial review of the selection process on behalf of the Middle Quinton objectors. The shortlist of proposals had altered considerably since first being published in April, with some schemes dropping out and others emerging. Only one (Rackheath) had a grade A rating in sustainability appraisal, and one (Western Otmoor) had grade C. All the others had grade B, meaning they would be suitable for eco towns, subject to meeting specific planning and design objectives. These were: Middle Quinton, Newton-Bingham, Ford, Bordon-Whitehill, St Austell China Clay Community, Rossington, North East Elsenham, Pennbury, Marston Vale and North West Bicester (an alternative to Weston Otmoor). Subsequently, the government announced only four schemes to go forward with the outside possibility that others might be supported.

The Killian-Pretty Report

The new Housing and Planning Minister, Margaret Beckett, welcomed the publication of the Killian Pretty Report at the end of November, vowing that 'when the economy begins to recover people will find a reinvigorated and leaner planning system' (Beckett, 2008). There was much to welcome in the report (Killian and Pretty, 2008), which aimed to increase substantially the number of small-scale commercial developments and other minor non-residential developments that could be treated as permitted development, so as to reduce the number of applications going through the system, with the result that more time and effort could be focused on major developments. But more significant was what the report did *not* recommend. There was no return to a presumption in favour of development, nor disregarding con-sultation responses that were not delivered on time. Generally, the report contained exhortations for everyone to try harder, and the suspicion was that in formulating a response civil servants would yet again introduce more complexity. The government promised yet more consultation on the proposals.

Third Runway at Heathrow

In January 2009, proposals for a third runway at Heathrow faced more hurdles as objectors (including Greenpeace and Tory environmental spokesman Zac Goldsmith) revealed plans to obstruct the planning process by purchasing a plot of land north of Sipson Village, which would be bulldozed for the expansion. Greenpeace sought to resist compulsory pur-chases on the land by selling portions of it across the world, and said it would represent millions of people at any planning inquiry. But the Planning Act 2008 allowed the IPC, which was likely to determine the application, to disregard representations thought frivolous or vexatious. The Tories insisted they would scrap the IPC and the third runway if they won the next election. Meanwhile, London Mayor Boris Johnson, who was pushing for an airport in the Thames Estuary, was among those set to mount a legal challenge if the runway was approved. Transport Secretary Geoff Hoon endorsed a third runway and sixth terminal at Heathrow. Even the government's own watchdog on sustainability branded the move highly irresponsible. Hoon's package of proposed sweeteners failed to appease opponents such as the 2M Group of 22 councils working with the London Mayor on a legal challenge.

There was opposition to the expansion from rebel Labour MPs as well as Tories and Liberal Democrats.

Opposition to the expansion of Heathrow threw together an unlikely coalition of protestors from the London Mayor to Labour MPs, the Conservative Party, actors, environmental campaigners, local residents, the National Trust and more radical groups such as 'Plane Stupid'. One of their leading activists, Leo Murray, was the grandson of the late Lord Greenwood, Housing and Planning Minister in Harold Wilson's Cabinet. The Tory proposals were to use Heathrow as a rail hub connecting the principal English cities such as Birmingham, Manchester and Leeds by new high-speed rail links with London.

The government asked the airport owners BAA to submit a planning application as soon as possible with a view to opening the new runway and terminal as early as 2015. The £9 billion expansion would increase capacity by 50 per cent, and would be one of the first projects considered by the new IPC. Meanwhile, Boris Johnson appointed Douglas Oakervee, the senior engineer behind the Hong Kong island airport, which was built on reclaimed land, to carry out a feasibility study for a Thames Estuary airport.

Regionalism

That same month, five new Regional Leaders' Boards (RLBs) were set up in readiness for the transfer of regional planning powers from the eight out-going RDAs. Following the sub-national review in the autumn, the government confirmed that RDAs and RLBs would jointly draft and implement single regional strategies, which would combine spatial and economic plans. At that time, only the Leaders' Forum for the North West was in operation. Now, the South East, South West, West Midlands and Yorkshire and Humber also finalised their working structures. Discussions continued in the East of England, the East Midlands and the North East. There was no requirement for a Board in London.

London's Crossrail

Crossrail had been on the drawing board for almost 20 years before it finally got the go-ahead. It had originally fallen victim to the recession in the early 1990s, and the London Mayor appeared determined not to let it fail this time round. The revised London Plan would include provision for a Section 106 levy specifically for Crossrail, and it was envisaged that £200 million could be gained in this way. The most difficult task in the future will be to decide which developments will be covered by this levy – those near the new stations, or throughout London. There are parallels between this concept and the financial contribution given to the construction of the Jubilee Line by the developers of Canary Wharf. The other controversial aspect of the Crossrail decision was the decision taken by the London Mayor to scrap a number of transport projects in the capital, so as to focus on the delivery of Crossrail. These included the Thames Gateway Bridge, the Cross River Tram, the Croydon Tramlink Extension, the Oxford Street Tram, and the DLR Dagenham Dock rail link. Concerns were raised by the supporters of Thames Gateway who viewed some of these projects as vital to its success.

Judicial Go-ahead for Eco Towns

Campaigners against the government's eco town drive lost their judicial review, as the High Court decision vindicated the legality of the DCLG's plans meaning that it could continue its consultation on the draft policy statement, which was to run until April. Opponents of the Middle Quinton eco town proposal in Warwickshire had brought the case to the High Court. The judgement continued a long-standing reluctance of the judiciary to intervene in the political decision-making of the planning process, and more recently articulated in the Alconbury decision. Less encouraging was the report of the House of Commons Communities and Local Government Committee (2008) which reported in February, and advised that the eco towns policy was clearly in some difficulty. Only one site had been fully approved, and that offered fewer than the original minimum 5,000 new houses required under the scheme. The plans for a generation of ten new eco towns were further undermined by a further report that only three of the proposals were likely to be financially viable. Even more daunting was that these three (Weston Otmoor in Oxfordshire, North-East Elsenham in Essex and Middle Quinton in Warwickshire) probably faced the greatest public opposition of any of the schemes. The ambition of the government that a total of 100,000 homes would be constructed looked highly unlikely to be achieved. The eco town programme, even if successful, would make no great contribution to the very significant problem of housing supply, concluded the committee.

Returning Power to Local Communities

In February, David Cameron launched a major review (Cameron, 2009) of planning and local government. The document, entitled *Control Shift: Returning Power to Local Communities*, was a wide-ranging commentary on New Labour's modernising programme for local government and planning, and promised a radical decentralisation. Pointing out that over the last century Britain had become one of the most centralised countries in the developed world, and that this trend had accelerated under New Labour, the document contrasted this top-down, central control with the technological advances of the 'post-bureaucratic age' that had placed greater power with the citizen who could now share information and knowledge freely without constraint. The changes would involve abolishing regional planning, revoking all regional spatial strategies, including regional building targets, and repealing the national planning guidance that related to regional planning. Except in London, the Tories would abolish RDAs and transfer all regional, housing and planning powers back to local authorities. Councils would be encouraged to form their own 'local enterprise partnerships'.

The Conservatives committed themselves to scrapping the HPDG and replacing this by matching the Council Tax raised by each council for each new house built for each of the six years after that house was constructed in order to incentivise councils to meet housing needs. A major change would be to scrap the power of central government to cap rates which had been introduced by Chris Patten in the last Conservative government and give local people the power to veto large Council Tax rises through local referendum. The paper also confirmed the Conservatives' plan to abolish the IPC, and instead speed up planning inquiries. These would focus on material planning considerations instead of questioning the project in principle. National policy statements would remain for major infrastructure. One of the key features was to hold a referendum on the introduction of a mayoral system in 12 of the largest English cities. The London Development Agency, already run by the Mayor of London, would be kept, but the Government Office for London would be abolished, and its powers transferred to the mayor or boroughs. The review was likely to provide a platform for the Conservatives' manifesto for the next general election anticipated in May 2010, but was also well timed for the English county elections in June 2009.

The Shard to be Built

At the end of February, the developer Sellar Group announced that it had let the £400 million contract to the Mace Group to build the Shard Tower. Planned to replace the 1970s Southwark Tower by London Bridge and designed by Renzo Piano, it would include a hotel, offices and flats. One of the few major towers being developed in London during the property slump, it is expected to be completed by 2012. A number of rival schemes including the British Land 'Cheesegrater' and Land Securities' 'Walkie Talkie' office buildings had been shelved due to a lack of debt funding and concerns over demand for space, and the *Evening Standard* newspaper reported (Carmichael and Bar-Hillel, 2009) that 21 property schemes involving high buildings in London could be scrapped or dramatically shrunk. The construction of the Shard in the midst of a recession brings to mind the building of The Empire State building in New York in the 1930s in similar circumstances.

Left or Right on the Economy?

By the spring of 2009, with probably little more than a year to the next general election, for the first time in more than a decade there was a clear choice between Left and Right on how to govern the economy through the recession. On 15 September 2008, the US bank Lehman Brothers had filed for bankruptcy. The decision of the then US Treasury Secretary Hank Paulson to let Lehmans go bust unleashed six weeks of mayhem in the financial markets, and the beginning of the global downturn, which had its origins in the US sub-prime mortgage market crisis, which subsequently impacted on house-building in the UK and the liquidity of the banks. The Prime Minister had authorised a huge increase in public borrowing to mitigate the effects of the recession, through increased spending on public services and state infrastructure. This included the new Homes and Communities Agency, and initiatives to revive house-building by councils. This could be done by allowing them to keep the receipts from rental income and sales through the Right to Buy. Since 1980 they had to give back 75 per cent of receipts to the Treasury, and council-house building had been at a low level since Margaret Thatcher had to all intents and purposes abolished housing subsidies. The Conservatives were concerned that a rising fiscal deficit in 2011 would mean a return of inflation, and therefore rising interest rates which would hamper economic recovery.

The Debate About the Role of Spatial Planning

Gordon Brown, in his speech to the United States Congress on Wednesday 4 March 2009, set out the goals for both Britain and the United States, led by the new President Barack Obama: 'Our task is to rebuild prosperity and security in a wholly different economic world, where competition is no longer local but global and banks are no longer just national but international' (Brown, 2009). Despite the undoubted success of the Prime Minister's speech and standing ovations from Congress, one political commentator saw an uncanny similarity with Jim Callaghan's return from the Guadeloupe summit, and Margaret Thatcher's return from Brussels before their respective falls from office (Watkins, 2009). The policies introduced by Gordon Brown in response to the economic downturn were a return to Keynesian economics, and a retreat from a liberal belief in a market economy introduced to Labour by Tony Blair. Yet since the advent of New Labour, the policies underpinning its modernising planning agenda had essentially been Keynesian: the new Homes and Communities Agency (HCA) took equity stakes in schemes, front-funding infrastructure and purchasing sites, and the Growth Areas programme and Thames Gateway, where nearly £10 billion of state investment had been spent to date, were examples of pump priming by the public sector, so that in the realm of spatial planning there was no fundamental change. Under Gordon Brown, the old socialist dream of an economy whose commanding heights would be publicly owned was probably nearer to realisation than ever before in peacetime. In a capitalist economy, the commanding heights are the financial services and banking, in which government now had a stake. The debate about the future objectives and principles of spatial planning had now begun for real, as at last the Tories had a coherent and arguable narrative. It would be between the Keynesian philosophy of Gordon Brown, with its belief in regional planning and targets, and the bottom-up localism now articulated by David Cameron and his team who had abandoned Thatcherism – their role models were Macmillan and Rab Butler. What was now apparent was that after more than ten years, Labour's centrally planned and controlled system had failed to deliver the housing that it planned, and their arguing that what was needed was more targets and more agencies would now fall on deaf ears. The Conservatives realised that without real local participation, these proposed levels of housing were not achievable in a modern, information- and knowledge-based society that could quickly and efficiently muster opposition to unwanted schemes. The challenge for the Tories was how to harness the undoubted electoral appeal of their approach to a programme for sustained economic recovery, which would rely on a significant contribution from the construction and development industry. The risk for them was a reversion to nimbyism as the less attractive flipside of localism (Norris, 2009).

Moves to reject a parliamentary culture that put a distance between citizen and government were given additional momentum by the parliamentary crisis over MPs' expenses. Just weeks before the European and shire county elections and a year before a possible May 2010 election, the disclosures by the *Daily Telegraph* threatened the hegemony of the three principal parties implicated and offered the smaller parties a chance to dramatically increase their share of the popular vote. Suddenly, the future of the political system and how it would impact on the shape and appearance of England looked much less certain.

The Future of the IPC

The future of the IPC, introduced by the Planning Act 2008 under its chairman Sir Michael Pitt, would depend on who won the next general election. The Conservatives were concerned that local communities would have less opportunity to make their voices heard and would keep some elements of the new system, such as the national policy statements, which would be subject to a vote in both houses, and the principle of single applications, but would transfer the work of the IPC to a strengthened Planning Inspectorate. Perhaps the Tories' strongest point was that the claims to speed up the planning process for key infrastructure projects could be illusory if planning decisions made by the IPC experienced legal challenges in the UK or Europe.

Civic Trust Closes After Fifty Years

Hit hard by the squeeze on local authority spending in the current economic climate, the Civic Trust announced in April 2009 that it was closing because of a lack of funds. Founded in 1957 by the influential Conservative politician Duncan Sandys, its campaigns had been taken on board by successive governments. One of the most important elements of the Trust's work was its awards scheme and its support for more than 700 civic societies across England. Various initiatives had been canvassed to continue its work but a new organisation working within its means and building gradually from the grass roots seemed the only realistic way forward. The National Trust announced that in conjunction with the Royal Institute of British Architects (RIBA) and the CPRE it was setting up the Civic Society Initiative to help establish a new collective voice for civic societies.

New Single Planning Policy for Economic Development

The proposed Planning Policy Statement 4, *Planning for Prosperous Economies*, published in May 2009, aimed to replace a whole plethora of planning advice by a single document which detailed planning policies relating to the economy in one place. The document repeats the 'town centre first' principle first pronounced by John Gummer when Environment Secretary in John Major's Cabinet, but the recession which brought most town centre schemes to a standstill raised a question over the credibility of this policy. Town centre schemes are long term, and the major food stores, particularly anxious to maintain their market share, would cast envious glances at existing edge-of-town retail parks where new retail development could more quickly be realised.

Latest Green Belt Statistics

Published in May 2009, statistics showed that about 13 per cent of the land area of England was designated as green belt, but there were areas where new plans showed a decrease. The following month two councils, Guildford and South Oxfordshire, announced that they were lodging legal challenges to the newly-adopted South East Plan, because of the plan's proposals to build in the green belt around Guildford and Oxford.

Prince Charles Defends Views on Architecture at RIBA Lecture

Some 25 years after his 'carbuncle' attack on modern architecture, Prince Charles told an audience of architects that he spoke out on architecture because 'the built environment affects us all'. He also highlighted the brutal destruction wrought on towns and cities in the 1960s, claiming that much of the urban realm was becoming depersonalised and defaced. Only a month later, he was again at the centre of controversy when the developer behind the redevelopment of Chelsea Barracks in London withdrew the planning application and scheme designed by Lord Rogers from Westminster City Council, and which had been publicly criticised by the Prince. In response, the architect called for a public inquiry into the Prince's constitutional powers, and lamented the loss of some 5,000 construction jobs in the middle of a recession. Only time will tell if Charles' intervention was justified but looking back at the history of controversial projects in London such interventions have probably been too infrequent rather than the reverse.

More Ministerial Changes

A day before the European and shire county elections to be held on Thursday 4 June 2009, Hazel Blears, embroiled in the MPs expenses controversy and sporting a silver brooch which read 'Rocking The Boat', announced her resignation as Secretary of State for Communities and Local Government. Her place was taken by John Denham, and his appointment was welcomed by both the RTPI and the TCPA, who pointed to his experience as an environmental campaigner and local government councillor.

Election Campaign 2010

As a newspaper leader writer shrewdly observed, at the end of the first week in June Gordon Brown had survived both a palace coup and a peasants' revolt. A month later, he to all intents and purposes began New Labour's campaign for the 2010 election with the publication of a document entitled *Building Britain's Future* which was strongly redolent of the National Plan produced by George Brown during Harold Wilson's premiership 30 years previously. The most expensive element of the plan was the goal to build 20,000 affordable houses in the next two years. Also included was a proposal for a new Bill to prepare the country for a future where the climate would be more unpredictable and to address the effects of climate change such as droughts and flooding, with new responsibilities for the Environment Agency. Critics asserted that by focusing on headline-grabbing initiatives, the government was trying to avoid addressing the most important issue in politics: the fiscal crisis. Missing too was any commitment to give local government more financial autonomy. Unlike the Liberal Democrats, who, had long maintained the need for a local income tax, New Labour and the Conservatives still hung on to spending controls on local government so that 80 per cent of their spending was dependent on central government sanction. This exposed a fundamental contempt for local democracy among the country's political class. The MPs' expenses scandal aroused the electorate who were unlikely to tolerate this contempt for much longer.

So What Comes Next?

Eric Hobsbawm (2009), in a persuasive article in the *Guardian*, pointed to the demise of the two ways of thinking about modern industrial economies in terms of two mutually exclusive opposites, capitalism or socialism, and the need for a more progressive policy that saw economic growth and the affluence it brings as a means and not an end. Such a policy would mean public non-profit initiatives, even if only in redistributing private accumulation of wealth, so as to achieve a collective social improvement. This, he asserted, would be particularly important in tackling the environmental crisis, and would mean a major shift away from the free market and towards public action, on a scale not yet envisaged. It is against this background that spatial planning, reared in the welfare state but maturing in a market economy now facing enormous global challenges, has to position itself. The look and shape of England in a hundred years time will reflect that struggle.

References

Beckett, M. (2008) Government welcomes the Killian Pretty report, press release 24 November.

Blears, H. (2008) An end to the waiting game for planning decisions, press release 25 March.

Brown, G. (2009 Speech to US Congress, *Guardian*, 5 March, p. 11.

Cameron, D. (2009) *Control Shift: Returning Power To Local Communities.* London: The Conservative Party.

Carmichael, S. and Bar-Hillel, M. (2009) London's faltering towers, *Evening Standard*, 4 March, p. 13.

Giddens, A. (2007) It's time to give the Third Way a second chance, *Independent* 28 June.

Hobsbawm, E. (2009) Socialism has failed, now capitalism is bankrupt, so what comes next? *Guardian*, 20 April.

House of Commons Communities and Local Government Committee (2008) *Communities and Local Government's Departmental Annual Report 2008, Second Report of Session 2008–2009.* London: The Stationery Office, pp. 20–21.

Killian, J. and Pretty, D. (2008) *Planning Applications: A Faster and More Responsive*

System. Final Report, Executive Summary and Recommendations: Report for Communities & Local Government. London: DCLR.

Norris, S. (2009) Popularity of local power must not blind the Tories to the risks, *Property Week*, 6 March, p. 45.

Watkins, A. (2009) A standing ovation for a fallen man, *Independent*, 8 March, p. 45.

13

The Five Persistent Themes and Afterwards

A Paradigm Shift in British Politics

This book has surveyed the political origins of the system of spatial planning in England since its inception in 1909, and how this has influenced the appearance of the country over the last century. A child of the first Liberal government, and its programme of social reforms, particularly the need for affordable housing, championed by intellectuals in the inter-war period as a curb on the growing urbanisation of England, maturing during the Second World War when its strategic value was recognised, it became a key element of the post-war welfare state and the political consensus. Like other elements of the welfare state, it was challenged during the Thatcher era, while in the Blair premiership it became a key part of the Third Way.

At the end of the first decade of the twentieth-first century, the problem of global warming poses ideological challenges to all the political parties, and the role of spatial planning to reduce emissions is now firmly on the political agenda. Conversely, at a time of global recession, many political and business interests view spatial planning as a brake on necessary economic development. A vital debate is emerging between New Labour, which has rediscovered Keynesian economics, and the Conservatives and the Liberal Democrats with their focus on localism and neo-liberal economics. Each party is trying to develop a narrative that reflects the paradigm shift that is taking place in British politics. The look and shape of England, as we approach the second decade of the twentieth-first century, reflects that political history, and in this chapter the five persistent themes that have characterised that history are examined to provide a guide to how the politics of planning will alter, and with it England's appearance. These are firstly the controversy over attempts to recoup some of the financial gains made by development to the state; secondly sustainability and global warming and the need to reduce carbon emissions; thirdly the need to increase the amount of

231

house-building and to find land for this construction; fourthly the governance of planning and whether it should be more rooted in local communities; and finally the future of green belt policy and whether it still has a role 60 years after its introduction.

Development Betterment and Planning Gain

If we exclude its use by Charles II to help rebuild London after the Great Fire, there have been five serious attempts to try and capture some of the betterment (best described as recouping the increase in private site value caused by public works), starting with the Liberal Party's Finance Act 1909, usually referred to as Lloyd George's 'People's Budget' in which he wanted to see a 20 per cent tax on land value increases where land in urban areas increased in value, and which led to the rift with the House of Lords and the Parliament Act. There then followed Lewis Silkin's development charge contained in the Town and Country Planning Act 1947, the Land Commission Act 1967 and the development levy, the Community Land Act 1975, and the development land tax, followed by the 2008 Planning Act with its Community Infrastructure Levy (CIL). This has transmogrified from the original idea of a tariff on development, then the planning gain supplement, through to its current much modified form where it will be determined in relation to the economic viability of a scheme. Originally to be levied against the increase in land value after planning permission had been granted, it was criticised as impossible to enforce, and too similar to the previously proposed PGS, which was scrapped in 2007 after massive opposition from the development industry. The final revision was not opposed by Conservative MPs who withdrew the amendments that had threatened to defeat the Bill.

Briefly, its pedigree was a recommendation in the Barker Report that a PGS should operate alongside Section 106 agreements. This was an attempt to replace the original idea of a tariff which was modelled on the infrastructure tariff used in Milton Keynes, where developers paid flat-rate sums based on the number of houses or the amount of commercial floor space they wanted to develop. Critics said that this might work in clearly defined expansion areas made up of greenfield land, and where the infrastructure costs were relatively easy to identify, but it would not work in more complex schemes such as mixed-use developments on brownfield sites with decontamination costs and other problems. Paradoxically, New Labour finally got the CIL onto the statue book as the recession gathered pace, and this has been the recurring feature of all these attempts by the Labour Party to recoup betterment: they have occurred on the cusp of a recession. The levy will be optional as local planning authorities can continue to use Section 106 agreements, as the Mayor of London is doing with contributions to Crossrail.

One might ask what was wrong with Section 106 agreements, which have been used for many years to negotiate a proportion of development gain for necessary infrastructure investment. The development industry complained that they were too slow and unpredictable, and local authorities said they lacked confidence in their ability to negotiate complex agreements with more experienced developers, and that not enough money was being obtained for necessary social and physical infrastructure work. Frankly, in comparison with the disruption that any tax change will bring, these criticisms do not amount to very much, and could be remedied to bring about a transparent and workable system. The real issue has been in fact one of ideology which has opposed the pragmatic use of Section 106 agreements, despite the support of the courts for their use.

The town planner in this country is governed by three themes that have provided the existing framework in which he or she operates. First, the tradition of reform from the eighteenth century to the present day has led to improved legislation in the fields of housing, public health and the construction of ideal communities; secondly, a concern for the countryside dates from the work of the eighteenth-century landscape architects; and thirdly, and in recent years increasingly, the view is current that planning the use of scarce resources is more rational than relying on market forces to meet demand.

Objections to Planning Gain

A primary objective of the spatial planner is to try to influence the market tendency. The feeling that the market, acting uninterrupted, will not provide the social cultural and welfare goals thought essential to the well-being of our cities and countryside is immediately recognisable in the objectives and aims spelt out in any planning document. The paradoxical situation exists that planners, traditionally hostile to the market, must operate within the market system. Planners and developers are, in truth, two sides of the same coin. Planning objectives are often thwarted by increasingly high land costs and by the difficulties of site assembly. Developers, unrestrained by planning controls, might put up buildings satisfactory in aesthetic and marketing terms, but there would be scant reference to local amenity, traffic, public transport and a host of other planning factors, as is evident in parts of the developing world.

Such bargaining has been criticised as contrary to the ideal which is supposed to govern planning – the pursuit of the 'public interest'. The 'planning gain' agreements made possible by the property boom of the late 1960s and early 1970s and again in the 1980s and 1990s were attempts to obtain some benefits for the community from the very large profits. As a consequence, the expression 'planning gain' has increasingly come to be used in connection with conditions attached by a local planning authority to a grant of planning permission and also in connection with the execution of a legal agreement. This approach is criticised on several counts. Local planning authorities may seek to impose illegal or invalid conditions on planning permissions. Unreasonable haggling over proposals may delay development even more than usual. The incorporation of residential units and public facilities as part of development projects may be somewhat arbitrary and conflict with comprehensive planning. In particular circumstances, any of these criticisms might be valid, but the great value of the 'planning gain' approach to development is that it forces the planner to confront the rigours of the market in terms of what is or is not possible. Unlike the developer, profitability is not the planner's only consideration. The central problem of town planning is to decide what value, or how much weight, should be given to each particular objective. Is it worthwhile reducing employment in the centre of cities at the expense of a large loss in land values, in order to provide more people with homes in central areas and thus reduce traffic congestion or, alternatively, to attract people back to inner-city areas at great financial cost in terms of the infrastructure improvements required? The market acting alone could not choose between these conflicting objectives.

Although much criticised, planning gain has a long tradition in planning negotiations. The use of planning agreements is not new. Their origins can be traced back to the Housing & Town Planning Act 1909. There was concern even in those days as to their use. In 1943, legislation was introduced to allow ministerial supervision of planning agreements.

Definitions of Planning Gain

But before getting too far into this area, which is a quagmire of conflicting ministerial pronouncements and judicial authority, it is well to try and find a working definition. In April 1983, the RTPI endorsed a definition which read as follows:

A Planning Gain is a benefit which accrues when in connection with the obtaining
of a planning permission, a developer incurs some additional expenditure or other
liability beyond that required to meet normally accepted planning standards in
providing a benefit he would not otherwise choose to provide, but which the
Local Planning Authority has justifiable planning grounds for seeking to achieve.

(RTPI, 1983)

The planning profession has tried to widen the definition of planning gain
to include community benefits rather than be tied down to the narrow
requirements of access or drainage to a site. Government has sought to try
and restrict the definition by setting down precise criteria. Conversely, the
courts, through judicial authority, have ever widened the scope of planning
gain and planning authorities, taking their cue from the courts, have striven
to introduce extensive shopping lists of planning gain through planning
policies.

In earlier guidance, Circular 16/91, *Planning Obligations* the then DoE tried
to actually ban the use of the expression 'planning gain'. At paragraph B2 of
Annex B2 of the Circular, the authors state: 'The term "Planning Gain" has
no statutory significance and is not found in the Planning Acts'.

Despite the strictures of the then DoE, the expression has not been lost
from the planning negotiations between developer and local planning
authority. The planning system is adversarial and planning gain has a justification to both applicant and authority. In addition, government itself has
become an enthusiastic promoter of planning gain. This approach was
endorsed by Circular 16/91 (*Planning Obligations*) which in setting down the
tests of the reasonableness of seeking a planning obligation from an applicant for planning permission included 'or to secure the implementation of
local plan policies for a particular area of type of development'.

The government has sought to encourage the legitimate transfer of
responsibility for the cost of traditional and non-traditional off-site infrastructure from the public to the private sector. The present provisions are
much wider than their predecessors. The courts have endorsed this
approach and, increasingly, planning documents through their policies
sought maximum developer contributions to various forms of
infrastructure.

Current Practice

Local planning authorities are now completely uninhibited from seeking the maximum financial contribution possible. By way of example, Fenland District Council, in a district plan published some years ago, advised: 'All new public infrastructure needed as a direct consequence of proposed new development will be sought from the developer at no cost to the public purse'.

At Red Lodge, between Newmarket and Thetford, Forest Heath District Council are promoting a 1,500 dwelling expansion of the existing village on the A11 trunk road. Having steered the concept through structure and local plan inquiries and prepared a master plan, they are ambitious for planning gain. Endorsed by the local plan inspector, they sought land for a two-form county primary school, a multi-purpose community centre, outdoor special facilities, a wildlife area, environmental improvements, off-site road improvements, on-site infrastructure costs, social housing provision and village centre and construction costs for most of this.

What is a Planning Obligation?

The Planning and Compensation Act 1991 made new statutory provisions for planning obligations, substituting by amendment new Sections 106, 106A and 106B into the 1990 Act. These introduce the concept of planning obligations which may be entered into either by means of:

- an agreement between a developer and the local planning authority; or
- a unilateral undertaking by a developer.

Such obligations may restrict the development or use of land; require the land to be used in any specified way; or require payments to be made to the authority either in a specified amount or by reference to a formula; and require periodic payments to be made indefinitely or for a specified period. One effect is to widen considerably the express ambit of planning obligations. It permits the greater use of private capital for 'off-site infrastructure costs' which were formerly borne by the public sector alone. The case of R. v. Plymouth City Council, Plymouth and South Devon Co-Operative Society Limited, 28 May 1993, cast a great deal of light on the way in which the courts should approach cases in which the legal validity of planning obligations is in issue. From it and the other leading authorities cited in the judgement, the following three propositions were derived:

1   The legal validity of a planning obligation depends on whether it is material to the proposed development and fulfils Viscount Dilhorne's three tests in the Newbury case (1981 A.C. 578 at p. 599).

2   Whether a benefit by way of planning gain fairly and reasonably relates to a proposed development is a matter of fact and degree in every case.

3   There is an important public interest in not permitting planning permissions to be bought and sold in exchange for benefits which are not legitimate considerations or do not relate to a proposed development: even if the proposed benefit is of a type which can properly be regarded as material, it must not be so disproportionately large as to include a 'significant additional benefit' over and above that which could properly be considered to be material (relying on the judgement in Safeway Properties Ltd *v.* Secretary of State for the Environment 1991, 3 P.L.R. 91 at p. 96 C/D).

The latest government advice concerning planning obligations is set out in Circular 05/05 (*Planning Obligations*).

When is a Planning Obligation Required?

The Secretary of State's policy requires planning obligations to be sought only where they meet the following tests:

- relevant to planning;
- necessary to make the proposed development acceptable in planning terms;
- directly related to the proposed development;
- fairly and reasonably related in scale and kind to the proposed development; and
- reasonable in all other respects.

Planning obligations can therefore relate to any form of development, residential or commercial, which meets these tests and can relate to land, roads or buildings outside the application site, provided that there is a relationship between the two. Like planning conditions, planning obligations are only valid if they fulfil a planning purpose and are not so unreasonable that no planning authority could require them. The use of planning obligations must be governed by the fundamental principle that planning permission must not be bought or sold.

Superstore Wars in Witney

The legal position of what developers can offer and local planning authorities legitimately accept was clarified in a judgement delivered on 11 May 1995 when the House of Lords rejected Tesco's appeal against the Secretary of State's decision to turn down its application for a superstore in Witney, Oxfordshire. The issue revolved around the question of whether the Secretary of State should have given more weight to Tesco's offer to build a £6.6 million link road and bridge to alleviate any increase in traffic produced by its proposed new premises. Unfortunately, in turning down Tesco, the opportunity was lost for in-depth analysis of the role of planning gain. The Tesco case began in the early 1990s when three companies applied to the local planning authority for permission to build a retail food superstore in Witney, each one on a separate site. Tesco's was described as the Henry Box site; Tarmac/Sainsbury's was known as the Mount Mills site. (The third application was quickly dropped.)

A local planning inquiry had accepted the need for a retail food superstore – preferably on the Henry Box site – and endorsed a new river crossing, the West End Link (WEL), to relieve resultant traffic congestion. The inspector produced a policy statement arguing that the superstore developer should contribute to the cost of the WEL. This seemed to favour Tesco, which offered to pay for the link road. Tarmac made no such offer. On 26–28 July 1992, an inquiry into the applications by Tarmac and Tesco was held, and the inspector recommended that the latter be chosen. On the third and last day of the inquiry, Tesco entered into an agreement with Oxfordshire County Council to pay the Council £6.6 million if planning permission was granted.

On 16 April 1993, however, the Secretary of State issued a decision letter in which he rejected the inspector's recommendation and threw out the Tesco scheme. At the same time, he approved Tarmac's scheme. There were three reasons for this: Tesco's offer to fund the link road was not sufficiently related to its retail scheme; the recommendation of the local planning

238

inspector should receive only limited weight; and Tarmac's site at Mount Mills was preferable on planning grounds.

Tesco successfully appealed to have the Secretary of State's ruling overturned in the High Court on 7 July 1993. But, ten months later, the Court of Appeal reinstated the judgement on 25 May 1994.

The Law Lords decided that:

- A planning obligation that has nothing to do with the proposed development, apart from the fact that it is offered by the developer, is plainly not a consideration. It can only be regarded as an attempt to buy planning permission.
- If a planning obligation had some connection which is not *de minimis*, then regard must be had to it. But the extent, if any, to which it should affect the decision is a matter entirely within the discretion of the decision-maker and, in exercising that discretion, he is entitled to have regard to his established policy.

The Secretary of State had not regarded Tesco's offer to fund the link road as immaterial. On the contrary, after giving it careful consideration, he allowed it little weight in the final decision.

The Use of Agreements

Research has shed light on the form of development included in these agreements. In 1993, Oxford Brookes University and the Association of District Councils analysed the use of planning agreements in non-metropolitan district councils in England and Wales.

Some 202 authorities responded. The agreements related to three development types: 'large office development', 'superstore/supermarket development' and 'residential development of 100 plus units'. Analysis shows that:

- highway items always figure prominently, compared with public transport contributions which hardly appear at all;
- water and sewer contributions were being collected by local authorities to quite a large extent at that time;
- green issues were not a priority; neither were art or heritage issues;

- 'social housing' was achieved by only 12 per cent of authorities, even in the potentially favourable context of large residential development.

One implication of this analysis is that agreements may reflect those items that are easiest to quantify (e.g. highway and parking measures compared to the equivalent public transport contribution for the same amount of development in the same location). Road and parking solutions may also be preferred by developers and investors.

South Northants Local Plan

One of the most interesting approaches to date is that of the South Northants Local Plan. Made famous by the Court of Appeal decision in October 1994, R. *v* South Northamptonshire District Council, David Wilson Homes Ltd, *ex parte* Crest Homes Plc. The decision supports a local plan policy which seeks from developers a set percentage of the enhanced land value of a given site – i.e. the difference in values of the site with and without the permission. For residential development the contribution was to be 20 per cent. The money is paid into an account out of which the local authority can fund infrastructure.

The council's chief planning officer described the background:

Towcester had grown significantly during the 1960s and 70s, so much so that it was being asked to provide a level of service and a number of amenities for quite a large resident population. The local council was unable to provide out of its own funds, so we came to the decision that any further development in the town would need to bring with it community facilities and amenities to meet the needs of the incoming population, and to some extent to redress the imbalance from the past. Through our own local knowledge, it was quite clear that there were three particular concerns – for example, that the people in Towcester needed to see, overcome firstly the heavy traffic on the A5, the trunk road through the town, so the need was there for a trunk road bypass; secondly further car parking in the town centre; and lastly the provision of open space that is not just simply a little square foot of grass at the back of someone's house. So those are perhaps just three of quite a long list of items that made up the shopping list totalling £18 million. Having looked at what Towcester needed to accommodate development, the proposition was put to the agents, or the landowners themselves, that if you wanted to play ball, you needed to contribute to the relief of the strain in the town and they all agreed.

At the time of the Appeal Court judgement, the *Monthly Bulletin of the Encyclopedia of Planning Law and Practice* commented:

> The Court of Appeal's decision reflects a new willingness on the part of the judiciary to find ways of adapting the legal framework of planning control to the changing economic realities of development. They have interpreted the introduction of planning obligations in 1991 as giving a new legal basis for securing infrastructure contributions, but at the same time signalling that a crude attempt to tax out local increases in land values will be unlikely to succeed. The key to ensuring a lawful approach to developers' contributions is the properly drawn up scheme which estimates total costs, and apportions them in some economically logical and therefore defensible way. There is no standard formula itself, whether, as in this case, by reference to a proportion of land value increase, or as a proportion of estimated or actual costs, assessed in terms of type and/or density of permitted development. One variant of that approach might be the American 'impact fee' approach, under which developers are commonly assessed for contributions per dwelling (or other unit of development) to be constructed in accordance with the infrastructure needs generated by the development (such as fire services, water, sewerage, highways and so on).
>
> *(Encyclopedia of Planning Law and Practice*, 1994)

In Circular 1/97 the then DoE was at pains to ensure that the Towcester approach was not repeated and the following footnote appeared:

> In R *v* South Northamptonshire DC and others *ex parte* Crest Homes plc [1994] 3 PLR 47; [1995] J.P.L. 200; the Court of Appeal considered a series of planning obligations which included a formula based on the enhanced value of the land. On the facts of the case, the planning obligations were held to be lawful, but this should not be interpreted as providing a justification for similar arrangements in other circumstances. As Lord Justice Henry explained, the facts of the case were crucial 'because they legitimise a formula which, if used in other factual contexts, could be struck down as an unauthorised local development land tax'.

However, Edwards and Martin, in an article in *Estates Gazette* on 17 June 1994, took a more tolerant view of the Towcester case:

> The judgement of Henry L.J. gives clear guidelines to a local planning authority faced with a situation such as that existing in Towcester and anxious to withstand legal challenge. Provided that it has a local plan policy which is regarded both as lawful and in accordance with departmental guidance, then a method of implementation in line with that adopted by South Northamptonshire District Council should be upheld.

Perhaps the vital aspects are openness in relation to reports and minutes, consultation throughout with interested parties on the developer's side, a scientific approach to aiming at an equitable contribution scheme (so that it can be argued that a serious attempt has been made at achieving a genuine pre-estimate of each developer's proper contribution to the related infrastructure), and the absence of anything to suggest that overall an attempt is being made to raise more than the cost of the related infrastructure. On this basis, if there is no obvious workable alternative, a formula related to enhanced land value should be acceptable.

Once, however, an authority steps outside these judicial guidelines Henry LJ's warning that the formula chosen may be struck down as an unauthorised local development tax must be heeded.

(Edwards and Martin, 1994)

Drawbacks of Agreements

John Walker, the then director of environmental services at Oxford City Council, described the disadvantages of planning gain as firstly the distortion of agreed programmes by the emergence of unforeseen planning gain offers, secondly the uncertainty involved in building a capital programme based on developer contributions, particularly when market conditions are volatile and agreements may have to be re-negotiated; and thirdly the disproportionate amount of time and money, both public and private, that needs to be committed to resolve complex negotiations compared to the relative simplicity of earlier divisions of labour – developer builds the houses, council builds the community centre (Walker, 1996).

Despite these criticisms, given that local authorities have seen their method of raising money reformed, their ability to spend capital receipts circumscribed and their powers in general cutback, it is inevitable that they will continue to be encouraged to finance their programmes in other ways, and the most obvious route for some councils is planning gain. The impact of the recession in 2009 has seen local authorities thwarted because financial contributions from Section 106 agreements have dried up, but there is the scope to renegotiate these in return for a guaranteed start date on development, and/or a clawback procedure for when market conditions improve.

The Way Ahead

The Nolan Committee on Standards in Public Life turned its attention to local government, including specifically the operation of the planning system.

The Committee's Statement of Issues and Questions contains the following paragraphs on town and country planning (Nolan, 1997):

55. We shall also want to consider the safeguards against local authorities buying or selling planning permission in return for what is known colloquially as 'planning gain', and to the Department of the Environment as 'planning obligations'. This is when a Council which grants planning permission secures agreement from the developer that it will fund other works of community benefit.

56. The Department's advice on this is that 'planning obligations' must relate to the proposed development, must only be sought when they are necessary to make a project acceptable in land-use terms, and must have a direct relationship with the development. The House of Lords has recently ruled that this guidance is lawful. We shall want to consider to what extent the advice is being followed, and whether the general principles underlying the advice are consistent with what the Department describes as 'the fundamental principle that planning permission may not be bought or sold'.

Planning featured prominently in the recommendations of the Nolan Committee, published in July 1997. The Committee commented that planning is probably the most contentious matter with which local government deals and is the one on which we receive by far the most submissions from members of the public: 'We have no doubt that there have been serious abuses of the planning process . . .'

The Committee felt that there were some specific areas where action is needed:

We believe it is important that members of planning committees should be trained in planning procedures and planning law. We have particular concerns about planning gain and about local authorities granting themselves planning permission; we believe that there are changes which can help to reduce the potential for planning permission being bought or sold; and we believe that there should be greater openness in the planning process. We also believe it important that the relevant Secretary of State should be notified of all planning applications involving the local authority's own property or land which contravene the local plan or excite a substantial body of objections. Consideration can then be given to which applications should be called in for decision.

As a commentary on the recommendations of the Committee, it is revealing to reproduce the quotation from Harry Deakin, a town planning consultant, and formerly county planning officer to Kent County Council, which is included in the Committee Report:

> I think that short of abandoning planning gain – which I do not offer very seriously – short of that, I come back to my old favourite, openness coupled with . . . a significant speeding up of the appeal system. I think those two – openness and a good appeal system – would go a long way to remedying the worst incidences of malpractice.

This, in fact, appears to have been very much the approach of the Nolan Committee to the question of planning gain.

Planet Newbury

Vodafone's campus HQ on the outskirts of Newbury is referred to as 'Planet Newbury' by wags in the mobile phone industry, but this enormous complex on a 17-hectare site employing about 3,000 people with 2,000 car-parking spaces and built in 2003 not only caused a major planning controversy which split both the town and the council but demonstrated the pros and cons of a Section 106 agreement. Formerly occupying more then 50 offices in New-bury, Vodafone began its global growth in 1999 when, under the leadership of Sir Chris Gent, it bought Air Touch of America, and then acquired the mobile arm of Bell Atlantic and the German company Mannesmann, and in that year indicated that it wanted to build a new headquarters on a greenfield site on the edge of the town. Planning negotiations centred around a Green Travel Plan, and the housing implications of additional workers in Newbury, which would result from the office space vacated by Vodafone being taken by new firms. To mitigate this latter problem the council's proposed solution was as part of the Section 106 agreement to ask Vodafone to put £5 million into buying sites with existing consents for employment use which could be redeveloped for housing. The company saw this as buying the application, refused to agree these terms, and threatened to relocate from Newbury if the application was turned down. The application was considered at a planning committee meeting on 27 April 1999 with the council's planning officer Jim Sherry recommending refusal, and in the early hours of the following morning, after a lengthy and tense debate, the application was approved by a single vote with the ruling Liberal Democrats being split and the majority carried by Conservatives voting with the council's leader and his supporters.

Christopher Marriage, then chairman of the environment committee who supported the planning officer and voted against the application commented, 'Vodafone refuses to accept its downstream, or social responsibilities for the privilege of obtaining permission for a site which is not only outside planning boundaries but exactly where it wanted to go, on the 'front seat' site at the gateway to the town' (Marriage, 1999). Negotiating Section 106 agreements can be messy, but in this case Tim Brett, a planning partner at consultancy Barton Willmore, which advised Vodafone, estimated that the agreement would cost the company some £12 million to implement, so Vodafone were making a major contribution to the off-site costs, particularly through the Travel Plan (Blackman, 1999). A levy might have been simpler, but there is no knowing whether that would have tipped the balance, and persuaded Vodafone to contemplate a global HQ in San Francisco, which was a possibility mooted after the acquisition of Air Touch (Simpkins, 1999).

Future Initiatives

After the experiments of Betterment Levy, development gains tax and development land tax, and now the CIL, Labour governments do not appear to realise that attempts to impose special taxes on development are very unsuccessful. For the foreseeable future, planning gain through the lawful medium of local plan policies has been legitimised, and should continue to be the main means of funding social and physical infrastructure. The Section 106 system is largely a matter of negotiation and allows a deal to be struck which reflects the viability of the scheme. In uncertain times it is the only realistic way forward.

Planning gain survived Nolan. However, the perennial questions remain: can planning gain be made more precise and predictable? Are developers being asked for too much? But the answers are not susceptible to a generalised response and the likelihood in the future, as in the past, is that planning gain is very much a negotiating tactic that is a function of the character and viability of a specific planning proposal, at a particular time in the development history of a locality.

Political pressures from central government to curb capital expenditure at local government level have forced local authorities to use the planning system to secure more planning gain. The courts have responded to these trends sympathetically and attempted to set down appropriate procedures and protocols. The government has responded to criticism of the CIL by bringing it forward as an enabling mechanism that local authorities can decide to use rather than a compulsory tax, but there is still a yawning gap between the Labour Party and the Tories on the issue of betterment, and development tax still remains a leitmotif for the Labour Party.

Sustainability and Global Warming

The notion of sustainable development was popularised by the Bruntland Report in 1987. During this first phase there was a move away from the more traditional reactive methods of solving environmental problems towards the prevention of harm. By the middle of this decade there was a realisation of the need for a more holistic approach, but this has only taken place on a wide-ranging group of policies since 2005. We can therefore distinguish two stages. There was an initial stage which drew extensively on the 1987 Brundland Report of the World Commission on Environment and Development and culminated in the 1995 Environment Act going on to the statue book and the setting up of the Environment Agency. There then followed increasing pressure from environmental groups for a more over-arching policy across all arms of government. The legislative process required a series of step changes:

- the 1990 White Paper, *This Common Inheritance*, which underlined the commitment to a planned development of environmental policy;
- the 1990 Environmental Protection Act;
- the June 1992 Rio Earth Summit and the promotion of Agenda 21;
- the January 1994 White Paper on *Sustainable Development*;
- the 1995 Environment Act which included setting up the Environment Agency which is the lead agency to procure sustainable development, and the principal adviser to government.

The Government saw the planning system as an effective way of implementing sustainable policies and published in 2005 a paper that set a framework for incorporating sustainable development within the planning system. Further advice followed on climate change and since then there has been considerable legislative activity to ensure that a sustainable approach is taken across all sectors of planning, construction and development. Environmental groups have been instrumental in pressing for legislative changes and once all party political support was broadly obtained, the legislative pressure has increased. The second phase has been marked by an acceleration of legislative changes so as to achieve an integrated approach to sustainable development Over the period 2005–07 there was a wealth of policy advice that is now consolidated in a series of documents.

Reducing Carbon Emissions

In February 2005, PPS1 *Delivering Sustainable Development* set out the government's objectives for the planning system while in March the policy document *Securing the Future* was published aimed at an integrated approach to protect and enhance the physical and natural environment, and to use resources and energy as efficiently as possible. These documents were accompanied by planning policy statements on key issues such as the protection of biodiversity and geological conservation, sustainable development in rural areas, waste management, renewable energy and flood risk. The May 2007 White Paper, *Planning for a Sustainable Future*, was followed by a keynote speech in November by the Prime Minister Gordon Brown setting out a wider environmental agenda for the government, and in the same month Climate Change Minister, Phil Woolas, encouraged councils to reduce carbon dioxide emissions, both through their own actions and by setting an example to the wider community. He also confirmed action on the issue would be included in part of the framework used to assess local government performance from April 2008.

In December 2007, a Bill was introduced giving councils the right to implement the 'Merton rule' on renewable energy. The aim was to enshrine in law the right of councils to insist that development meets a certain amount of their energy needs from onsite renewable sources. The policies, which had at that time been proposed by about 100 councils, are based on an initiative by Merton Council in south London. That same month the *Supplement to Planning Policy Statement 1* was published, entitled *Planning and Climate Change*, and sets out how planning should contribute to reducing emissions and stabilising climate change, taking into account the unavoidable consequences. Tackling climate change is a key government priority for the spatial planning system, and there is now a firm basis of planning policy to guide local planning authorities and developers, but what is needed now is delivery of sustainable development.

The rate of construction in the UK is set to increase. The government's Sustainable Communities Plan seeks to accelerate the current house-building programme and increase the house-building target by about 200,000 on top of the 900,000 new homes planned between 1996 and 2016 in the South

East. However, the energy used in constructing, occupying and operating buildings represents approximately 50 per cent of greenhouse gas emissions in Britain. This new emphasis on growth should represent an opportunity to shift development towards delivering more sustainable homes and construction. There are little or no policy differences between the main political parties on climate change. Where differences could occur is on delivery, and policy towards specific projects such as airport expansion and nuclear power stations. The Conservatives and the Liberal Democrats have opposed the expansion of Heathrow, and the latter have pledged an end to the development of coal and nuclear power stations. New Labour has adopted a top-down policy-led approach but critics assert that practical delivery and management of sustainable buildings is being held up by these myriad policies, regulations, tools and standards (King, 2009). Despite all the changes to policy and legislation, New Labour has shied away from asserting a presumption in the planning system to the delivery of sustainable development, and that remains a principle for the Conservatives to adopt as a cornerstone of their approach to spatial planning that would signify a policy difference between the two parties.

Housing Land and House-building

Since large-scale housing began after the Housing and Town Planning Act 1919, when council subsidies were first introduced, there has been an ideological divide between Labour and the Conservatives about the delivery of new housing, with Labour wanting to see the housing programme led by the public sector, whereas the Tories wanted the private sector to lead. Aneurin Bevan insisted that the public sector should be the principal house-builder, but Harold Macmillan was more pragmatic, and during the 1950s more than 200,000 council houses were built in each year, but as we have seen, many were poor quality, prefabricated houses built in tower blocks. The Housing Act of 1980, which included the Right to Buy, changed everything, and with limited subsidies, councils ran down their housing programmes, leaving it to the Housing Associations to build affordable housing. These, together with the private sector, particularly the large-volume house builders, were expected to build the necessary new houses. This was the approach to delivery supported by Gordon Brown, both as Chancellor and Prime Minister. The main difficulty perceived was the planning system, which was thought to be an obstacle to house-building, and the economist Kate Barker was to review, and to make recommendations as to how to increase the flow of housing. The financial crisis and the shortage of liquidity for the banks and its effect upon mortgage applications has broken that delivery model.

House-building in England recovered from the slump of the 1990s to peak at nearly 170,000 dwellings in 2006–07 (DCLG, 2009), but has now dramatically fallen, and in 2009–10 there may be little more than 50,000 dwellings built. First-time buyers have fallen from 503,000 in 1997 to 300,000 in 2007 (Halifax, 2007), and it is estimated that there are more than 4.5 million people in England on council waiting lists (*The Times*, 2009). The situation is dire. New Labour now wants to kick-start house-building by councils and to do this, to change the public sector borrowing requirements so that money lent for building does not have to be treated as public debt, and to allow councils to keep the receipts from rental income and sales through the Right to Buy. New targets have been set, which would mean some 70,000 social homes a year built by 2010–11, and yet only 20,000 were built in 2008. The big question is, where will all these new homes be located?

Hopes have been pinned on the growth areas and Thames Gateway, but an infrastructure bill of at least £1 billion for flood protection work in that area, and increased concerns that sea levels are predicted to rise twice as fast as formerly forecast, means that the contribution of Thames Gateway to house-building must be reappraised. A high proportion of the dwellings built in recent years have been flats, as their number has trebled since 1997–98 (DCLG, 2008), but these dwellings have experienced the sharpest falls in house prices during the financial crisis and this also needs to be re-examined. New thinking is required on where the houses should be built. There are many smaller cities and towns in England that would benefit from additional housing, which will support their town centres and services. If the idea of the Conservatives to encourage local authorities to welcome new housing by providing them with a financial incentive could work, then the housing needs could be met by a large number of smaller sites.

Council house-building has a role to play, and the Conservatives need to adopt the pragmatic stance of Harold Macmillan, if not his tolerance of tower blocks, and support house-building by councils. Evidence that the volume house builders have deliberately banked their housing sites so as to ration the supply of new houses has been difficult to identify, but it is more likely than not, that the volume house builders have squeezed out of the housing land market the smaller house builder and contractor. Council-led house-building would provide a market for these firms which would boost local employment. The other area where government needs to act is to boost rented housing by tax incentives, which would provide a further boost to house-building, as well as taking households off the council waiting list. Housing production for more than 30 years has been plagued by ideology, but if nothing else a historical review indicates constructive pointers for the future.

Governance

We have seen during its 100-year history that spatial planning has been subject to a raft of different theories, processes and objectives, but the three themes of strategy, management and delivery have been constant. Central to the role of spatial planning has been the relationship between central and local government. Walker (2008) has identified that local government traditionally undertakes activities on behalf of central government – it does not possess power over its own affairs. This situation contrasts with the majority of European systems where local government possess power under the doctrine of general competence and is subject to less interference from the centre, provided local administrations are able to undertake their functions. By contrast, in Britain local government is an agent of central government and its roles and responsibilities change over time. Over the last century, England has become one of the most centralised countries in the developed world. This centralisation continued under Thatcherism, when local government was perceived as an executive arm of central government, and has gained momentum under New Labour. The irony is that New Labour inherited a system of local government traumatised by the Thatcher years, and has helped local government to regain its confidence, but 'modernising planning' as a central theme of its thinking on planning since election success in 1997 threatens to marginalise the role of many councillors and raises important questions of local autonomy. Planning decisions are part of the bedrock of local democracy. Many councillors come into local government because of an interest in a planning proposal or because of a previous involvement in a planning issue or controversy. There is now a huge tension between on the one hand the search for new forms of local governance, and on the other speed and efficiency.

Community politics also poses a threat to the role of elected councillors but from a different direction. Early attempts at public participation by local authorities in the 1970s now look contrived and patronising. The revival of the Liberal Democrats since that date owes much to community politics and their willingness to campaign on doorstep issues. New Labour, with its wish to embrace additional stakeholders in local governance, has not thought through clearly the threat that this could pose to the role and responsibilities of elected members.

Now, on the approach to the next general election, the Conservatives have contributed to the debate by publishing their policy paper on returning power to local communities: *Control Shift* (Conservative Party, 2009). A key narrative in the document is that Britain has moved into a 'post-bureaucratic' age, where technological advances have put information within reach of every citizen. People now expect greater power over the things that matter to them, and influence their lives, and they expect institutions to share knowledge and information freely and without constraint. The government has to adapt to these changes. The Conservatives set out their intentions, if elected, to introduce a new planning bill which will disband the RDAs. That was expected, but what is new is the intention to introduce a new general power of competence which gives local authorities an explicit freedom to act in the best interests of their voters, unhindered by the absence of specific legislation supporting their actions. No action – except raising taxes, which requires specific parliamentary approval – will any longer be 'beyond the powers' of local government in England, unless the local authority is prevented from taking that action by the common law, specific legislation or statutory guidance. Contrast is drawn with the Local Government Act 2000 and the power that the Act gave to local authorities to do anything which they consider likely to promote or improve the economic, social or environmental well-being of any part of their area. However, because the scope of action permitted to councils under this power is not clear, many local authorities have not used it all. The Conservatives therefore want to go much further, and argue that the implications of this new statutory presumption are intentionally vast, and that it will usher in a new attitude among both councillors and their voters, and make the system of local government in England more akin to that in France, Spain, Sweden and Denmark where, it is argued, decentralising power and control to local communities has successfully revived civic life.

This approach contrasts with the attempts by the government to simplify the regime of regional planning by integrating regional, economic and spatial plans, which will be carried out by RDAs, who in turn will be overseen by a new suite of parliamentary regional committees. To overcome the democratic deficit, ministers have proposed that the involvement of so-called local authority Leaders' Boards will ensure that the democratic link with spatial strategies will be maintained. A report by the Commons Business, Enterprise and Regulatory Reform Committee indicated the concern of MPs both as to how the Boards would operate and how disagreements between the boards and the RDAs would be resolved, and whether the parliamentary committee would have the resources to scrutinise all this.

A further aspect of governance that the present government wishes to see is a stronger link between the LDF and the Community Strategy. A principal reason for this is that both are concerned with the achievement of sustainable development. LDFs will act as the land use and delivery mechanism for the objectives and policies set out in the Community Strategy. LDFs will need to express, in appropriate land-use planning terms, those elements of the Community Strategy that relate to the development and use of land. By way of example, the Core Strategy envisaged at the heart of the LDF will set out the key elements of the planning framework for the area and comprise a vision and strategic objectives, together with the spatial strategy, core policies, and a framework for monitoring and implementation. In this way, the Core Strategy can much more readily than in the past reflect the corporate objectives of the council. After a shaky start, the majority of councils appear to have grasped the importance of the Core Strategy, and these documents are probably one of the most important and useful innovations that have emerged from yet another fundamental review of the planning system. Whatever the political changes ahead, these, as a fundamental component of the governance of spatial planning, should be retained.

Green Belt Policy

The first green belt scheme was launched by the London County Council in 1935, and adopted by Abercrombie in his Greater London Plan of 1944. It was subsequently given statutory protection by the 1947 Act. The Labour Party can claim the credit for that, but most policy development has come from the Conservatives. In August 1955, Duncan Sandys issued his circular giving firm government backing to green belts. It was regarded as a milestone in English planning history and at the time was seen as a great victory for the CPRE. The last principal government advice was in January 1995, during John Major's premiership, when a revised version of PPG2, *Green Belts* was published, and has proved to be one of the longest serving policy documents. Even during the Thatcher era, green belt policy was not seriously challenged, but Labour ministers appear to think that building homes in the green belt is a test of their political muscularity. Dick Crossman, who allowed Birmingham City Council to build a large housing estate at Chelmsey Wood in the Warwickshire green belt in the 1960s, boasted in his diaries of the tough decision he was prepared to take, while John Prescott at the beginning of his time in office allowed a major housing scheme in the Newcastle green belt. The journalist Lynsey Hanley in her wryly sardonic book, *Estates*, writes about Chelmsey Wood where she grew up with her parents, and the decision by Crossman:

> He never quite went as far as to say that the green belt was a bourgeois luxury, but the eagerness with which he signed off great tracts of virgin land to local authorities who only a few years earlier had had their planning applications refused by the Conservative government suggested that he felt as much.
>
> (Hanley, 2007)

Green belt policy seems to have two faces. Local politicians and local residents see the restrictions on development in green belts as permanent. Councillor Jerry Patterson, a former leader and planning committee chairman of the Vale of White Horse District Council, Oxfordshire, writing to the *Oxford Times* in July 2006 about the prospect of a review of the green belt boundaries around Oxford opined, 'That is a dangerous suggestion as the whole point of a green belt is that it should be as good as permanent to ensure that it safeguards the individuality of communities and avoids urban sprawl'. He concluded, 'Once you start to review it, where do you end?' (Patterson, 2006). But professional planners see it differently. Paul Hudson, who at the time was chief planner at the Department for Communities and Local Government, in an interview in 2006 observed:

> The function of green belts is principally to prevent sprawl and coalescence of urban settlements. It's not for countryside protection though these two coincide. Green belt policy provides for exceptions in tightly defined circumstances. Once housing takes place, it risks undermining the original policy. But reviewing green belt boundaries, particularly inner boundaries, must be a function of the forward planning process.
>
> (Hudson, 2006)

The Oxford Green Belt

The review of the Oxford green belt is a contemporary struggle which says much about the attitudes to the green belt of the two major parties and is being fought out to the south of Oxford. The planning history of the evolution of the Oxford green belt is worth a brief examination because it demonstrates the conflicts and political differences that New Labour's

253

In August 1955 Duncan Sandys issued his circular giving firm government backing to Green Belts.

© Building Magazine

planning governance, based on the regional spatial strategies, has brought to a Conservative-run shire county, which at its centre has Oxford and its dreaming spires run by the Labour Party.

The genesis for Oxford's green belt lies in Thomas Sharp's 1948 report to Oxford City Council, *Oxford Replanned*, which recommended the relocation of the motor industry out of the city, that its population be kept below 100,000 and that no further development other than for rural purposes be allowed in a belt of countryside around the city some ten miles wide. It was not until 1958 that formal proposals were submitted to the minister following the publication of Circular 42/55. The process was torturous, and in 1961 an inquiry was held and in 1975 the concept of a green belt for Oxford was approved as an amendment to the approved County Development Plan. The belt was narrower than Sharp had recommended, and was only six miles at its widest. Also, the inner boundaries had still to be finalised, and it would be many years before these were firmed up. Nonetheless, for nearly 30 years there was widespread support for the Oxford green belt. During that time there was major employment growth in the south of the county, in an area bisected by the A34 trunk road from the West Midlands to Portsmouth and Southampton, which now boasts the strapline 'Science Vale UK', and includes the Culham Science Centre, Milton Park and the Harwell Science and Innovation Centre. The Vale is the home to thousands of jobs, many in high-tech industries and research. In March 2006, the local authorities who made up the South East Assembly submitted the South East Plan to the Secretary of State. A central feature of the plan was a Central Oxfordshire sub-region centred on the city but including a large area to the north and south, which was to accommodate the employment and housing growth. An independent panel of experts examined the plan and were impressed by the case put forward by Oxford City Council, the Oxford colleges who owned land to the south of the city, and business interests, that land had to be released from the Oxford green belt to accommodate the housing needs of what had become one of the strongest growth areas in the country. They reported in August 2007 and recommended an urban extension of Oxford, which would require a selective review of the green belt and joint working between Oxford City Council and South Oxfordshire District Council within whose purview the proposed development area was situated.

At the end of July 2008, Communities Secretary Hazel Blears backed plans for 4,000 dwellings south of Grenoble Road, on green belt land near the Kassam Stadium, home to Oxford United and once owned by Bob Maxwell. Blears charged Oxford City Council and South Oxfordshire District Council to identify land to be removed from the green belt to facilitate an urban expansion of Oxford. The announcement was couched in contemporary terms that extolled the regenerative benefits for Oxford, but in truth it was a good old-fashioned land grab by a Labour council into the shire county, reminiscent of those by Birmingham and Manchester in the 1950s and 1960s.

Oxford City Council, in their representations to Hazel Blears in October 2008 on the proposed alterations, expressed their concern that the urban extension was not being delivered through a joint development plan document (DPD). They felt that this approach weakened their position and allowed South Oxfordshire District Council to continue without full involvement of the City Council, even though there would be a need to integrate into Oxford city. The City Council had discussed with the other landowners, Thames Water and Magdalen College, the need to work together. Angie

Paterson, South Oxfordshire District Council's cabinet member for planning, pledged that her council would continue to fight the scheme (Patterson, 2008), and South Oxfordshire District Council in its draft core strategy has identified an area of search for the urban expansion, but this excludes the area of land owned by the Oxford City Council.

The panel report had suggested that the urban extension to the south of Oxford should be delivered through a DPD produced jointly by Oxford City Council and South Oxfordshire District Council, but the proposed changes put forward by Hazel Blears did not specifically endorse the use of a joint DPD but referred to the local authorities 'working collaboratively'. South Oxfordshire District Council probably took the pragmatic view that it would not get its core strategy endorsed by an independent inspector without the inclusion of the urban extension of Oxford. Supporters of regional planning will see politically opposed city and district councils working together, however tentatively, on an urban extension as a demonstration of the power of the regional spatial strategy to deliver controversial proposals despite local political differences. The difficulties will come with delivery. The District Council is already heavily involved with a similar level of growth at Didcot, in the south of the county, where the A34 trunk road meets the Paddington-Bristol rail line, together with a major town centre redevelopment scheme. Originally earmarked in 1944 for growth in Abercrombie's Plan, Didcot's time has finally come, but resourcing both growth centres will prove a burden for a small district council.

In many ways, the plan-making involved in the urban extension is the relatively easy part. The real question is what will be the delivery vehicle. South Oxfordshire District Council will remain the local planning authority to negotiate the Section 106 agreement and the CIL. The EiP (examination in public) into the final core strategy will be after the general election, and at that stage South Oxfordshire District Council will have to indicate how the urban extension will be delivered as the inspector will be concerned not only with the soundness of the strategy, but whether it can be delivered. A further complication has arisen as CPRE have suceeded in their legal challenge to the Green Belt Review and the Secretary of State has conceded that insufficient consideration was given to alternative sites. The strategy for Oxford will have to be reconsidered.

This episode raises the question of how the government, and the EiP panel ever thought that the urban extension could be delivered. The politics of this seems to have been overlooked. The panel concluded that by the time the RSS was adopted, there should be sufficient confidence for Oxford City Council and South Oxfordshire District Council to move straight to a joint

Area Action Plan (AAP) if they had completed their LDF core strategy by then. This proved to be hopelessly over-confident and ignored completely the political differences between the two councils.

The Oxford experience bears out that around Bristol observed by Walker (2008). He concluded that the operation of the new planning system lessened the control of local politicians over strategic planning, and that this goes conceptually against what the government's broader local government reforms are trying to achieve and adversely affects the ability of communities and councillors to make the most of their place-shaping role, or to debate the scale of housing growth.

Birmingham Builds in the Green Belt

There are parallels with Birmingham City Council's wish to build in the Warwickshire green belt at Chelmsley Wood following Richard Crossman's decision, when Housing and Planning Minister in 1964, that the City Council could go head and build nearly 16,000 dwellings in an unspoilt area best known at the time for its bluebell wood. The houses were built in record time using system-building techniques, and as we have already observed the scheme included many ten-storey tower blocks. The area became part of Solihull Borough in 1974 after local government reorganisation, although Birmingham City Council retained control of the houses until they were transferred to Solihull MBC in September 1980. The borough has embarked on an extensive refurbishment of the area's shopping centre, which is the third largest in the borough, which should be complete by 2010, and includes a new library, bus station interchange and a large new food store. The original design was a Radburn layout with a large concrete raft with shopping on the upper level and undercover.

There is still a rawness about the appearance of the 'Wood' estate, nearly 40 years after its completion. In less than an hour, a car journey along the M6 motorway northwards leads to Telford New Town, which was designed and built at the same time as Chelmsley Wood. Admittedly larger in scale and ambition, it now has a maturity and confidence about its design, enhanced by attractive landscaping. The difference is in the governance. Chelmsley Wood was planned and designed by Birmingham City Council's architects department in what was hostile territory as the local councils had bitterly opposed the city's expansion. Telford had the benefit of a Development Corporation and a dedicated professional team, along with supportive local authorities who saw the benefits of development to what had been a blighted

Chelmsley Wood: Dick Crossman made the original planning decision to allow Birmingham City Council to build a large housing estate in the Warwickshire Green Belt.

© Nigel Moor

industrial area. The designated area included Ironbridge on the River Severn which had been the birthplace of the industrial revolution. The record of the past 50 years is that planned overspill from cities into the surrounding shire counties without the governance of a Development Corporation is extremely difficult, and beyond the resources of local planning authorities.

In 2006, the DCLG commissioned Oxford Brookes University (Oxford Brookes University and the DCLG, 2006) to identify lessons from the new towns programme that might be transferable to the Growth Areas Initiative. This was particularly important as the Growth Areas would be the largest programme of state government sponsored development sine the new towns. Part of the research examined the key lessons on governance. In respect of power and responsibility, the consultants advised that clarity of responsibilities for delivery and related governance in the Growth Areas would be essential, especially so since delivery partnerships would be far looser entities with more diffused power structures than those which characterised the new towns programme. Their further comments were

258

particularly perceptive. They advised there may be a need for a conscious trade-off between strong leadership of the delivery bodies and local democratic accountability, and that diffused partnership structures would not automatically be more democratically accountable than were the new town Development Corporations if the real location of power and responsibility was mystified by the partnership itself.

These doubts about the governance of the Growth Areas programme have proved uncannily accurate. Delivery in the Growth Areas has been compromised by competing and overlapping agencies and partnerships, and a new government must revisit the programme and its governance if it is to achieve its original housing and development objectives.

To further consider this important question of governance, we turn for a moment again to Chelmsley Wood. Solihull is the most polarised borough in the country, and the 40,000 people who live in the three northern wards, including Chelmsley Wood, on nearly all social and economic indicators face worse life chances than those living in the south around Solihull. The Birmingham comedian Jasper Carrot may poke fun at the apparent pretentiousness of the title but the North Solihull Partnership is making a determined effort through a 15-year programme to improve the quality of life of the northern area of the borough that has been hard hit by the industrial contraction of the Midlands in the last 30 years. Sliced through by the M6 motorway, the scores of tower blocks that announce the 'Wood' are most people's first visual experience of the Birmingham conurbation as they travel north on the motorway. In truth, Solihull Borough Council are having to tidy up after Crossman's decision to give Birmingham the go ahead to build in the Warwickshire green belt. In his memoirs, when discussing the planning decisions that arrived on his ministerial desk, Crossman (1975) explained 'I find these decisions easy, pleasant, and I take them in a fairly light-heated way'. Although he lived in leafy Oxfordshire near Banbury, Crossman was an MP who represented a Coventry constituency, and he was always prepared to back the big cities in their housing expansion plans. Unfortunately, Chelmsley Wood, where people from central Birmingham were rehoused and faced a long and awkward bus journey from the city centre, was not one of his best decisions, and the consequences have taken more than a generation to tackle.

The IPC

One other area of governance that has split the political parties is the introduction of the IPC and national policy statements (NPSs). The government has set out a timetable for how it plans to set up the IPC and consult on the detailed regulations and NPSs to implement the new system, but it is worth examining the justification for this dramatic change. One third of Britain's electricity-generating capacity needs replacing, fuel bills are rising and we become more dependent on imported energy as supplies from the North Sea decline. The new regime will create an integrated planning system for major infrastructure. Ministers will set out NPSs detailing national infrastructure priorities for the country in areas such as energy, aviation, road and rail transport, water and waste, and the decisions as to whether to allow individual projects to go ahead will then be taken independently by the IPC operating within the framework set by ministers. Developers will be required to consult local communities and other stakeholders prior to submitting applications, and to conduct environmental assessments when required by EIA (Environmental Impact Assessment) regulations. There will also be consultation on the NPSs. By streamlining consent procedures and rationalising the different regimes that currently exist (eight at the present time), improving inquiry procedures and imposing statutory timetables on the process, the government expects the time taken from application to decision to fall to under a year in the majority of cases.

The new regime is ambitious and understandable given the need to improve infrastructure and reduce carbon emissions, but the Conservatives have pledged to repeal the Planning Act 2008. They maintain that the IPC is liable to be subject to challenges through judicial review, the European Court of Human Rights and the European Court of Justice and the likelihood is that the IPC will actually slow down the planning process. The Tories would keep the NPSs but would ensure that they are subject to parliamentary approval in both Houses of Parliament. As for improving and speeding up inquiry procedure, they point out that a private or hybrid Bill in Parliament provides a sensible timescale and point to the Crossrail Act 2008 as an example of a fast-track planning process for the complex Crossrail scheme. Much of the Felixstowe Dock expansion, which was within a sensitive Area of Outstanding Natural Beauty in Suffolk, was achieved by means of a hybrid Bill before this procedure was discouraged in favour of public inquiries.

In an interview (Donatantonio, 2009), the Conservative planning spokesman, Bob Neill, a relative newcomer to the House of Commons but someone with a long background as a councillor in London local government commented,

> We want the practical ideas from an NPS, but not a separate quango. With the Heathrow Terminal 5 inquiry, for example, too much time was taken up with the philosophy of the planning arguments. All an inquiry needs to say is: 'Here is the practical evidence as set out in an NPS, now we will deal with the local objections". People will feel that there is much more accountability. So why have a quango to enforce it?

As an ex-barrister, Neill should understand how an inquiry should be shortened, and he has written to the new chairman of the IPC advising him that the Conservatives, if elected, will repeal the 2008 Act.

What Future for Regionalism?

Following the sub-national Review of Economic Development in 2007, the government announced that spatial and economic strategies would be replaced by single integrated strategies. These would be produced by the RDAs and the Regional Assemblies were to be withdrawn. To address the democratic deficit, regional Leaders' Forums have been introduced which will work with the RDAs to produce the new integrated strategies. At the end of January 2009, the DCLG issued a policy document setting out the principles for integration which will be included in the Local Democracy, Economic Development and Construction Bill which should receive Royal Assent late in 2009. These changes have produced a hiatus as the RDAs, fearful of legal challenge, have been reluctant to make a start on the new strategies.

Further doubts arise because of the commitment of the Tories if elected in 2010 to withdraw the RDAs and hand their economic development responsibilities and budgets, which total £2.2 billion a year for the next three years, to new Enterprise Partnerships established by local authorities for areas that reflect a common local agenda. These are likely to be less extensive than the Regional Assemblies such as SERPLAN, originally set up by the Conservatives, which might prove too large to adopt a common economic agenda. Clearly much hinges on the outcome of the next general election, but it may be that after just over a decade, John Prescott's Economic Development Agencies, which took over most of the previous regeneration budget such as City Challenge and the Single Regeneration Budget (SRB), will have come to the end of their lifespan.

Planning and Politics

This book has shown that politics and planning are inseparable. The 'P' in planning does stand for politics. But planning is about more than making strategies and plans. It is ultimately about delivery. The Development Corporations used by Labour for the successive waves of new towns, and by the Conservatives for inner-city renewal, have proved the most effective means of delivering comprehensive planned development, but they came with a democratic deficit. Now we have Development Corporations set up for the growth areas and Thames Gateway but to ensure democratic accountability they are shadowed by consultative groups and procedures, and have become bogged down as a result. They lack the drive and focus which was such a characteristic of the original Development Corporations. Conversely, the Conservatives and the Liberal Democrats promise localism, which they argue can deliver sustainable development because communities will become empowered. Which of these models will prevail depends on the ballot box, and with it the look and shape of England through the rest of this century.

References

Blackman, D. (1999) Common ground for an ambitious plan, *Planning*, 7 May.

Conservative Party (2009) *Control Shift: Returning Power to Local Communities*, Policy Green Paper No. 9 London: The Conservative Party, p. 4.

Crossman, R. (1975) *The Diaries of a Cabinet Minister, Volume One: Minister of Housing 1964–66*. London: Hamish Hamilton, p. 99.

DCLG (2008) *Housebuilding: Permanent Dwellings Completed by House and Flat, Number of Bedrooms and Tenure*. London: DCLG.

DCLG (2009) *New House Building Statistics*. London: DCLG.

Donatantonio , D. (2009) Maintaining opposition: interview with Bob Neill MP, *Planning*, 20 March, p. 15.

Draft South East Plan EiP Panel Report (2007) *Central Oxfordshire Sub Region*. London, August, p. 349.

Edwards, M. and Martin (1994) Implications of the Towester case, *Estates Gazette*, 17 June.

Encyclopedia of Planning Law and Practice (1994) Monthly bulletin, October. London: Sweet & Maxwell.

Halifax (2007) First time buyers, press release, 22 December.

Hanley, L. (2007) *Estates: An Intimate History.* London: Granta Books, p. 27.

Hudson, P. (2006) Interview with Chris Griffin, *Axis*, May/June, pp. 6–7.

King, P. (2009) Report of the UK Green Building Council (UKGBC), *Planning*, 6 March.

Marriage, C. (1999) Industry should pay its social bill, *Planning* 21 May.

Nolan Committee (1997) *Third Report of The Committee on Standards In Public Life*, Volume 1, Cm 3702. London: HMSO.

Oxford Brookes University and the DCLG (2006) *Transferable Lessons from the New Towns.* London: DCLG.

Paterson, A. (2008) Council attacks Secretary of States's proposal for 4,000 homes in the green belt, Crowmarsh, South Oxfordshire District Council press release, 18 July.

Patterson, J. (2006) Dangerous, *Oxford Times*, 20 July.

Simpkins, E. (1999)Vodafone HQ move in balance, *Estates Gazette*, 14 August.

The Times (2009) Council house building, 30 January, p. 8.

Walker, J. (1996) Disadvantages of planning gain, *The House Builder*, April.

Walker, R. (2008) *Planning Perspectives on the Governance of the Housing Growth Agenda*, MA Town & Country Planning Thesis, April, UWE, Bristol.

Index

Page references in *italic* refer to illustrations.

265